HOW WE THINK AND LEARN

Theoretical Perspectives and Practical Implications

Written in a conversational and engaging manner, *How We Think and Learn* introduces readers to basic principles and research findings regarding human cognition and memory. It also highlights and debunks twenty-eight common misconceptions about thinking, learning, and the brain. Interspersed throughout the book are many short do-it-yourself exercises in which readers can observe key principles in their own thinking and learning. All ten chapters end with concrete recommendations – both for readers' own learning and for teaching and working effectively with others. As an accomplished researcher and writer, Jeanne Ellis Ormrod gives us a book that is not only highly informative but also a delight to read.

Jeanne Ellis Ormrod received her AB degree in psychology from Brown University and her MS and PhD degrees in educational psychology from The Pennsylvania State University. She was Professor of Educational Psychology at the University of Northern Colorado until 1998 and is now Professor Emerita in the university's School of Psychological Sciences. Although she no longer conducts her own research on learning and cognition, she remains an avid reader of psychological and educational research, stays in touch with many of her professional colleagues around the world, and continues to update her popular college textbooks in human learning, educational psychology, and research methodologies. *How We Think and Learn* is her first book with Cambridge University Press.

How We Think and Learn

Theoretical Perspectives and Practical Implications

Jeanne Ellis Ormrod

University of Northern Colorado

CAMBRIDGE
UNIVERSITY PRESS

CAMBRIDGE
UNIVERSITY PRESS

One Liberty Plaza, 20th Floor, New York, NY 10006, USA

Cambridge University Press is part of the University of Cambridge.

It furthers the University's mission by disseminating knowledge in the pursuit of education, learning, and research at the highest international levels of excellence.

www.cambridge.org
Information on this title: www.cambridge.org/9781316616840
10.1017/9781316691458

© Jeanne Ellis Ormrod 2017

First published 2017

Printed in the United States of America by Sheridan Books, Inc.

A catalogue record for this publication is available from the British Library.

ISBN 978-1-107-16511-3 Hardback
ISBN 978-1-316-61684-0 Paperback

CONTENTS

ACKNOWLEDGMENTS

Although I am listed as the sole author of this book, I have hardly written it alone. In particular, I must thank the countless psychologists and other scholars who have conducted the research studies and developed the theoretical perspectives that have shaped my thinking about human learning and cognition over the past 50 years. If I were to list all of them in the footnotes and reference list, this would be a very long book indeed.

I must also thank four individuals who have helped me turn my ideas into the concrete reality that is *How We Think and Learn*. Dave Repetto at Cambridge University Press recruited me to write the book, and together we conceptualized a work that can (we hope) appeal to a broad audience of readers. Megan Ferrara created several arts that illustrate certain ideas in delightful visual form. And with their attention to both the big picture and many nitty-gritty details, Joshua Penney at Cambridge and Sathish Kumar at Integra transformed my manuscript into the final product you see before you.

A special shout-out goes to Adrienne Starrs, who has, over the past 15 months, doggedly and yet graciously persisted in her efforts to stretch my mind and fingers in new musical directions. In doing so, she has not only enabled me to improve my piano-playing ability but also expanded my conceptions of what expert instruction and effective learning are all about.

Finally, I will be eternally grateful to my husband, Richard, who has been my cheerleader throughout this and previous book-writing projects, and to my children and grandchildren, who have given me many great examples of human cognition and learning in action.

The General Nature of Human Cognition and Learning: Probably Not Quite What You Think It Is

We human beings are hardly alone in our ability to learn from our experiences. Even snails and earthworms can acquire and remember new behaviors as their environmental circumstances change, and many mammals and birds can learn new skills simply by observing and modeling what their human or nonhuman companions do.[1] Yet as members of the species *homo sapiens* – Latin for "wise man" or "wise human" – we have several capabilities that far exceed those of our fellow residents on Planet Earth.

Key among our exceptional talents is an ability to communicate with one another using a grammatically complex and very flexible *language*. Our language provides a critical means through which we learn from other people's experiences and guidance. For example, if you want to fix a broken bicycle or bake chocolate chip cookies, you can ask other people – or read books or websites that other people have written – to guide you through the process. In addition, as you'll discover in Chapter 3, language also provides an important resource for *thinking* about our experiences.

Another thing that sets us apart is the fact that virtually all of us humans live within a certain *culture* that not only helps us learn new things but also serves as a repository of what we have collectively learned as a group.[2] Consider our many books, museums, universities, and Internet websites; all of these serve as shared "memories" of what various civilizations have learned over the ages.

Finally, much more so than is true for any other species, we human beings can *self-reflect* about the things we have learned and about our thoughts in general.[3] For example, we can mull over and evaluate our own and other people's ideas about, say, social or political issues, and we can integrate the many tidbits of information we've obtained from various sources to draw conclusions, speculate about implications, and solve new problems.

Such mental self-reflection is known as *metacognition*, a topic we'll explore in depth in Chapter 7. But in fact, this entire book is the result of countless researchers' attempts to reflect on and try to explain the nature of human thinking and learning. In this short book, we can only skim the surface of what has become a complex, multifaceted, exponentially increasing field of scientific inquiry. Nevertheless, as your author, I'm hoping that by the end of the book, you'll have a better understanding of how we humans think about, learn, and remember aspects of our day-to-day experiences – and why we often *don't* think about, learn, and remember them. I'm hoping, too, that you'll be able to apply your new knowledge both in your own future learning activities and also in your efforts to help others learn effectively – whether such efforts be in a role as parent, teacher, workplace supervisor, journalist, website designer, or general member of our society and culture.

WHAT WE USUALLY *DON'T* AND *CAN'T* DO WHEN WE THINK AND LEARN

In my own experiences as a psychologist, teacher, parent, friend, consultant, and citizen, I've found that many people have significant misconceptions about what our minds can do for us. I'll be presenting common misconceptions throughout the book – 28 of them altogether – and again in the Appendix that immediately follows Chapter 10. For now, I want to alert you to three especially pervasive ones.

Misconception #1: That our minds mentally record every piece of information we encounter

Many people mistakenly believe that somehow we absorb and mentally "keep" everything we see and hear. But as you'll see in upcoming chapters, and especially in Chapter 4, we really don't have the hardware and software to save every tidbit that comes our way. Much as we might like them to be, our minds aren't video cameras or audio recorders. Ultimately, we probably capture only a tiny fraction of the environmental stimuli that bombard us at every waking moment.

Misconception #2: That our minds record information exactly as we receive it

Quite the opposite is true. Right from the get-go, we humans mentally *do* something with much of the information we get: Our minds change and condense it in ways that enable us to remember it more effectively. Thus, we should never assume that our recollections of information and events are accurate ones. Nor should we assume that other people's recollections are accurate, no matter how confidently and self-assuredly those individuals describe the "facts" of the matter.

Misconception #3: That occasional forgetfulness is a sign that something is wrong with our mental hardware

No, not at all. Some absent-mindedness is perfectly normal in people of all ages. Usually the problem isn't one of forgetting something altogether, but rather of failing to remember it *when we need it* – for example, completely forgetting about errands we've wanted to complete or appointments we've made for later in the day.

Chronic forgetfulness can sometimes indicate significant mental impairment or decline. But especially if we lead complicated lives with many distractions, virtually all of us occasionally forget something we've really wanted to remember. I'll talk more about this problem, including strategies for addressing it, in Chapter 6.

WHAT WE TYPICALLY *DO* DO WHEN WE THINK AND LEARN

Over our long history of evolving to become the species *homo sapiens*, we have ingeniously adapted to the limitations of our biology-based mental equipment. Two general principles characterize key strategies we use to make the most of our experiences. First, *we summarize and try to organize the information we obtain from our environment.* We seem to be predisposed to find patterns and consistencies in what we observe. This inclination toward identifying regularities in our world appears quite early in life, and it's undoubtedly a central reason why we acquire language as quickly and easily as we do.[4]

To see this summarizing/organizing principle in action, look at Figure 1.1. I doubt very much that you see only black marks scattered randomly about. Instead, you probably see several rows of circles, and you probably also see the larger circles forming two diagonal lines that crisscross each other in the middle. Perceiving all of these things – the circles, the rows, the diagonal lines, and the crisscross – reflects your own mental efforts to organize what you're looking at.

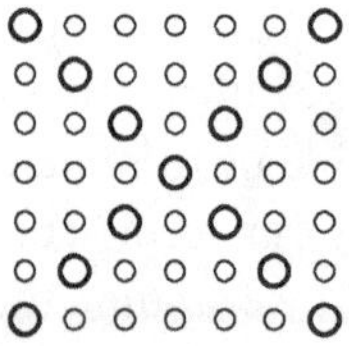

FIGURE 1.1. What do you see here?

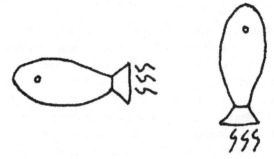

FIGURE 1.2. Here are two views of the same object. What might this object be?

I'm guessing that, in addition, you see the letter *X* in Figure 1.1, which illustrates a second general principle: *We try to impose meaning on the information we obtain.* As a rule, we humans seem determined to make some sort of sense of our experiences. At our very core, we are meaning makers. To see what I mean, look at Figure 1.2, which shows the same object in two orientations, one being a 90-degree rotation of the other. What is this object? Give it a label of some sort.

If you focus your attention on the left-hand version of the object, you might think that it's a fish or submarine going through water. If, instead, you look more closely at the right-hand version, you might perhaps think that it's a rocket ship launching into space. In each of these cases, you might interpret the three squiggly lines as indicating some sort of *movement* of the object. Alternatively, you might think of the squiggly lines in the right-hand version as reflecting the movement of *air* – perhaps as a vacuum cleaner sucks up dirt from a carpet. The object isn't necessarily a fish, submarine, rocket, or vacuum cleaner, of course; it could be something else altogether, or it could be just a collection of black marks that have no meaning whatsoever.

Sometimes most of us can agree on the meanings we attach to certain objects or events. For example, if we see objects of a particular shape moving in a particular way in a lake or river, we might all agree that those objects are "fish." And we'd probably all agree that we're looking at a "vacuum cleaner" if the object makes an irritating noise and if a person is moving it slowly and systematically across a carpet.

On other occasions, we might have trouble reaching consensus about what something means. For instance, people's body language can be notoriously ambiguous and hard to interpret with certainty. What does it mean when a person *smiles* at you? Is the person simply feeling happy? offering a gesture of friendship? feeling smug about winning a highly competitive event? trying to manipulate you in some way? It could be any of these things.

EMPIRICAL AND THEORETICAL BASES FOR THE BOOK

As I continue to talk about human cognition and learning in the pages ahead, I'll be basing my statements on research findings in psychology, neuroscience, and such related fields as neuropsychology and the learning sciences. (These fields overlap considerably, with various theorists often disagreeing about where one field ends and another begins.) Although I'll occasionally be able to describe specific processes that occur in the brain, for the most part I'll be relying on studies of observable, measureable human behaviors. Such is the nature of psychological inquiry: to observe what people *do* and then draw reasonable inferences about how people *think*.

If you have some background in psychology, you may notice that I don't cite my sources in parentheses within the text. Thus, I don't use the writing style that the American Psychological Association (APA) recommends. Instead, I cite my sources in "Endnotes" sections at the end of each chapter. My reasoning for this departure from APA format is simple: Lists of many names and dates within a paragraph can be quite a distraction for readers whose primary goal is to *understand* what I'm saying. By all means, please make use of the sources I cite in the endnotes to learn more about particular points I make in the book.

DEFINING BASIC TERMS

Before we go any further, you and I need to be on the same page regarding the meanings of certain words. Following are a few terms that are central to the entire book.

First, consider the title of this first chapter: "The General Nature of Human Cognition and Learning." Psychologists often use the term **cognition** to encompass all the internal mental processes that occur in our heads as we go through our daily lives. Many psychologists also make an implicit distinction between *brain* and *mind*. The **brain**, of course, is our basic thinking hardware; it provides the neurological underpinnings for everything we do mentally. By the term **mind**, psychologists are often referring to *psychological* phenomena either in addition to or instead of *physiological* phenomena. For example, the concept of mind encompasses the many memories we experience, the many mental strategies we use to help us learn and remember things more effectively, and our general awareness of ourselves as thinking, remembering, and forgetting individuals.

Is the mind nothing more than a collection of brain-based processes – that is, are mind and brain one and the same – or do our minds also involve processes that in some way transcend our physical brains? And what about our general awareness of ourselves as thinkers – that is, our consciousness? Such existential questions are likely to remain unresolved for the foreseeable future.[5] Thus, I'll largely ignore them in this book, although I'll touch briefly on the concept of consciousness in Chapter 4.

Two other key concepts are *learning* and *memory*. For purposes of this book, the word **learning** refers to a long-term change in mental representations or associations as a result of experience. Three parts of this definition are important to note. First, learning involves a *long-term change*: It has an impact for quite a while, although not necessarily forever. Second, learning involves a change in *mental representations or associations*; in other words, it's an internal, mind- or brain-based phenomenon.[6] And third, learning is a *result of experience*; it isn't a change due to, say, mood swings, fatigue, mind-altering substances, or the onset of mental illness.

Meanwhile, the word **memory** can be used in either of two ways. In some instances it refers to a general ability to retain information or skills over a lengthy period. In other cases it refers to a specific "location" where ideas and skills are saved – for example, in "working memory" or "long-term memory." Keep in mind, however, that these supposed "locations" aren't really discrete parts of our brains; rather, they're psychologists' labels for different components of our complex memory system (more about this point as well in Chapter 4).

BEING STRATEGIC

Our brains don't come with owners' manuals. And without such manuals, most of us tend to be quite naive and ill-informed in our approaches to new learning and teaching situations. The next two misconceptions illustrate the problem:

> Misconception #4: That we intuitively know how we can best learn and remember something new

> Misconception #5: That we intuitively know how we can most effectively teach other people new knowledge and skills

Sadly, many people of all ages think that the best way to learn a new fact is simply to repeat it over and over. And some teachers seem to emphasize drill-and-practice exercises in their instructional methods. As you'll see in the discussion of automaticity in Chapter 5, repetition and drill-and-practice do have their place, but as a general rule they're *not* terribly effective ways to either learn or teach new knowledge and skills.

By and large, effective learning and effective teaching require conscious, intentional, planful *strategies*. Sometimes we develop such strategies on our own, but we typically do so only after we've undergone a fair amount of trial and error with relatively mindless approaches. Fortunately, with appropriate guidance and support from others, we can acquire many good strategies, the result being that we become far more successful and efficient learners and teachers. In other words, we can greatly enhance our own and others' brainpower.

Consistent with my optimism about what we *can* do if we use the right strategies, each chapter in this book has a "Being Strategic" section that includes both (a) self-strategies for enhancing thinking and learning in your own everyday life and (b) formal and informal instructional strategies for enhancing thinking and learning in other people. Those other people might be students (if you're a teacher), employees (if you're a boss or supervisor), or readers of your work (if you're a writer or Internet blogger). I'll often use the word *students* in my instructional strategies, but I urge you to interpret the word quite loosely to encompass virtually anyone who might benefit from your guidance and support.

At this point in the book, we haven't yet delved into the nitty-gritties of human cognition. Even so, we can derive a few implications from the ideas and principles we've discussed so far.

Enhancing Your Own Thinking and Learning in Everyday Life

- **Self-Strategy 1.1: Be realistic about how much you can learn and remember in any given time period**. You will never remember everything you see and hear. Don't even try. However, you might find some comfort in the fact that if you become a more strategic learner, you can enhance your memory quite a bit.
- **Self-Strategy 1.2: Focus on making reasonable sense of various information and events you encounter**. Remember, we humans are predisposed to find meanings in the things we see and hear. For the most part, your meaning-making tendencies will work to your advantage, although they'll sometimes lead you astray – a problem I'll discuss in greater depth in Chapters 3 and 8.
- **Self-Strategy 1.3: Look for patterns in what you observe**. On average, organizing what you see and hear can help you remember it better. There's an important caveat here: To the extent that you organize it incorrectly – perhaps by lumping two or more very different entities into a single category that doesn't accurately represent them, or perhaps by identifying a cause-and-effect relationship that doesn't really exist – your understanding of a situation might be way off the mark. Chapter 8 will address this problem as well.
- **Self-Strategy 1.4: Never trust your memory to be a complete, accurate record of your experiences**. No matter how convinced you are that you saw an event unfold in a particular way or that you heard somebody make a particular statement, your memory might not be a good representation of what actually happened. If you want to remember something accurately, it's best to rely on an external record of the event – say, by taking notes in a lecture class or making a video or audio recording of an important interview or other conversation.

Enhancing Other People's Thinking and Learning
in Instructional Settings

- **Instructional Strategy 1.1: Help people find productive meanings in what they see and hear**. Especially when people are novices in a particular activity or subject area, they don't always know how to make reasonable sense of what they're observing. One way to help them make better sense is to draw their attention to noteworthy aspects of a situation. For example, if you're using a map of Europe to teach high school students about Napoleon Bonaparte's rise to power in the late 1700s and early 1800s, you might point out how controlling certain rivers, ports, and other locations on the map were critical for Napoleon's conquests. And if you're coaching a soccer team (this would be a "football" team if you were anywhere other than in the United States or Canada), you might draw team members' attention to the footwork techniques that professional players use to keep the ball away from their opponents. Another way to help people in their sense making is to attach meaningful labels to what they're observing – for instance, by explaining how people's experiences on some amusement-park rides illustrate *centrifugal force* or by identifying various trees on a nature walk as being either *deciduous* or *evergreen*.

- **Instructional Strategy 1.2: Provide one or more organizational structures to help people make sense of new information and synthesize it into larger, more integrated understandings**. For example, if you were to introduce a visitor to a large city you know well, you might (in New York) provide a simple map of key subway lines in downtown Manhattan or (in Boston) explain how streets in one popular part of the city are labeled alphabetically from east to west – first Arlington and then Berkeley, Clarendon, and so on up to Hereford. And as a 60-something woman who has been at the receiving end of piano lessons this year, I've been quite grateful for the many times my teacher has pointed out certain repetitive patterns in what have initially struck me as arbitrary series of notes on the page.

- **Instructional Strategy 1.3: Foster meaning making not only in how you teach others but also in how you assess their final knowledge and achievements**. If you currently teach or plan to teach in a formal educational setting, you should keep in mind that students are apt to focus their efforts on mastering the things they expect you to test them on. For example, if you tell students that you want them to *understand* a topic but then give them a hastily constructed exam that requires word-for-word recall of specific, unrelated facts, they'll quickly figure out that they can get the best grades if they devote their studying efforts more to rote memorization than to genuine meaning making. You must think of any quizzes, exams, and other assessment methods you use as being *integral parts* of your instruction – not as separate, unrelated activities – because they'll give students clear messages about what things are most important for them to learn and remember.

NOTES

1. Aplin et al., 2015; Datta, 1962; de Waal, 2016; Heyes & Galef, 1996; Samarova et al., 2005.
2. Some research has detected primitive forms of a "culture" in certain other species as well (e.g., see Aplin et al., 2015; Boesch, 2012), but nothing that approaches the sophistication of human cultures.
3. For examples of self-reflection in other animals, see Foote & Crystal, 2007; Kornell, 2009.
4. Chomsky, 2006; Dewar & Xu, 2010; Mandler, 2007; Quinn, 2007.
5. For varying perspectives, see Dehaene, 2007; Fernández-Espejo et al., 2011; Kaku, 2014; G. A. Miller, 2010; Paller, Voss, & Westerberg, 2009; Siegel, 2012.
6. If you have a background in psychology, you might realize that this part of the definition conflicts with traditional behaviorists' view of learning, which involves a change in observable behavior rather than a change in a mental entity.

2

The Human Brain: The Hardware of Our Thinking and Learning

The human brain is such an incredibly complex organ that researchers have only begun to get a handle on the intricacies of its structures and functioning. For a long time, much of what researchers knew about the brain came either from animal research or from observations and (sometimes) postmortem autopsies of people who had sustained brain injuries, undergone neurosurgical procedures, or had other brain abnormalities. Fortunately, recent advancements in technology now enable neuroscientists to examine brain structures and functioning of presumably normal human beings in varying circumstances. One technique is to place electrodes at strategic locations on a person's scalp and record patterns of the brain's electrical activity. The result is an *electroencephalogram (EEG)* record that can reveal different patterns of brain waves for different activities (e.g., for sleep versus wakefulness). Researchers have also been using *neuroimaging* technologies to take pictures of blood flow or metabolism rates in various parts of the brain as people do certain things; examples are positron emission tomography (PET), computerized axial tomography (CAT), magnetic resonance imaging (MRI), and functional magnetic resonance imaging (fMRI). And as neuroscientists have increasingly recognized that two or more parts of the brain often work *together* even in the simplest of everyday activities, they have begun to use functional connectivity MRI (fcMRI), a technique that enables them to determine which brain regions consistently work together in one task or another.

You and I will draw on all of these sources of information as we explore the human brain in this chapter. We'll start with the brain's most basic components – its countless tiny cells and their many, many, *many* interconnections. We'll then look at larger structures within the brain and at the developmental changes that the brain undergoes across a typical lifespan. Finally, we'll get strategic, using what we've learned about the brain to identify ways of enhancing brainpower in both ourselves and others.

BASIC BUILDING BLOCKS OF THE BRAIN: GRAY MATTER
AND WHITE MATTER BOTH *MATTER*

A typical human brain is made up of a mind-boggling number of cells –
several *trillion* of them. Using numerical symbols, one trillion means
1,000,000,000,000 cells, so now multiply that number by 3 or 4 or 5.
Perhaps 100 billion of these cells (100,000,000,000) are brownish-grayish
neurons that are collectively known as *gray matter*. Accompanying neurons are a few trillion whitish-colored glial cells, which are known as *white
matter*.

Neurons and Their Interconnections

Neurons – which in everyday speech we sometimes refer to as *nerve cells* –
are cells that specialize in receiving and transmitting messages. Neurons
are located all over the body, including in the skin, eyes, ears, tongue, and
internal organs (e.g., lungs, stomach, and intestines). However, most of
them are located either partly or entirely in the central nervous system –
that is, in the brain, spinal cord, or both.

All neurons have several features in common (see Figure 2.1). First, each
neuron has a cell body that contains the cell's *nucleus*, which holds the cell's
DNA and other genetic material. Every neuron also has a number of
branch-like structures, or *dendrites*, that receive messages from other
neurons. And an especially prominent feature of any neuron is its *axon*,
a long, armlike extension that sends messages along to still other neurons,
some of which might be close by and others of which might be a fair
distance away. As illustrated in Figure 2.1, the axons of many neurons have
a white, fatty coating known as a *myelin sheath*; this sheath is typically
broken up into a series of separate little "jackets."

When a neuron's dendrites are stimulated either by a sensory organ or
(more often) by one or more *other* neurons, the dendrites acquire an
electrical charge. Once the total charge has reached a certain level, the
neuron "fires," sending an electrical impulse along its axon. If the axon has
a myelin sheath, the impulse zips along quite rapidly because it essentially
leaps from one gap in the myelin to the next; axons without any myelin are
much pokier. In either event, the charge eventually reaches the *terminal
buttons* at the axon's far end, which then, in turn, transmit the message
along to one or more other neurons. In Figure 2.1, the direction of message
transmission is shown by the curvy arrow at the bottom – in this case, from
left to right.

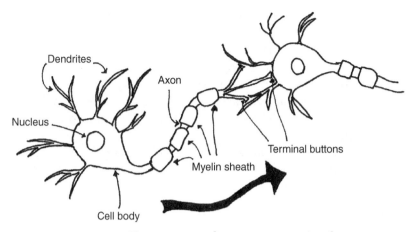

FIGURE 2.1. Two neurons and a synapse connecting them

Although neurons regularly communicate with one another, it may surprise you to learn that they don't actually touch one another, nor do they send their messages electrically. Instead, they communicate *chemically* across tiny gaps, or **synapses**. More specifically, when an electrical impulse reaches an axon's terminal buttons, it triggers the release of certain substances known as **neurotransmitters**; examples of such substances are dopamine (which influences our ability to experience pleasure), epinephrine (which causes increases in heart rate and blood pressure), and serotonin (which can impact mood or sleep). Those neurotransmitters stimulate the dendrites of one or more subsequent neurons in the pipeline, which in turn react electrically.

Especially in the brain, a neuron is apt to have synaptic connections with hundreds – perhaps thousands – of other neurons.[1] Some neurotransmitters increase another neuron's electrical charge, whereas others reduce its charge. Whether a particular neuron ultimately fires, then, is the result of how much its many neighbors either "encourage" or "discourage" it.

Like muscles, synapses need regular exercise to keep them in good working order. The more often that Neuron A activates Neuron B, the stronger the synapse between them becomes. And if, for whatever reason, Neuron A no longer has any occasion to stimulate Neuron B, their synaptic connection weakens and may eventually disappear. The maxim "Use it or lose it" definitely applies here.

Much of our learning probably involves changes in the interconnections among neurons – more specifically, in the formation of new synapses or in the strengthening, weakening, or disappearance of existing ones.[2] We don't necessarily need to mourn those lost synapses. Sometimes our brains behave in ways that aren't in our best interests. For example, such would be the case if we mistakenly keep calling a new neighbor Maria when her name is actually Marjorie, if we keep misspelling the word *separate* as "seperate," or if we blurt out offensive four-letter words every time we get frustrated in a professional setting. Some synapses really do need to be tossed in the trash.

Changes in synapses don't explain all of our learning, however. Changes in the neurons themselves also come into play, which brings us to another common misconception:

Misconception #6: That we are born with virtually all the neurons we will ever have

A few decades ago, it was widely believed that we acquire all of our neurons – all the ones we will ever have – within the first few weeks of our prenatal lives. But in the meantime, some researchers have discovered that, quite the contrary, we continue to form new neurons throughout our lifespan – a process called **neurogenesis**. New learning experiences nurture these young neurons and encourage them to survive and thrive; otherwise, they may slowly die away.[3]

Some neurons seem to have a particular subspecialty in helping us learn. These **mirror neurons** fire either when (a) their owners perform a particular action themselves or (b) their owners see *someone else* perform the action.[4] It appears, then, that our brains might be prewired to make connections between what we see and what we do, thereby enhancing our ability to learn new skills from our fellow human beings.

Yet there's even more to learning than changes in synapses and neurons, as you'll see now.

Glial Cells and Their Roles in Brain Functioning

The vast majority of cells in our brains are whitish-colored **glial cells** – also known as *neuroglia* or simply *glia* – that surround and protect our neurons. Glial cells seem to serve several essential functions. Some of them control blood flow to the neurons, others are garbage collectors for unwanted debris, and still others work to fight infections or repair injuries. And remember those myelin sheaths that many axons have? We have glial cells to thank for them.

Recently some researchers have found evidence that certain star-shaped glial cells known as **astrocytes** are just as important as neurons in learning and memory. For us humans, astrocytes outnumber neurons by a ratio of at least 10 to 1, a ratio much larger than that for laboratory animals. Astrocytes are chemically interconnected with many of their neighbors and also with nearby neurons; here I'm talking about an even more mind-boggling – truly countless – number of interconnections. Our brains typically create many new astrocytes throughout our lives, and they appear to be quite influential regarding what neurons do and don't do and how much they communicate with one another.[5]

The Process of Consolidation: Learning and Memories Need Time to Firm Up

The neurological underpinnings of new memories usually need some time to stabilize enough that they can endure over the long run. This **consolidation** process occurs in at least two distinct phases, each of which involves a different subprocess. In the first phase, *synaptic consolidation*, relevant neurons increase their ability to transmit and receive the chemical substances (neurotransmitters) that make cross-neuron communication possible. In the second phase, *systems consolidation*, neural networks are gradually reorganized in such a way that they eventually take on a broader and more permanent quality. Synaptic consolidation typically takes a few minutes or hours, whereas systems reconsolidation is apt to continue for weeks, months, or even longer.[6] Although neuroscientists haven't pinned down the precise nature of these consolidation processes, one or both of them may possibly involve some sort of low-level, unconscious repetition of relevant connections. When the process is interrupted – as can happen when people temporarily lose consciousness as the result of a serious head trauma – events that have recently occurred can essentially disappear from memory.[7]

LARGE STRUCTURES OF THE BRAIN: THE WHOLE IS MORE THAN THE SUM OF ITS PARTS

Despite their sophisticated capabilities, our 21st-century brains are rather clunky contraptions that reflect many millennia of evolution and adaptation to life's daily challenges. Some brain structures emerged quite early in our evolutionary journey, with others appearing later and piggybacking on their predecessors in ways that no reasonable

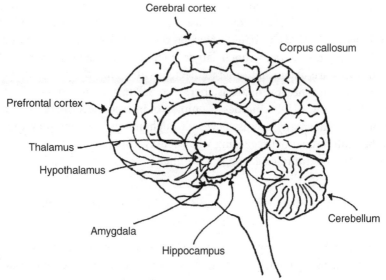

FIGURE 2.2. Vertical cross-section of a typical human brain

human or super-human being would have ever engineered in advance.[8] Remember, the evolution of any species involves unpredictable genetic mutations, considerable trial and error, and the building of one better-than-before-but-not-necessarily-ideal change on top of another.[9] Yet somehow our brains work pretty well for us most of the time.

Figure 2.2 presents a vertical cross-section of the brain that illustrates some of its key structures. The oldest and most primitive part of the brain – yet also the most critical one for our survival – is the *hindbrain*, located in the lower back when the spinal cord enters the skull. Its subparts are responsible for basic activities that keep us alive, including breathing, sleeping, swallowing, and regulating our beating hearts. One especially noteworthy subpart is the **cerebellum**, which helps to coordinate our sensory input with our motoric output – that is, with such behaviors as walking, riding a bicycle, and swinging a baseball bat.

Next to come along in our evolutionary travels was the *midbrain*, a relatively small area located slightly above and to the front of the hindbrain. One of its subparts regulates our sleep and wakefulness and alerts us to new and potentially important or threatening events in our immediate environment. Other parts support our vision and hearing, for instance by controlling and coordinating our eye movements.

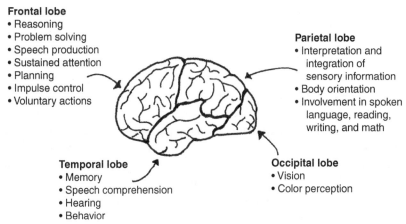

Frontal lobe
- Reasoning
- Problem solving
- Speech production
- Sustained attention
- Planning
- Impulse control
- Voluntary actions

Parietal lobe
- Interpretation and integration of sensory information
- Body orientation
- Involvement in spoken language, reading, writing, and math

Temporal lobe
- Memory
- Speech comprehension
- Hearing
- Behavior

Occipital lobe
- Vision
- Color perception

FIGURE 2.3. The four lobes of the cerebral cortex

The newest and biggest part of the brain, the *forebrain*, rests on top of and surrounds much of the hindbrain and midbrain. Its most prominent subpart is the **cerebral cortex**, which looks like a thick, lumpy toupee. The cortex is largely – although not entirely – divided into two *hemispheres*, one on the brain's left side and the other on its right side. Each hemisphere has four distinct lobes that specialize in somewhat different functions, as illustrated in Figure 2.3. The two hemispheres are connected by the **corpus callosum**, a large bundle of more than two million axons that regularly transmit messages back and forth across the divide.

Although the various lobes of the cerebral cortex constantly communicate with one another, the left and right frontal lobes seem to house much of our conscious thinking – that is, our general awareness of ourselves and of the outside world. The frontal lobes are largely responsible for our sense-making capabilities, speech, logical reasoning, problem solving, and general ability to keep our mental attention focused on whatever it is we need to accomplish. The frontal lobes are also primarily responsible for our ability to inhibit irrelevant and counterproductive thoughts, control impulses, and productively plan future actions. At the very front of the frontal lobes, right behind the forehead, is the **prefrontal cortex (PFC)**, which seems to be "command central" in our conscious, controlled, planful thought processes.

Other structures in the forebrain, all lying nestled in the middle of the brain under the cortex, are key players as well. Intricately connected to the cortex is the *limbic system*, a cluster of structures that are actively involved in learning, memory, emotions, and motivation. One structure is the

hippocampus,[10] which plays central roles in attention and learning, especially for things that we consciously study and try to remember. A good deal of that neurogenesis I mentioned earlier – the formation of new neurons – takes place in the hippocampus.[11] Close by is the **amygdala**, which is at the heart of such unpleasant emotions as fear, stress, and anger and can trigger certain physiological reactions (e.g., increases in heart and breathing rates) and fight-or-flight behaviors (e.g., aggression or running away). The amygdala also helps us connect our experiences with our emotional reactions to them – for example, by helping us learn and remember not only that an icy patch on the sidewalk can make us slip and fall but also that we really *don't like* slipping and falling on ice. Although Figure 2.3 shows only one hippocampus and one amygdala, we actually have two of them, one on each side of the brain.

Two other limbic-system structures are worth mentioning here as well. The **thalamus** integrates the messages it receives from various sensory neurons and passes the results along to relevant parts of the cortex; it also alerts the amygdala to potentially threatening situations. Located right below the thalamus, the **hypothalamus** is responsible for producing the kinds of hormones that regulate basic physiological functions, including hunger, thirst, sleep, body temperature, and general body metabolism.

You may have noticed some redundancy in the preceding descriptions of various brain structures. For example, the hindbrain, amygdala, and hypothalamus are all involved in regulating the basic physiological activities that enable us to survive. And the midbrain, cortex, amygdala, and thalamus all play key roles in triggering and sustaining our attention to critical environmental events. To some degree, these apparent duplications of effort might be the result of the haphazard one-thing-building-on-another process that is evolution.[12] But mostly the various structures of the brain work in a complementary, collaborative manner to help us maximize our chances of survival and success.

The Left and Right Hemispheres: Inseparable Partners in Whole-Brain Thinking

In your readings of books, magazine articles, or Internet posts written by self-proclaimed experts, you've probably seen discussions of "left-brain thinking," "right-brain thinking," or "teaching to the left [or right] brain." Sadly, the "experts" who write such things are spreading an especially preposterous misconception:

Misconception #7: That the brain's left and right hemispheres have very different functions and can be independently trained and nurtured

Researchers have indeed found some differences in what the left and right hemispheres do. Contrary to what might seem logical, the left hemisphere controls the right side of the body, whereas the right hemisphere controls the left side. In addition, the two hemispheres seem to specialize a bit in different aspects of human cognition. For most people, the left hemisphere is in charge of language skills, including speech production, comprehension of spoken language, and reading. And in general, the left hemisphere is the more analytical and detail-oriented of the two; for instance, it tends to dominate in mathematical calculation skills and in analyzing music.[13] Meanwhile, the right hemisphere takes the lead role in processing visual and spatial information – for instance, in perceiving objects within their overall spatial contexts, conjuring up mental images, estimating quantities, and interpreting people's facial expressions, gestures, and other nonverbal body language. The right side is also much better than the left side at synthesizing information into multifaceted, meaningful wholes. In other words, the right hemisphere is better at seeing the big picture – it's more likely to see the overall forest in situations in which the left hemisphere is being distracted by some of the trees.

Yet thanks to the corpus callosum that connects them, the two hemispheres of the brain constantly collaborate in even the simplest of daily activities. Let's take language comprehension as an example. Although the left hemisphere might handle the nitty-gritty details of syntax and word interpretation, it tends to take what it hears and reads quite literally. The right hemisphere is better able to put the words in their larger contexts – for instance, to interpret metaphors, detect sarcasm, and find multiple possible meanings in words.[14] To see what I mean, try to make logical sense of the following three sentences *in combination*:

> Time flies.
> I can't.
> They go too fast.

These three sentences go together only if you think of the first sentence as a *command* rather than as a common expression regarding how quickly time can whizz by. Get it? If you're still puzzled, then imagine that I'm a biologist conducting lab research with fruit flies. You're my research assistant, and I want you to measure how quickly the little critters are zipping around in their container. The first sentence is what I ask you to do – to time my flies – and the second and third sentences comprise your frustrated response. Your right hemisphere enables you to think outside the box about what "Time flies" might mean in this situation.

So, can you think only with your left brain? Can you train yourself to be a predominately right-brain thinker? Nope, not a chance. Except in cases of serious brain injury or neurosurgical procedures that disconnect the two hemispheres (often to control debilitating epileptic seizures), there's really no such thing as "left-brain" or "right-brain" thinking.

Just one more point about the relative abilities of the left and right hemispheres: They don't apply to all of us. Only about 80% of us divvy up our cognitive abilities in the ways I've just described. For example, although the left hemisphere plays the dominant role in language for more than 90% of right-handed people, it does so for only about 60% of left-handed people. We also differ in how "lopsided" our thinking is: Some of us regularly think in a fairly balanced, two-sided manner.[15] And if for some reason a very young child loses the use of most or all of one hemisphere, the other hemisphere will sometimes take over many of its functions.[16]

Human Cognition as a Distributed Process: Nothing Happens in a Single Spot

Remember those 100 billion (100,000,000,000) neurons that are in the human brain. And remember that each neuron might have hundreds or thousands of synaptic connections with other neurons. All these synapses – we're talking about numbers in the trillions or quadrillions here – make the brain an inconceivably complex and interactive mechanism. Messages go every which way. Some go from "lower down" in the system (i.e., from places where sensory information first reaches the brain) to "higher up" (i.e., to areas that synthesize and interpret information or to areas that choose and control behavioral responses). Others go in the opposite direction, from "top" to "bottom" – for example, from interpretive areas that say, "Hey, there's a problem out there, and we need more information about it" to areas that redirect our attention to additional environmental input. And still other messages go to and fro among diverse areas that can collaboratively contribute to our sense-making efforts.

Related to the preceding paragraph is a misconception that I've occasionally encountered when talking with my own students:

Misconception #8: That each tiny bit of knowledge is located in a particular spot in the brain

Again no, not true. The process of learning or thinking about virtually any tiny thing in our lives – even a single word – is distributed across many parts of the brain.[17] As an example, take the word *horse*. That simple word probably involves brain regions related not only to how the word sounds, how it's pronounced, and how it's spelled, but also to what you've observed and can remember about the word's concrete equivalents – actual horses.

And here's another misconception that I must emphatically refute:

Misconception #9: That most of us don't use more than 10% of our brain capacity

Oh, for Pete's sake. I mean, *really*??!! I can't recall where this idea originally came from – from some self-proclaimed "brain expert," no doubt – but it's completely bogus. Think about it: The human brain has several trillion cells that are interconnected in more ways than we can count. How could anyone possibly calculate a "percentage" of what's being used? Besides, as we've seen, unused neurons and synapses (and presumably also glial cells) gradually wither away. It's inconceivable that 90% of anyone's brain is just sitting there idly with nothing to do.

DEVELOPMENT OF THE BRAIN: ALWAYS A WORK IN PROGRESS

Not only are the numbers of neurons, glial cells, and interconnections in the human brain far beyond our comprehension, but so, too, are the genetically driven processes through which this marvelous organ develops. Given the infinite ways in which the development of the brain might possibly go wrong, it's amazing that it usually goes *right*. There are exceptions, to be sure, but for the most part, our brains work quite well for us.

The human brain begins its development soon after conception, but it also continues to develop for many years after birth. In fact, it doesn't really stop changing until we die.

How It All Starts: The Prenatal Period

About 25 days after conception, the brain emerges as a tiny tube that quickly grows longer and starts to fold and divide into its major parts. Many neurons and glial cells rapidly sprout up within this tube. For example, approximately 50,000 to 100,000 new neurons form *per second* between the 5th and 20th weeks of prenatal development.[18]

In the second trimester, those many neurons and glial cells migrate to various locations in what now has a roughly brain-like shape. When the neurons arrive at their final destinations, they reach out to one another with their dendrites and axons in an effort to make synaptic connections, with the glial cells supporting them in their efforts. Those neurons that make productive contacts begin to organize themselves and take on particular functions. Those that don't – maybe half of them – gradually wither away. These latter neurons are pretty useless, actually, and they'd be a nuisance if we kept them.[19]

In the third trimester, the brain becomes capable of learning and remembering a few things about its world.[20] For example, in one research study,[21] pregnant women read aloud an excerpt from a children's book (e.g., Dr. Seuss's children's book *The Cat in the Hat*) twice a day for the last six weeks of their pregnancies. Then, at some point within the first few days after birth, the babies were given pacifiers, and their sucking rates (either fast or slow) controlled whether they heard a recording of their mother reading the prebirth story or, instead, a different story. Even though the infants were only two or three days old, they began to adjust their sucking rate so that they could hear the familiar story – the one they'd previously heard only in the womb!

How It Continues after Birth: Infancy and the
Early Childhood Years

With the birth of a full-term infant comes a virtual explosion of new astrocytes, followed soon thereafter by the rapid formation of many new synapses.[22] Thanks to this process of genetically driven synapse creation – **synaptogenesis** – young children have many more synapses than adults do. Eventually, the proliferation of synapses slows down and comes to a halt, with the slowdown occurring at varying times for different areas of the brain. For example, synapses reach their peak in some areas of the cerebral cortex within the first year, but they continue to increase in the prefrontal cortex well into the second and third years of life.[23]

As children experience new and recurring events in their daily lives, some of their synapses come in quite handy and are used repeatedly. Those that aren't terribly relevant or helpful gradually fade away in a process known as **synaptic pruning**. In some areas of the brain, much of this pruning occurs fairly early – for instance, in the preschool or early elementary years. In other areas, it begins later and continues until well into adolescence.[24] Unfortunately, widespread knowledge of this developmental phenomenon has spawned yet another misconception:

> Misconception #10: That parents, teachers, and other adults need to do everything they can to minimize the loss of synapses in young children

This misconception has been translated into many efforts to inundate babies, toddlers, and preschoolers with as much stimulation as possible. Parents enroll their young children in intensive academically oriented daycare programs, sign them up for weekly violin lessons, and engage them in computer games that give them practice in eye–hand coordination, focusing attention, and basic reading and counting skills. In moderation, such interventions can be beneficial.[25] But parents' attempts to make their offspring as intelligent as possible sometimes get pretty ridiculous. And please don't fall for all those ads declaring that certain software or Internet-based programs can "train the brain" and significantly "enhance IQ," possibly turning a typical young child into a "genius." There's very little evidence to back up their claims.[26]

As I said earlier, not all synapses are useful ones – some can actually be counterproductive. What Mother Nature seems to have done here is to program us to create many more synapses than we'll ever need; she then lets us discover on our own (a) which ones can best help us adapt to the particular circumstances we find in our physical and social environments and (b) which ones we should toss aside. Synaptic pruning, then, may be Mother Nature's way of enhancing our brains' efficiency and effectiveness.[27]

A third genetically preprogrammed process – **myelination** – contributes to the brain's efficiency as well. As previously noted, many neurons have axons coated with myelin, which enables messages to travel along the axons as much as 100 times faster than they would otherwise.[28] Some myelination takes place near the end of the prenatal period (especially in areas related to basic survival skills), but a good deal of it occurs in the first few years after birth. This proportional increase in myelin (i.e., white matter) in early childhood probably underlies much of the improvement in our cognitive functioning in the early years.[29]

How It Gradually Matures: Middle Childhood, Adolescence, and Early Adulthood

Following is one final misconception about the human brain, this one relevant to its development:

Misconception #11: That the brain reaches full maturity within the first few years of life

Once again, *no!* Synaptic pruning continues into middle childhood and adolescence, especially in the cortex, and myelination continues at least into the middle twenties. Especially noteworthy is the fact that the prefrontal cortex – that part of the brain that is most centrally involved in our abilities to maintain attention for lengthy periods, plan ahead, and control impulses – undergoes a good deal of synaptic pruning and myelination in adolescence and early adulthood.[30]

In other respects, too, the adolescent brain is definitely *not* an adult brain. The onset of puberty brings changes in hormone levels, in certain neurotransmitters, and in dendrites that receive those neurotransmitters. All of these changes can adversely affect brain functioning, at least for a few years.[31] Also accompanying puberty are significant changes in areas of the brain that crave pleasure and heighten a teenager's desire to engage in enjoyable activities – perhaps drinking alcohol, taking dangerous drugs, driving at high speeds, or having unprotected sexual intercourse.[32] Not until the late teens or early twenties does the prefrontal cortex kick in to counterbalance such pleasure seeking with more rational decision making and self-restraint.[33]

The adolescent brain is often more interested in seeking immediate gratification than in working toward long-term goals.

The Brain's Plasticity: For Many Ideas and Skills, It's Never Too Late

Unless we have Alzheimer's disease or another seriously debilitating neurological condition, our brains can continue to learn and remember new ideas and skills throughout our lives. In the lingo of psychologists and neuroscientists, our brains maintain their **plasticity**. For example, we form new astrocytes well into old age, and – especially when we learn new things – those astrocytes might divide to create even more astrocytes. Furthermore, if we tackle new tasks in our adult years – say, juggling or driving a taxi – we might even restructure our brains in ways that neuroscientists can document.[34]

Certainly we do slow down a bit as we get older. Those myelin sheaths on our axons can start to wear thin as early as our 30s. And in our later adult years, the prefrontal cortex isn't as effective as it previously was in coordinating and controlling our thoughts and actions. As a result of such changes, our reaction times tend to increase, and we acquire new information and skills at somewhat slower rates.[35] Even so, old dogs can definitely learn new tricks.

BEING STRATEGIC

The human brain is possibly Mother Nature's most sophisticated creation, but it needs regular maintenance to keep it in good working order. Following are a few recommendations for keeping it in tip-top shape.

Enhancing Your Own Thinking and Learning in Everyday Life

- **Self-Strategy 2.1: Continually seek out new intellectual challenges.** Whether you're 8 or 80, you should give your brain regular exercise. Venturing into new mental territories can be especially beneficial – for example, studying Japanese or Swahili, learning how to play the marimba, or tackling cognitively challenging new puzzles and board games.[36] Being a couch potato is an absolute no-no.
- **Self-Strategy 2.2: Stay physically active.** Physical exercise helps keep your brain healthy, especially if it includes aerobic activities such as jogging, dancing, or kickboxing. A particular benefit of physical exercise is its positive impact on your ability to pay attention to and concentrate on those intellectual challenges I just mentioned.[37] Here, then, is a second reason to avoid couch-potato-hood.

- **Self-Strategy 2.3: Get lots of sleep**. As you well know, a good night's sleep can help you stay mentally alert. But in addition, extended periods of sleep seem to be essential for neurologically firming up recently acquired memories – that is, for *consolidating* new knowledge and skills.[38] Sleep also provides a time for sorting through various new synapses and discarding those that aren't likely to be helpful over the long run.[39]

Enhancing Other People's Thinking and Learning in Instructional Settings

- **Instructional Strategy 2.1: Engage young children in stimulating activities, but don't overdo it**. Children certainly need regular stimulation in order to learn and develop. For example, they won't learn language unless the people around them often talk to them and engage them in conversation, and they can't possibly learn much about their physical environment if they don't have opportunities to interact with it and watch what happens as a result.[40] But bombarding them with a lot of stimulation every waking minute of the day is counterproductive. Not only might it be "TMI" (too much information), but it can actually stress them out.[41] Furthermore, the human brain seems to need some mental downtime when it can rest and reflect on its experiences.[42] As is true for many things, moderation is the key here.

- **Instructional Strategy 2.2: Also engage older children and adolescents in enriching experiences**. Given what you now know about the brain and its development, this strategy should go without saying, but I think I need to say it anyway. Some well-meaning "experts" are so concerned about preserving all those early-childhood synapses that they put undue emphasis on preschool education while giving short shrift to what happens later. Yes, children can benefit a great deal from enriching preschool programs, but the gains they make in such programs are likely to peter out unless they continue to have stimulating experiences throughout their school years.[43]

- **Instructional Strategy 2.3: Steer adolescents into safe, productive activities**. Remember, adolescent brains are *not* adult brains, especially when it comes to choosing their safety and long-term well-being over alluring and immediate (but possibly dangerous) alternatives. Teenagers are especially enticed by what they think might be fun and what their not-terribly-prudent peers are doing.[44] Thus they're apt to throw caution to the wind and common sense out the window, regardless of any stern lectures their parents and teachers might give them. A more fruitful approach is to offer them safe yet appealing options – perhaps structured athletic events after school or all-night after-prom parties. As an example, when my daughter Tina was in her last year of high school, she desperately wanted to go to a popular Mexican resort town for spring break. "All my friends are going," she told her father and me. Knowing that the trip would be a week of alcohol and poor decision making and also knowing that telling her no wouldn't deter her in the least, we planned a trip to Puerto Rico for the week, portraying the island as *the most exotic place ever*. Fortunately, Tina agreed and came with us.

○ **Instructional Strategy 2.4: Be optimistic about what people of all ages can learn to do**. People often become quite proficient in topics or skills they don't begin to tackle until they're adults. For example, as I write this chapter, I think about the week of intensive Spanish instruction I recently had in Seville, Spain. For five hours each day, my teacher, two classmates, and I spoke almost entirely in Spanish – well, okay, not entirely in Spanish, given that my classmates and I had come into the class with almost *zero* knowledge of Spanish vocabulary and grammar, but we did speak rudimentary Spanish a good part of the time. I certainly didn't become fluent, but by the end of the week I was able to converse with hotel and restaurant staff in Seville and elsewhere in ways that they understood. I'm well into my 60s now – not exactly a spring chicken – and yet in my Spanish lessons I sometimes picked up on ideas more quickly than my 29-year-old and 56-year-old classmates did.

From a neurological standpoint, our brains retain their ability to adapt to new situations and challenges throughout our lifespans. For most topics and skills, the door never closes on our ability to learn.

NOTES

1. C. S. Goodman & Tessier-Lavigne, 1997; Lichtman, 2001; Mareschal et al., 2007.
2. For example, see Hebb, 1949; Lichtman, 2001; Posner & Rothbart, 2007; Trachtenberg et al., 2002.
3. Leuner et al., 2004; C. A. Nelson, Thomas, & de Haan, 2006; Shors, 2014; Spalding et al., 2013.
4. Arbib, 2005; Gallese, Gernsbacher, Heyes, Hickok, & Iacoboni, 2011; Lu et al., 2012; Murata et al., 1997; Rizzolatti & Sinigaglia, 2008.
5. Han et al., 2013; Koob, 2009; Oberheim et al., 2009; Verkhratsky & Butt, 2007.

6. Bramham & Messaoudi, 2005; Roediger, Dudai, & Fitzpatrick, 2007.
7. Bauer, DeBoer, & Lukowski, 2007; Rasch & Born, 2008; Siegel, 2012; Wixted, 2005.
8. For an excellent discussion of this point, see Marcus, 2008.
9. The classic work on this topic is, of course, Charles Darwin's *On the Origin of Species by Means of Natural Selection*, first published in 1859.
10. *Hippocampus* is the Greek word for "seahorse," which this brain structure's shape loosely resembles.
11. Shors, 2014; Spalding et al., 2013.
12. Marcus, 2008.
13. Booth, 2007; Byrnes, 2001; Ornstein, 1997; Ratey, 2001.
14. Beeman & Chiarello, 1998; Goel et al., 2007; Ornstein, 1997.
15. Ornstein, 1997; Siegel, 2012.
16. For example, see Immordino-Yang & Fischer, 2007.
17. Chein & Schneider, 2012; Gonsalves & Cohen, 2010; Pereira, Detre, & Botvinick, 2011; Shimamura, 2014.
18. Diamond & Hopson, 1998; Koob, 2009.
19. Diamond & Hopson, 1998; Goldman-Rakic, 1986; Huttenlocher, 1993; Koob, 2009.
20. DeCasper & Spence, 1986; Dirix, Nijhuis, Jongsma, & Hornstra, 2009.
21. DeCasper & Spence, 1986
22. Koob, 2009.
23. Bauer et al., 2007; Byrnes, 2001; Huttenlocher, 1979, 1990.
24. Huttenlocher & Dabholkar, 1997; C. A. Nelson et al., 2006; Reyna, Chapman, Dougherty, & Confrey, 2012; Steinberg, 2009.
25. Brooks-Gunn, 2003; Case & Okamoto, 1996; Hyde et al., 2009; Pianta, Barnett, Burchinal, & Thornburg, 2009; Rothbart, 2011; Neville et al., 2013.
26. For example, see Unsworth et al., 2015.
27. Bryck & Fisher, 2012; Haier, 2001; C. A. Nelson et al., 2006.
28. Giedd et al., 2012.
29. Gogtay et al., 2004; Jung & Haier, 2007; Lenroot & Giedd, 2007.
30. Bauer et al., 2007; Bryck & Fisher, 2012; Luna & Sweeney, 2004; McGivern, Andersen, Byrd, Mutter, & Reilly, 2002; Reyna et al., 2012; Sowell, Thompson, Holmes, Jernigan, & Toga, 1999; Steinberg, 2009.
31. Bauer et al., 2007; Kolb, Gibb, & Robinson, 2003; Shen et al., 2010; Steinberg, 2009; Walker, Shapiro, Esterberg, & Trotman, 2010.
32. Dodge et al., 2009; Galván, 2012; Galván et al., 2006; Nell, 2002.
33. Figner & Weber, 2011; Luna, Paulsen, Padmanabhan, & Geier, 2013; Somerville, Jones, & Casey, 2010.
34. Draganski et al., 2004; Koob, 2009; Maguire et al., 2000.
35. Gorus, De Raedt, Lambert, Lemper, & Mets, 2008; Hertzog, Kramer, Wilson, & Linderberger, 2009; Lenroot & Giedd, 2007; Poston, Van Gemmert, Barduson, & Stelmach, 2009.

36. Hertzog et al., 2009; Koob, 2009; Verghese et al., 2007; Wilson, Scherr, Schneider, Li, & Bennett, 2007.

37. Castelli, Hillman, Buck, & Erwin, 2007; Erickson et al., 2011; G. E. Smith, 2016; Tomporowski, Davis, Miller, & Naglieri, 2008.

38. Dinges & Rogers, 2008; Kirby, Maggi, & D'Angiulli, 2011; Ólafsdóttir, Carpenter, & Barry, 2016; Payne & Kensinger, 2010; Rasch & Born, 2008.

39. I. Feinberg & Campbell, 2013; Tononi & Cirelli, 2013.

40. L. B. Cohen & Cashon, 2006; Risley & Hart, 2006.

41. Bruer, 1999; Keogh, 2003; Lundberg & Forsman, 1971; Rothbart, 2011; Thompson & Nelson, 2001.

42. Barron, Riby, Greer, & Smallwood, 2011; Immordino-Yang, Christodoulou, & Singh, 2012; Ratey, 2001.

43. Bronfenbrenner, 1999; Brooks-Gunn, 2003; McCall & Plemons, 2001; Ramey & Ramey, 1998.

44. Albert, Chein, & Steinberg, 2013; Galván, 2012; Knoll, Magis-Weinberg, Speekenbrink, & Blakemore, 2015.

3

Cognition and Learning as Constructive Processes: Finding Order in Chaos

As you learned in Chapter 2, the human brain has several trillion cells – including 100 billion neurons – that are interconnected in countless ways. At any single point in time, a great many neurons are apt to be busily firing away and chemically communicating both with one another and with their supportive glial cells. Some of this brain action is instigated by outside forces, such as the light rays that hit our eyes, the sound waves that hit our eardrums, the airborne chemicals that float up our nostrils, the substances that land on our tongues, and the many objects our bodies touch as we move about. Internal stimuli – perhaps a growling stomach, an achy joint, or a persistent feeling of anxiety – can also get our brains in motion.

Not only are our brains constantly being stimulated, but in fact it appears that our brains *need* physical stimulation to keep them working properly.[1] For example, in a classic research study conducted in the 1950s,[2] college students were paid $20 a day (quite a tidy sum in the '50s) to do absolutely nothing. In particular, they were asked to lie on a bed in a small room for as long as they could, with only very short breaks for eating and other basic biological necessities. The students wore visors that let in light but otherwise prevented them from seeing anything, and they wore thick sleeves and gloves that prevented them from feeling or manipulating anything. And the only noise in the room was the dull, repetitive hum of an air conditioner. Most students spent the first few hours catching up on their sleep, and after they woke up, many of them thought a bit about their schoolwork or personal issues and, eventually, talked to themselves, sang songs, or recited favorite poems. As time went on, the students became increasingly confused and disoriented. They began having hallucinations, such as hearing a nonexistent choir or seeing a procession of eyeglasses marching down a street. And after emerging from their physical and social isolation a few days later, perception of their outside reality was quite

distorted: Flat surfaces appeared to be curvy, objects seemingly kept changing their sizes and shapes, and everything seemed to be in constant
motion.

We human beings really don't like being bored.[3] But neither do we like
having so much stimulation that we feel confused and overwhelmed by it
all. Just as Goldilocks liked her porridge not too hot, not too cold, but "just
right," so, too, do we want our environments to be not too much, not
too little, but just the right, middle-of-the-road amount.[4] And when our
environments are at this just-right level, our brains seem to be predisposed
to find order in the apparent chaos of what we're seeing, hearing, and in
other ways perceiving. As previously noted in Chapter 1, we typically try to
organize new information in some way and to *find meaning* in it. We rarely,
if ever, take what we get at face value.

GOING BEYOND THE PHYSICAL FACTS: THE CENTRAL ROLE OF ENCODING

Those neurons that reside in our sensory organs don't keep external
stimulation in the exact form in which they get it; all messages from the
outside world are immediately changed into electrical impulses that rush
off to the brain. Our brains synthesize those impulses into larger patterns of
electrical and chemical activity, and almost immediately we try to make
enough sense out of them that we can respond appropriately. From the
very beginning, then, we are **encoding** information – that is, we're changing its form into something we can more effectively use.

As we humans have physically and culturally evolved over many millennia, we've acquired increasingly sophisticated ways of encoding new
information. One critical way in which we encode some information is to
attach one or more verbal labels to it. For example, imagine that you see
a large object moving quickly across a field. The upper, horizontal part of
this object is long and roundish, almost like a cylinder. Attached to one end
of the almost-cylinder is an upside-down sock-shaped thing with stringy
stuff coming out of the top. Attached to the other end is more of that
stringy stuff, which hangs down in a roundish cluster. The whole thing is
held up by four spindly things that keep moving in a steady, rhythmic
manner. Occasionally the front edge of the upside-down sock-like part
opens to emit a loud "neighing" sound. Rather than remember all the
details of this mysterious object, you simply think of it as a *horse*. The sock-
shaped part is its *head*, the cluster of stringy stuff at the other end is its *tail*,
and those four spindly things are its *legs*. Thinking about a horse is far more

FIGURE 3.1. How well might you remember this drawing?

efficient than thinking about a large cylindrical object with appendages at two ends (one shaped like a sock, the other consisting of a bunch of stringy stuff), four more appendages extending down to the ground, and a strange sound occasionally emanating from the sock-like part.

Here we see a second very important role that language plays in our lives. Not only does it enable us to communicate with one another (see Chapter 1), but it also provides a means through which we can encode our experiences and think more quickly and efficiently about them.[5] Attaching a meaningful label to something is especially helpful when we can't initially make much sense of what we're seeing. As an example, take a quick look at the drawing in Figure 3.1. *Spend only a few seconds looking at it*, and then cover it up so you can't see it anymore.

In the short amount of time you looked at the drawing, could you make much sense of it? How well do you think you might be able to recreate it in a week or so if you didn't look at it again in the meantime? But now look at it once again. Think of it as a giraffe bending over to kiss an elephant that's lying on its back. Suddenly those two large roundish things sticking out at the bottom become elephant ears, the parts halfway up become an elephant's truck and a giraffe's snout, the four small parts protruding at the top are giraffe horns and ears, and the four small black circles at the sides are two pairs of eyes. As a result of such meaning-making, your chances of recreating the drawing next week would increase considerably.[6]

We encode what we hear as well as what we see – a horse's neigh, an elephant's trumpeting call, a honeybee's buzz, a car horn's beep-beep – and we're often alarmed when we can't make reasonable sense of a loud noise (What was *that*??!!). When listening to other people talk, we immediately encode their speech in part by breaking a continuous string of sounds into discrete sections and recognizing each section as a particular word. We can do such things only if we know the language being spoken. For example, if you're a monolingual English speaker, you should easily understand the spoken version of

"Do you speak French?"

but would perceive

"Parlayvoofrahnsay?"

as complete gibberish. You wouldn't even hear the distinct words in the French question (which are actually "Parlez-vous français?"), let alone have a clue as to what they mean.

The words in any human language are *symbols*, in that they represent objects, events, or relationships without bearing much, if any, resemblance to the things they stand for. For example, why do we call that cylindrical object with the sock-shaped, stringy, and spindly appendages a "horse," rather than, say, a "cow," a "bulldozer," or an "appendectomy"? We also use nonlinguistic symbols to encode some of our experiences. For example, we count and calculate using *numbers*, we sometimes express trends and patterns as *graphs*, and we often represent spatial relationships as *maps*.

Language and other symbol systems are hardly the only ways in which we encode the things we learn. We remember many of our physical behaviors as exactly those – *actual behaviors* – or at least as the neurological representations of them.[7] Sports coaches and fitness trainers sometimes use the term "muscle memory" for our drilled-in knowledge of certain psychomotor skills, but they're actually talking about memories in the brain, not in the muscles.

Another common form of encoding is *imagery*, which involves thinking about how various events look, sound, smell, or feel out there in the nonmental world. As an example, close your eyes for a second and picture a red rose. Almost certainly you can conjure up a nice one. Now close your eyes again and try to smell that rose and then touch one of its thorny branches. Can you smell it? Can your fingers feel its prickly thorns? Probably so. Roses don't make noise, so try to imagine a dog's bark or a lion's roar. We humans encode many of our experiences partly in the ways in which our senses have detected them.[8]

Finally, deep down, we humans seem to be especially good at encoding life's events as general *meanings* – or *gist* – that might transcend particular words, actions, and images.[9] For instance, think about the good feelings you often have when you and many other people work together to make something important happen. You're all working together, sharing the load, and helping one another, and you all feel a sense of satisfaction and camaraderie that you might not get in any other way. English doesn't have a word for what you've experienced – you've encoded it more as a complex feeling with a deep, indescribable meaning. Several Bantu languages in southern Africa do have a word for it – *ubuntu* – but no single human utterance can completely capture it.

INDIVIDUAL CONSTRUCTION OF MEANING: MAKING SENSE ON OUR OWN

As a species, we all seem to be predisposed to organize our world in somewhat predictable ways. For example, in the early decades of the 20th century, research by certain German theorists known as *Gestalt* psychologists revealed consistent patterns in how we tend to perceive and organize visual stimuli.[10] Figure 3.2 presents four examples. The upper left box (Figure 3.2a) illustrates the principle of *figure-ground*. When you first look at this box, a black vase or goblet might pop out at you. But if you refocus your attention to look at the white areas on each side, you can instead see two faces. It's virtually impossible to perceive *both* the vase/goblet and the two faces at exactly the same time: When you're trying to make sense of and observe the details of the black part – the *figure* – the white areas fade into the background, or *ground*. When you switch your attention, the two faces come into focus (the figure) – you can see the noses, foreheads, chins, and so on – but the black becomes just a blur.

Now look at the upper right box (Figure 3.2b). Obviously you see 12 black squares, but the important thing to note is that you see them as three groups of four squares each. Here the principle of *proximity* comes into play: You're more likely to see things as a group when they're spaced close together. And when you look at the 15 shapes in the lower left box (Figure 3.2c), you're apt to mentally organize them as five columns rather than as five rows, illustrating the principle of *similarity*. (The letter *X* you "saw" in the rows of circles in Figure 1.1 reflects the similarity principle as well.) Finally, what do you see in the lower right box (Figure 3.2d)? I'm guessing that you integrate all those short dashes into a single wavy line. This principle of *closure* – the tendency to fill in the gaps in what we see to create one or more unified wholes – permeates a good deal of our everyday visual perception.

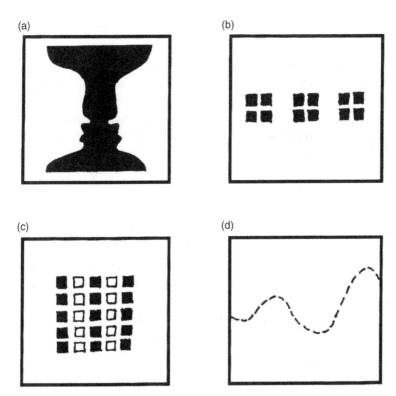

FIGURE 3.2. Examples of four basic Gestalt principles of perceptual organization

If you think about it, you might realize that these organizational principles often hold true for hearing as well as vision. The figure-ground principle kicks in whenever you're in a cocktail-party-type situation and need to listen to one conversation while ignoring others. You might take advantage of the proximity principle when you're listening to poetry: You're apt to hear a few close-together words as a single line, with a short pause indicating the start of the next line in the poem. The similarity principle sometimes applies when you listen to music; for example, in Beethoven's Symphony no. 5 – which you would definitely recognize as something you've heard before if I could play it for you now – the first three notes are all the same, followed by a much lower fourth note. It sounds a bit like this: "Bum-bum-bum BUM," with the first three notes sounding like a group and the fourth one being distinctly separate. And as for the principle of closure, consider what happens when someone is trying to tell you something in a very crowded and noisy room:

"Let's -ee if -ee -an fine . . . -eyet -ace . . . -alk!"

You might reasonably guess that the person is saying "Let's see if we can find a quiet place to talk" or something of that ilk.

But our inherited tendency to make sense of what we see and hear goes far beyond a few simple principles of perceptual organization. As soon as we have the physical capability to do so, we humans actively *seek out* new information and experiences in an apparent effort to learn more about our environment, and we actively manipulate nearby objects to discover some of their properties. We work hard to make sense of language-based information as well. To see how this can happen in your own head, read the following passage:

> Late one night, Jason stopped at a neighborhood convenience store to pick up some cigarettes. He stayed for a few minutes to talk with the pretty store clerk. A large man entered the store, rudely handed the clerk a large canvas bag, and insisted that she put the contents of the cash register into it. The man then sped away with the filled bag under his arm, leaving the clerk in tears, the empty cash register drawer still open, and Jason looking on helplessly.[11]

What happened at the convenience store? Was this a robbery? Maybe it was, but maybe, instead, the large, obnoxious man was the store's owner, who came by to pick up the store's earnings for the day. Also, was Jason a smoker? Maybe, but maybe not; possibly he was buying the cigarettes for a friend. Hey, we don't even know whether he actually *purchased* any cigarettes; maybe he completely forgot about his errand once he saw the pretty store clerk, or maybe he was a shoplifter who "picked up" a pack of cigarettes and stealthily put it in his coat pocket. And was there even *money* in the cash register? We know that it had "contents," but the story doesn't tell us what those contents actually were. (Yes, yes, I know, cash registers usually do have cash in them – that's what my students have always told me when I've presented this scenario – but there's no law mandating that they have to have cash in them.)

The most important thing to note here is that *our self-constructed understandings of the world aren't always accurate ones.* Perhaps we have insufficient prior knowledge to make appropriate sense of a situation. Such was the case when one 4-year-old dinosaur enthusiast learned that many dinosaur species died off as the Earth's climate became colder. He concluded that "they did not know how to put on their sweaters."[12] But perhaps, instead, our own observations lead us astray. For example, until we have formal instruction about how the Earth rotates on its axis (in one day) and revolves around the sun (in one year), virtually all of us think of the sun as doing the moving – for instance, we see the sun "come up" in the morning and "go down" at night. Of course, it doesn't help that in our everyday speech we all talk about the sun *rising* and *setting* – which brings me to my next point: A great deal of our meaning-making comes courtesy of our interactions with our fellow human beings, as you'll see now.

SOCIAL CONSTRUCTION OF MEANING: CO-CREATING UNDERSTANDINGS WITH OTHERS

Thanks in large part to our complex language, we can often put our heads together to make better sense of a situation than any one of us might do on our own. For example, imagine that you leave a class lecture a bit confused about some of the things the lecturer said. You and several classmates get together for a few minutes after class: "What did she mean when she said ... ?" "I'm not sure, but I thought she meant that ..." "Hmm, that's a possibility. But maybe instead she meant ..." "Oh, I have an idea. Here, let me draw it on paper. Is my diagram consistent with the stuff she said last week?" Possibly you all come away with a better understanding – or at least you think you do – about what the lecturer was trying to tell you. Sometimes two or more heads are better than one.

Some of our collective meaning-making efforts continue over very long periods of mental collaboration. Think of the academic disciplines with which you've become acquainted in your years of formal education. Mathematics, the physical and life sciences, history, geography, economics, psychology – all of these disciplines have evolved over many decades or centuries, with a great many theorists, researchers, and practitioners contributing pieces to various worldly puzzles. For example, building on Copernicus's and Galileo's 16th- and 17th-century proposals that the Earth revolves around the sun (rather than vice versa), thousands of astronomers have combined their research findings and insights to construct our current understandings of our solar system, galaxy, and universe.

This brings me once again to the importance of *culture* in making us such a cognitively advanced species. I'm not just talking about museums, concerts, and literature here; rather, the term **culture** includes the many typical behaviors and beliefs that a long-standing social group acquires and then passes along to future generations. Our culture includes not only our language but also our collective perceptions and understandings of our physical, psychological, and social experiences. Through our parenting practices, schools and universities, social institutions and agencies, and various media, we humans make a concerted effort to teach one another important elements of our culture – how to act, how *not* to act, what to believe, what *not* to believe, and how to interpret and make sense of puzzling events that regularly present themselves in the local environment. For example, we often help children make better sense of a puzzling object or event by giving it a label ("That's a triceratops – see the three horns on its head?") and presenting our culture's widely accepted explanation of it.[13]

Another important way in which our culture enhances our ability to survive and thrive in the world is by passing along the tools it has created to make our daily living more effective and efficient. Some tools are actual physical objects; for example, hammers help us build houses, scissors can cut paper and cloth, and protractors make it possible for us to draw geometrically accurate circles of varying sizes. But many others are **cognitive tools** that enable us to *think* in more productive ways.[14] Cognitive tools take a variety of forms, including concepts, symbols, strategies, procedures, and any other culturally constructed mechanisms that help us tackle life's mental challenges more efficiently and effectively. For example, our *system of numbers* – not only whole numbers but also fractions, decimals, and negative numbers – allows us to perform precise calculations related to building construction, engine design, and cooking. The *maps* we create help us find our way around new cities, subway systems, and shopping malls. Our *writing system* allows us to record our thoughts on paper or in computer documents. By the way, *computers* are cognitive tools as well as physical ones because they help us think in increasingly sophisticated ways. All of these tools are cultural creations – the results of many, many years of our collective ingenuity and meaning-making.

But just as we don't always come to the right conclusions on our own, we don't always make good sense of things when we work as a group. For example, until Albert Einstein came along with his theory of relativity, we all thought of *time* as being something that passes at the same constant rate. Now virtually all physicists acknowledge that Einstein was right; clocks move more slowly if they're rapidly zipping through space than if they stay put on our bedside tables.

Constructive groupthink is even more prone to inaccuracies when it involves a relatively small number of individuals. For example, you've undoubtedly seen Internet postings that advocate outrageous ideas – perhaps that Elvis is still alive, that astronauts didn't ever really land on the moon, or that all the evidence for our worldwide rising temperatures constitutes an elaborate "hoax" created and perpetuated by more than 95% of the world's environmental scientists. Even reasonable people sometimes disagree about the supposed facts, as they often do when the topic of discussion turns to politics, critiques of art and literature, or moral and ethical dilemmas.

Now that you've read the preceding discussions of both individual and social construction of meaning, you can better appreciate Misconception #2, which I presented in Chapter 1 – *that our minds record information exactly as we receive it.* It's now time to alert you to a related misconception:

> Misconception #12: That people who say things with a great deal of certainty and conviction are likely to be giving us accurate information

Absolutely not true. Quite the contrary, some people who are quite confident in their assertions are downright wrong.[15] Instead, self-confident certainty about a question or issue is often a sign of an unhealthy *need for closure*, in which people are more concerned about settling on the "truth" quickly than contemplating and evaluating various perspectives on the matter.[16] We'll revisit this need for closure in the discussion of dispositions in Chapter 9.

ORGANIZING OUR THOUGHTS: INTEGRATING LITTLE UNDERSTANDINGS INTO BIGGER, MORE INCLUSIVE ONES

We humans tend to organize our many little constructed meanings to create broader understandings of our world as a whole. Such integrated bodies of information and ideas can take a variety of forms. I'll describe five of the many possibilities: concepts, schemas and scripts, personal theories, and worldviews.

Concepts

You might think of a **concept** as being a mental grouping of objects or events that have something in common. That "something" may or may not be easy to observe. For example, we can quickly recognize a *ball* by its three-dimensional roundness, and we can identify a moving object as a *horse* by observing its size, head and body shape, gait, and occasional neighing. But it's virtually impossible to pin down an example of *justice* on the basis of observable physical characteristics; for abstract concepts such as this one, we need to look well below the surface to identify the underlying qualities that all group members share.

We seem to be genetically prewired to form concepts as a way of helping us organize our world. In fact, by the time we're two months old, we show an inclination to categorize our experiences.[17] We don't initially attach labels to our concepts; for example, we're likely to recognize *milk* when we drink it long before we know what it's called. But as the people around us repeatedly attach certain labels to certain kinds of objects or events, we gradually learn that some things are called *milk*, other things are called *balls*, still others are *kitties*, and maybe one particular individual in our life is *Mama*. At this point, we're starting to learn our culture's language. (If we're immersed in a multilingual environment, we might learn two or more sets of labels – something that most young children seem to be able to do without much trouble.[18])

Most of our early concepts (e.g., *milk, ball, kitty, Mama*) are concrete ones based on obvious physical characteristics, with abstract concepts emerging only as we increase our abstract reasoning capabilities and gain an expanding body of knowledge that we can use to label some of our experiences as reflecting, say, *justice, opinion*, or *deceit*. Furthermore, because our concepts are largely self-constructed, some of them will typically need revision over time. For example, when children first learn the word *doggie*, they might think that it applies to cows and horses, and when they first learn the word *animal*, they're likely to think that it encompasses only four-legged furry things.[19] More accurate understandings of these concepts are apt to emerge only after considerable experience or explicit instruction.

Schemas and Scripts

A **schema** is a closely connected set of ideas (including concepts) related to a specific object or event.[20] For example, you probably have a schema for what a typical *kitchen* is like. Many kitchens have a sink, a stove, a refrigerator, several storage cabinets, and one or more counters for preparing food; some may also have a microwave, other small appliances, and a small table with chairs around it. Likewise, you almost certainly have a schema for *horse* that expands on your more basic concept of horses: Not only do horses have a certain shape and sound, but in addition they like hay and carrots, are often seen in pastures or at racetracks, and sometimes wear bridles and saddles to accommodate their human owners.

When a schema involves a certain kind of event, it's sometimes called a **script**.[21] For example, what do you typically do when you go to McDonald's or some other fast-food restaurant? Unless you're using the drive-through window, chances are pretty good that you walk up to the counter, peruse the various options on the menu displays behind it, place your order with one of the staff members, and then pay the required amount. You might get your order almost immediately, or you might have to wait a bit until someone behind the counter calls out, "Quarter pounder, large fries, and chocolate shake!" After you've gotten what you ordered, you stop at a side counter to get some napkins and maybe some ketchup, a fork, or a straw. You find an empty table where you can sit down and eat. Later, after you've finished your meal, you take your plate, cup, napkins, and empty ketchup packets to a trash can. You don't leave a tip. This scenario regularly repeats itself in your life until – I hope – you start cooking more healthful meals in that kitchen of yours.

Some of our self-constructed schemas and scripts are specific to the environment and culture in which we live. For example, your horse schema is apt to depend, in part, on whether you have grown up in a city, on a small family farm, or in the thoroughbred racehorse–breeding region near Lexington, Kentucky. And your scripts for typical weddings and funerals are apt to vary considerably depending on whether you've grown up in the United States, India, or Palau.[22]

In any event, our self-constructed schemas and scripts can often help us make better sense of what might otherwise be confusing situations.[23] As an example, consider this situation:

> One Saturday afternoon, 6-year-old Sarah put on her favorite dress and some fancy shoes. Sarah's mother gave her a box wrapped in brightly colored paper and said, "Have fun!" Sarah carried the box down the street to her friend Mary's house. When she arrived, she found several other children there, and they, too, had brought brightly wrapped boxes. After playing a few games, the children watched Mary rip open the boxes to see what they contained. Later, Mary's father served a cake with seven lighted candles on it, and Mary blew them out while everyone else sang a song to her. After eating the cake and playing more games, all of Mary's guests said good-bye and left.

What happened here? Why did children bring boxes to Mary's house, and why did Mary rip them all open? Why did Mary's father put lighted candles on the cake? Did it matter that there were seven candles instead of, say, only one or two of them? Why did Mary blow out the candles? What song might the other children have been singing? You can easily answer these questions if – but *only* if – you have a script for typical children's *birthday parties*, especially those in Western cultures.

Schemas and scripts influence our learning in another way as well: They help us determine which elements of a situation we should focus our attention on and which elements we can reasonably ignore.[24] For example, if you eat at McDonald's, you should make sure that everything you've ordered is in the bag the staff member has given you, and your table selection should be based on relative cleanliness – you'd probably steer clear of benches with ketchup smears or puddles of melted ice cream. But there's no need to worry about exactly what people at other tables are wearing or exactly how many staff members are in the kitchen deep-frying potatoes.

Personal Theories

On a grander scale, it appears that we construct our own theories about a wide variety of physical, biological, social, and psychological phenomena, in part because we seem to have a keen interest in identifying cause-and-effect relationships in our world.[25] Like scientific theories, these self-constructed **personal theories** encompass a fairly coherent set of beliefs that include cause-and-effect relationships about, say, why the sun seemingly rises and sets every day, why raccoons give birth only to other raccoons – they never have baby elephants or giraffes – and why many of us humans can be so forgetful at times. The key difference between personal theories and more scientific ones is that our personal theories don't necessarily have research evidence to back them up. Hence they're often only partially correct, and some of them can be downright wrong.

Let's consider an example. When you were a young child, you probably envisioned the Earth as being a really large, relatively flat thing that you, other living creatures, and many buildings were "on top" of (see the left side of Figure 3.3). The sky, sun, clouds, moon, and stars were just "up there" somewhere, hovering above you. But then adults kept telling you that the Earth was round, not flat. So, you thought, maybe it's a hollow ball with you and everyone else living on a flat surface inside of it (see the right side of Figure 3.3).[26] The sky, then, would be a sort of wallpaper surrounding you on the inside of the ball's outer surface, with the sun, clouds, moon, and stars hovering in the air right below the sky. Yup, both scenarios were consistent with the "facts" that you knew at the time, but presumably you've revised your Earth theory quite a bit since your early childhood days.

As another example, adults are apt to hold various theories about what human *intelligence* is. In my own conversations with friends and

FIGURE 3.3. Two possible theories of what Planet Earth is like

acquaintances over the years, I've found that many people think that (a) intelligence is largely an inherited characteristic and (b) any individual is apt to have an "IQ" that is a specific, permanent number. The facts of the matter are that psychologists can't agree either on what intelligence *is* or on how best to measure it; they can't even agree on whether it's a single entity that can reasonably be measured at all.[27] Furthermore, although a traditional intelligence test can yield an overall, general IQ score, different tests are apt to give us somewhat different scores, and any single test might give us two different scores for the same person on two different occasions. And whatever intelligence is, it's the result not only of heredity but also of environmental influences *and* the continuing interplay *between* heredity and environment.[28]

Some personal not-quite-right theories are widely shared; the Earth-is-flat and intelligence-is-inherited-and-permanent theories just described are examples. But other personal theories might be unique to specific individuals. For instance, as a preschooler, I constructed my own theory of where babies come from. I won't bother you with all the details, but I will say that my theory involved (a) a God-supervised baby factory up on a cloud; (b) a collection point on Earth at which several dump trucks were parked; (c) transportation by a truck to a local hospital in order to repair the many bumps and bruises resulting from a long fall from the sky; and (d) a "baby store" at the same hospital, where parents could purchase the finished products. At the time, this theory helped me make sense of the fact that my mother and father came home from the hospital one day with a new baby brother, but I eventually learned that my hypothesized scenario left a lot to be desired. For example, although my son Jeff came from a hospital, it wasn't a dump truck that brought him there. Trust me, I know – I was at the scene when he arrived.

Worldviews

Whereas our personal theories tend to be related to particular entities or phenomena, our overall **worldviews** are our sets of beliefs and assumptions about reality *in general*. For example, we might think that:

- We can best secure our own, others', and our planet's well-being by applying scientific theories and research findings OR by faithfully appealing to a Higher Power that watches over us and makes the best decisions for us.
- Our successes and failures in life are largely the results of our own actions and efforts OR of predetermined, uncontrollable events (e.g., fate) OR of divine intervention.
- We should strive to master the forces of nature OR live in harmony with them.
- Our social world is ultimately fair and just – good deeds eventually bring rewards and misdeeds are eventually punished – OR isn't necessarily fair and just.
- Our own cultural beliefs and practices are superior to those of other cultural groups OR differing cultural perspectives might be equally valid and legitimate.[29]

For the most part, our worldviews are the result of our joint efforts to make sense of general worldly phenomena – perhaps increasingly unusual weather patterns, catastrophic physical events (e.g., volcanic eruptions), puzzling scientific findings, or best practices in government. We continually transmit our worldviews to one another and to future generations through our day-to-day interactions – for example, through our informal conversations ("This hurricane is punishment for our sins"), our educational institutions ("Our best decisions are based on solid research findings"), our religious teachings ("In the beginning God created the heaven and the earth"), and social media ("Climate change is a hoax").[30]

Our personal theories and worldviews are often such an integral part of our thinking that we take them for granted and aren't even consciously aware of them. But whether they're right, wrong, or somewhere in between, they can have a significant impact on how we interpret – or *mis*interpret –

new information and events. We'll explore this idea further in the discussion of misconceptions and conceptual change in Chapter 8.

BEING STRATEGIC

It should be clear by now that we don't just passively absorb new knowledge from our environment; by no means are we "sponges" that mindlessly "soak up" new facts and ideas. Instead, we individually and collectively *create* our knowledge by filling in gaps in the incomplete information we receive, identifying important patterns in what might otherwise seem to be random occurrences, and, in general, imposing meanings on our experiences. By and large, our constructive sense-making efforts enable us to live longer, healthier, and more productive lives than we would otherwise be able to do.

Yet on the minus side, our gap-filling, pattern-identifying, and meaning-making efforts can sometimes lead us astray, such that we misinterpret or misremember the actual facts of a situation. Furthermore, we don't always have the prior knowledge we need to make *any* reasonable sense of an experience. I'll talk more about such problems in upcoming chapters, but even at this point in the book, you should know enough about human cognition and learning to make sense of the following recommendations.

Enhancing Your Own Thinking and Learning
in Everyday Life

- **Self-Strategy 3.1: Come to grips with the fact that your own "knowledge" might sometimes be wrong.** I can't say this enough: We humans *construct* our knowledge and beliefs about the world. We so quickly and automatically impose our own interpretations and meanings on events that we regularly confuse what we *think* we saw and heard with what we actually *did* see and hear. Our self-constructed "realities" don't always represent the true state of affairs. So try to be a little more self-critical of your own understandings and opinions. As I'm sure some of your childhood teachers told you more than once, it's okay to be wrong once in a while. What *isn't* okay is to stubbornly and pigheadedly insist that you're right when you might actually be way off base.
- **Self-Strategy 3.2: Actively seek out other people's perspectives on controversial topics and issues.** One good way to keep any counterproductive *my-opinion-is-fact* attitude in check is to continually seek out other people's opinions about matters of importance – perhaps about

beneficial public policies, plausible scientific theories, or sound business practices. These other people should include a few individuals who are apt to offer viewpoints very different from your own. You can't grow personally or professionally if the only people you ask are those who simply confirm what you already believe.

- **Self-Strategy 3.3: Be careful not to overly categorize things; for example, be on the lookout for inaccurate and unfair stereotypes you may have formed about various kinds of people**. Remember, we humans are naturally inclined to form concepts that in one way or another help us synthesize and summarize our experiences. But we sometimes go too far, especially when it comes to drawing conclusions about the kinds of characteristics that different groups of people are likely to have. "Boys need to be strong," "girls are no good at math," "illegal immigrants just want to get free handouts from the rest of us." Such stereotypes are neither accurate nor productive, but they're so pervasive in our society that you must consciously – and *vigorously* – resist adopting them.

- **Self-Strategy 3.4: Resist making the assumption that your own worldview is in some way superior to the worldviews of others**. Your underlying beliefs and assumptions about the physical world and about human experience – that is, your current worldview – are almost certainly products of the culture in which you were raised and/or now live. And without a doubt they pervade many aspects of your day-to-day thinking. For example, are you in control of your own life journey, or have the Hands of Fate consistently put insurmountable obstacles in your path? Are there certain religious preachings that you hold sacrosanct? How much stock do you put in the findings and conclusions of scientific researchers? You're most likely to be aware of your own answers to such questions – and most likely to live peacefully and productively with your fellow humans – when you (a) discover that some people have very different answers to the same questions and (b) strive to understand *why* other people think as they do about such matters. Maybe your worldview is the best way to look at things. But then again, maybe other people have more fruitful vantage points.

Enhancing Other People's Thinking and Learning in Instructional Settings

- **Instructional Strategy 3.1: Explicitly teach important new concepts**. Explicit instruction can often speed up the concept-learning process, especially when the concepts in question are fairly abstract ones – for example, as is true for the concepts *metaphor* and *onomatopoeia* (in creative writing), *longitude* and *dispersion* (in geography), and *miter* and *plumb* (in carpentry). Following are several strategies that research-ers have found to be effective in teaching new concepts:

- Provide a verbal definition.
- Identify the important characteristics that most or all members of the concept category have.
- Show a typical example, or *prototype*, of the concept.
- Also show less prototypical examples – ones that show the variability of members of the category (e.g., when teaching the concept *bird*, you might show not only a sparrow-like prototype but also an emu, a kiwi, and a penguin).
- Show examples of close-but-not-close-enough *non*members of the category (e.g., bats are *not* birds, whales are *not* fish).[31]

- **Instructional Strategy 3.2: Also explicitly teach cognitive tools for specific subject areas and for life in general.** For example, algebra offers many strategies for determining the values of unknown quanti-ties. Knowing how to *separate and control variables* helps us identify cause-and-effect relationships in the physical and social sciences. The concepts *miter* and *plumb* help the home builders among us construct houses that won't easily fall down. And in our high-tech 21st-century world, we are increasingly using computer software programs and smartphone applications – word processing programs, text-messaging apps, and social media – to communicate with others about our thoughts and experiences.

- **Instructional Strategy 3.3: Help children and open-minded adults revisit and revise any personal theories that run counter to scienti-fically validated perspectives.** In their nonstop efforts to make sense of the world, growing children construct many personal theories to explain the physical and social worlds in which they live. For instance, they're apt to have some fairly naive ideas about why the sun seemingly moves across the sky each day, why dinosaurs might have gone extinct (e.g., they weren't wearing sweaters), and where babies come from. And the prevalence of Facebook, YouTube, and other social media in our modern lives continually alerts us to the fact that some of our fellow humans actively promote bizarre ideas that fly in the face of all logic, reason, and well-established scientific findings. Unfortunately, chan-ging other people's counterproductive beliefs is much easier said than done, for reasons we'll explore in Chapter 8. For now, I will say only that we well-informed (I hope) individuals must work hard to do it. One advantage of the next (final) strategy is that it can sometimes have an idea-changing effect.

○ **Instructional Strategy 3.4: Encourage respectful dialogue about complex or controversial topics.** As a general rule, people construct more sophisticated and accurate understandings of multifaceted topics when they talk about these topics with other individuals.[32] In addition to exposing people to perspectives very different from their own, respectful dialogues can have benefits such as these:

- ○ People must reflect on and clarify their thoughts well enough to explain and justify them to others; in the process, relatively vague notions can evolve into more precise and specific understandings.
- ○ In trying to explain their current ideas, people might actually embellish on them – for example, by thinking of new examples and applications.
- ○ People may discover flaws and inconsistencies in their thinking, thereby motivating them to seek more accurate explanations.[33]

However, as noted earlier in the chapter, group discussions don't always yield desirable results; for instance, group members may simply accept and build on other people's *mis*understandings. If you're using small-group dialogue in formal instructional settings, then you should closely monitor students' comments and conclusions and, if necessary, steer flawed perspectives in more productive directions – perhaps by pointing out fallacies in logic, asking probing questions ("What if someone were to challenge your claim by saying . . . ?"), or presenting evidence that clearly contradicts what group members are proposing. Without appropriate guidance from an expert, groupthink sessions can occasionally result in the blind leading the blind to who-knows-where.

NOTES

1. Solomon et al., 1961.
2. Heron, 1957.
3. Hsee, Yang, & Wang, 2010; Pekrun, Goetz, Daniels, Stupnisky, & Perry, 2010.
4. Berlyne, 1960.
5. For a classic book on this idea, see Vygotsky, 1934/1986.
6. Bower, Karlin, & Dueck, 1975.
7. Goldin-Meadow & Beilock, 2010; Goldin-Meadow, Cook, & Mitchell, 2009; Spunt, Falk, & Lieberman, 2010; Willems, Hagoort, & Casasanto, 2010.
8. Minogue & Jones, 2006; Palmiero et al., 2009; Reisberg, 1992.

9. Brainerd & Reyna, 1998, 2005; Kintsch, 1977; Payne & Kensinger, 2010.
10. For example, see Koffka, 1935; Köhler, 1929. The German word *Gestalt* can be roughly translated as "organized whole that appears to be more than the sum of its individual parts."
11. Adapted from "Human Memory, Part 2: Long-Term Memory," an interactive learning module hotlinked in Ormrod, 2015.
12. Linn & Eylon, 2011, p. 1.
13. Crowley & Jacobs, 2002; Feuerstein, Feuerstein, & Falik, 2010; John-Steiner & Mahn, 1996; Vygotsky, 1986.
14. For classic writings on the importance of cognitive tools, see Vygotsky, 1978, 1987.
15. Brainerd & Reyna, 2005; Perfect, 2002; Wells, Olson, & Charman, 2002.
16. DeBacker & Crowson, 2009; Kruglanski & Webster, 1996; Roets & Van Hiel, 2011.
17. Dewar & Xu, 2010; Mandler, 2007; Quinn, 2007.
18. Adesope, Lavin, Thompson, & Ungerleider, 2010; Bialystok, 2001.
19. Carey, 1985; Saltz, 1971.
20. Dansereau, 1995; Kalyuga, 2010; Rumelhart & Ortony, 1977; Schraw, 2006.
21. Cole & Cagigas, 2010; Dansereau, 1995; Schank & Abelson, 1977.
22. Pritchard, 1990; Reynolds, Taylor, Steffensen, Shirey, & Anderson, 1982.
23. Bower, Black, & Turner, 1979.
24. Ramsay & Sperling, 2010; Schraw, 2006; Sweller, 1994.
25. D. E. Brown & Hammer, 2008; Flavell, 2000; Gelman, 2003; Inagaki & Hatano, 2006; Keil & Newman, 2008; Rosengren, Brem, Evans, & Sinatra, 2012; Torney-Purta, 1994; Wellman & Gelman, 1992.
26. Brewer, 2008; Vosniadou, 1994.
27. For diverse perspectives, see Brody, 1992; Cattell, 1987; Gardner, 1999; Nisbett, 2009; Sternberg, 2005.
28. Ceci, 2003; Nisbett et al., 2012; Rutter, 1997; Scarr & McCartney, 1983; Turkheimer, Haley, Waldron, D'Onofrio, & Gottesman, 2003.
29. Atran, Medin, & Ross, 2005; Cole & Hatano, 2007; M. Feinberg & Willer, 2011; Furnham, 2003; Gifford, 2011; Koltko-Rivera, 2004; Lewandowsky, Oberauer, & Gignac, 2013.
30. Evans, 2008; Koltko-Rivera, 2004; Kuhn & Park, 2005; O. Lee, 1999; Lewandowsky et al., 2013; Mosborg, 2002.
31. Aslin & Newport, 2012; Kornell & Bjork, 2008a; Mandler, 2007; Rosch, 1978; Ross & Spalding, 1994; Tennyson & Cocchiarella, 1986.
32. Kuhn, 2015; Murphy, Wilkinson, & Soter, 2011; Tessler & Nelson, 1994.
33. Andriessen, 2006; Kuhn, 2015; Kuhn & Crowell, 2011; Murphy & Mason, 2006; Nussbaum, 2008; Reznitskaya & Gregory, 2013.

4

Key Components of the Human Memory
System: An Overly Simplistic Yet Useful Model

Taken as a whole, the tens of thousands of research studies that psychologists have conducted about human memory indicate that it's a very complex phenomenon indeed. Furthermore, it can work somewhat differently on different occasions and for different kinds of stimuli, activities, purposes, and contexts. Nevertheless, in their collective efforts to organize and find meaning in their data, psychologists have constructed a few theories about how memory might work in general.

In this chapter, I present a model of memory that summarizes a good deal – but not all – of the research data. To some degree, this model is based on a classic theory proposed by Richard Atkinson and Richard Shiffrin in the late 1960s,[1] but I've modified it considerably to account for more recent findings. The basic components of the model are shown in Figure 4.1 Although the model is an imperfect one at best – it greatly oversimplifies what we mentally do when we think, learn, and remember – it provides a good organizational scheme for the chapter and can help *you* organize what you learn as you read the pages ahead.

An important thing to note about the model right off the bat is that it is *not* meant to depict distinctly different parts of the brain; for example, I'm *not* saying that the sensory register is in one spot and that working memory is somewhere else. As you learned in Chapter 2, the human brain works as an integrated whole, with countless interconnections going every which way. What I'm saying instead is that we often *behave* as if the memory system has somewhat distinct components with somewhat distinct functions.

As we examine the various parts of the model in this chapter and then continue to rely on it in subsequent chapters, three terms will pop up over and over: encoding, storage, and retrieval. As you should recall from Chapter 3, **encoding** information involves changing information from

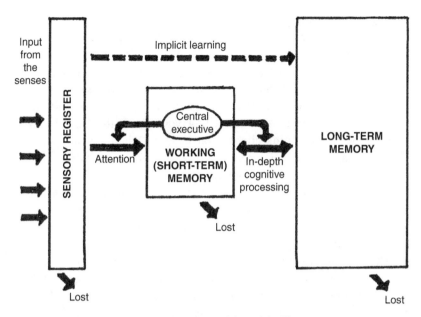

FIGURE 4.1. An imperfect yet useful model of human memory

one form to another – say, from the rose-like smell we might detect in someone's cologne to a mental image of a rose, or from complex visual input to the single word *horse*. When I use the word **storage**, I'm talking about the process of "putting" something in memory for future use. And **retrieval** is a process of "finding" information that has previously been stored somewhere in the memory system.

You might have noticed a parallel to computer lingo here: Computer scientists often talk about *coding, storage*, and *retrieval*. This isn't a coincidence. Many mid-20th-century models of memory were based on the idea that we humans think in much the same way that computers "think." Although many psychologists have abandoned the mind-as-computer analogy – because we rarely think and interpret information in the algorithmic, one-thing-always-leads-to-a-predictable-other-thing ways that computers do – some of the lingo has stayed with us.[2]

THE SENSORY REGISTER: A TEMPORARY MULTISENSORY HOLDING BIN

As we go through life, our brains seem to create a very temporary record of much or all of what we sense in our immediate environment.

They do so through several sense-specific areas of the brain that might collectively be called a **sensory register**.[3] For example, if you have ever played with a lighted sparkler on a festive holiday evening – as many people in the United States do on July 4th – then you've undoubtedly noticed the tail of light that follows the sparkler as you swish it about. That tail of light isn't "out there" in your environment; instead, this is your sensory register at work, telling you where the light has very recently been. And think about what happens when you find yourself daydreaming during a classroom lecture. As you mentally tune back in to what your instructor is saying, you might still be able to mentally "hear" the words that the instructor said within the preceding two or three seconds. As is true for the sparkler's tail, those words aren't lingering in the air around you; they're in your head – more specifically, in your sensory register.

The sensory register provides a way for us to record information in a relatively *un*encoded form; visual input remains as images, auditory input remains as it sounds, smells remain smelly, and so on. But this unencoded information doesn't last very long at all – especially if other, conflicting stimuli are coming our way.[4] Information about a visual stimulus begins to fade away within the first second or so, although rudiments of it may remain a little bit longer.[5] Information about an auditory stimulus may last several seconds, depending on how loud the stimulus was.[6]

In some instances, especially noteworthy information finds its way into long-term memory without us having to think much about it (more on this point in a later section on implicit learning). By and large, however, if we want to remember something for any length of time, we need to move it on to working memory, and we can do that only by paying attention to it. Otherwise, we're apt to lose it altogether, as indicated by the "lost" arrow below the sensory register in Figure 4.1.

MOVING INFORMATION TO WORKING MEMORY: THE ROLE OF ATTENTION

Notice the "attention" arrow going from the sensory register to working memory in Figure 4.1. By the word **attention**, I don't mean just focusing your eyes or ears in a particular direction. I also mean focusing your *mind* on what you're seeing or hearing. To see what I mean, try answering this simple question:

How long does information last in your sensory register?

If you can't answer my question, you weren't paying much mental attention to the paragraphs you think you just "read." Read them again, and this time *really* read them.

Certain kinds of objects and events just naturally draw our attention. Objects that are big, bright, colorful, or in motion almost always capture our eye. Exceptionally loud sounds – say the sound of gunshots or an explosion – can stop us dead in our tracks. Objects and events that are quite unusual or puzzling can be especially attention getting, and we're more likely to remember them as a result. For example, look at the four women in Figure 4.2. Which one keeps your attention the longest? Probably the modern-day Medusa – the one with snakes growing out of her head.

Psychological factors come into play in attention as well. For instance, we're more likely to pay attention to objects and events that evoke strong emotions, as an adorable puppy or a gory traffic accident might do.[7] We're also more likely to pay attention to things we find personally significant and important.[8] Events are especially attention grabbing when they have emotional overtones *and* are relevant to our personal lives.

A key reason why we seem to lose so much of what we've stored in our sensory register is that we can pay attention to only a little bit of information at a time; in other words, *attention has a very limited capacity.* For example, if you're walking through a flower garden, you can certainly see

FIGURE 4.2. Which one of these four women most easily captures and keeps your attention?

the wide display of shapes and colors all at once, but you can see details only if you stop and look at a particular lily, rose, or daffodil. And imagine that you're having dinner with several friends who are all talking at once about different topics. Although you can simultaneously hear all the chatter, you can probably focus in on and make sense of what only one of those friends is saying. In both the flower garden and dinner party scenarios, the *figure-ground* principle described in Chapter 3 is at work: You see or hear details in only a very small part of your environment, with the rest fading into the background.

Exactly how much we can pay attention to at once depends on the complexity of the various things we're dealing with.[9] For example, let's say that you're an experienced driver. You're driving along a major highway with a friend beside you in the passenger seat. It's a sunny day, the pavement is dry, and there's very little traffic to contend with. In this situation, it's probably pretty easy to carry on a conversation with your friend about, say, local politics or the latest juicy gossip. But maybe, instead, you're going through a heavy rainstorm, the road is slippery, and some of the drivers around you are dangerously zipping in and out of different lanes. In such circumstances, you need to keep your mental attention on the road and traffic – navigating safely is going to consume all of your mental capacity. This is definitely *not* the time to discuss the meaning of life or the nature of the universe.

WORKING MEMORY: WHERE THE WORK GETS DONE– BUT ONLY A LITTLE BIT AT A TIME

Working memory is the component of the human memory system in which we both (a) hold a little bit of information and (b) actively *think* about it. You might think of it as being the "awareness" or "consciousness" part of your memory.[10] For example, I'm hoping that as your eyes are moving down this page of the book, you're actively trying to make sense of the words you're reading. If so, the words and their meanings are in your working memory. If not – for instance, if your mind is instead making weekend travel plans or mulling over a bitter argument you recently had with a friend – I can guarantee you that nothing in this paragraph you're supposedly "reading" now will look familiar the next time you read it.

Earlier in the chapter I mentioned that the sensory register isn't really a single entity, that, rather, it encompasses several sense-specific areas of the brain. The same is true for working memory: It's comprised of several specialized brain entities that help us remember things for the short run.[11]

At a minimum, working memory seems to encompass (a) a subauditory system that can mentally "play back" what we've just heard or said; (b) a "computer screen" of sorts on which we can briefly display and manipulate visual images; and (c) a place where we can temporarily integrate, think about, and interpret multiple forms of input, usually drawing on information from long-term memory as we do so.[12]

Let's return again to the memory model depicted in Figure 4.1. Notice how the working memory box is much shorter (vertically) than the boxes for the sensory register and long-term memory. I've made the working memory box small to indicate that working memory doesn't have very much "room" in it; like attention, it has a *limited capacity*. As an illustration, try to solve the long-division problem shown in Figure 4.3 *entirely in your head*. I'm willing to bet that you can't do it unless you write down at least some parts of the problem or your solution. For example, you might start by trying to divide 47 into 168, getting an answer of "3" with some of that 168 left over ... so you need to figure out exactly how much is left over ... which is 27 ... and then you need to add the fourth number in the dividend to 27 to make a three-digit number ... and what was that fourth number again? (The solution to the problem is 359.)

Exactly *how* small working memory is depends on how we measure it. In the 1950s, one prominent researcher found that young adults can typically hold between five and nine randomly selected digits in working memory at any one time – a range he referred to as the *magic number 7, plus or minus 2*.[13] More recently, another prominent psychologist has proposed that adults can keep only about three to five *meaningful items* (e.g., very short sentences) in working memory – a capacity he has called the *magical mystery four*.[14] Given the limitations of today's research methods and technologies, it's virtually impossible to determine the exact capacity of working memory. How "small" or "large" it is depends both on what's in it and what we're trying to do with its contents as we actively process them.

So, then, both attention and working memory have limited capacities. This probably isn't a coincidence. Obviously, attention and working memory are closely linked. Some memory theorists have proposed that attention is actually an *integral part* of working memory, whereas as others

$$47 \overline{)16,873}$$

FIGURE 4.3. Can you do this long-division problem entirely in your head?

maintain that the two should be treated as separate phenomena.[15] You and I will leave the matter for future psychologists and neuroscientists to determine. The practical implications of our limited attentional and working-memory resources – which we'll zero in on at the end of the chapter – are pretty much the same either way.

Not only is working memory fairly "short" in terms of capacity, but it's also quite short in terms of duration. In particular, whatever we store in working memory typically doesn't last very long – maybe 30 seconds at most, and often for much less time than that.[16] Accordingly, an early term for working memory was *short-term memory*. Although this latter term still appears in some psychological literature, it has gone out of favor for at least two reasons. For one thing, it doesn't communicate the very active, "working" quality of this component of memory; it implies that it's only another passive holding bin for information.[17] Second, it has spurred another common misconception:

> Misconception #13: That information that can be remembered only
> for a few hours, days, or weeks is in "short-term memory"

No!! If we can't remember something for more than a few hours, we have a problem with *long-term* memory, not short-term, working memory. In our discussion of forgetting in Chapter 8, we'll explore reasons why we often lose information that we've previously stored in long-term memory.

There's one way we can extend the duration of *verbal* information in working memory just a little bit. In particular, we can repeat its contents over and over again – a process called **maintenance rehearsal**. For example, imagine that you want to call someone on your phone. You don't have the person's phone number in your contacts list, so you need to look it up somewhere. But when you find the number, your phone isn't handy, so you can't immediately dial it. What do you do to help you remember the number while you track down your phone's whereabouts? If you're like most people, you probably say it to yourself over and over again. This strategy works only if the number is quite short – maybe 7 or 8 digits – such that you can mentally still "hear" the first couple of digits while you're saying the last two or three.[18] Otherwise, you're out of luck, as reflected in the "lost" arrow below working memory in Figure 4.1. If you want to remember information that's longer or more complex than a seven-digit phone number, you can't just repeat it a few times; you need to do something more with it so that it works its way into long-term memory.

THE BEST PATH TO LONG-TERM MEMORY: PROCESSING INFORMATION IN DEPTH

In some parts of the world, phone numbers can be more than 10 digits long. For example, let's say that you want to remember this phone number: 56-78-987-654-3210. Even though it's 14 digits long, you can easily remember it by thinking: "It starts at five, counts up to nine, and then counts backward to zero." Identifying a logical pattern in a sequence of digits, or in some other way imposing meaning on it, makes it more memorable. For example, my home phone number ends in 1341. I remember it by thinking, "Start at one, go up two digits [to three], then up another one [to four], and then back to one." I have subsequently gotten a cell phone number that ends in 1261 – again, there's a start-with-1-and-end-with-1 pattern that helps me remember it. Notice how I've mentally changed my phone numbers – that is, I've *encoded* them – as a means of helping me make better sense of them.

Encoding information sufficiently that we can keep it for a while requires us to do a lot more than simply paying attention to it. We might find patterns in it, compare it with other things we've previously learned, draw conclusions and implications from it, or critically evaluate its accuracy and personal relevance for us. Or, as you might have done when you looked at Figure 3.1 in Chapter 3, we might simply attach a verbal label to it, such as "a giraffe kissing an elephant." We humans can be quite flexible and creative in how we encode and save information for the long run – so much so that I'm devoting all of Chapter 5 to what in-depth processing might entail. But for now you should know one important point about long-term memory storage. If you look at Figure 4.1 again, you can see that the arrow between working memory and long-term memory points in both directions. Making sense of new information in working memory typically requires us to make use of some of our "old" information – almost as if we're bringing a little bit of long-term memory's contents *back* into working memory.

LONG-TERM MEMORY: WHERE MEANINGS AND MEMORIES CAN LAST MUCH LONGER, BUT NOT NECESSARILY FOREVER

As its name implies, **long-term memory** is the component of the memory system that holds information and skills for a relatively long period – perhaps for hours, days, months, years, or decades. Unlike working memory, its capacity is essentially limitless. This brings us to another misconception:

Misconception #14: That long-term memory has an upper limit on how much information it can hold

If you ever hear someone suggesting that people may occasionally need to forget some things in long-term memory in order to make room for other things – and I myself have occasionally heard or read this very idea – you should quickly dismiss the message as complete hogwash. There is absolutely *no* evidence to indicate that we ever "run out of room" in long-term memory.

The neurological basis of long-term memory is distributed across much of the brain; it isn't the single, separate box that Figure 4.1 depicts. And the knowledge it holds takes many forms, including encoded versions of various symbol systems (e.g., words and numbers); perception-based images (e.g., visual imagery, memories of certain sounds and smells); behaviors (e.g., knowledge about how to use scissors or dribble a basketball); and under-lying, nonverbal meanings and gist (e.g., a general sense of the mood that Beethoven's *Moonlight Sonata* conveys).

Many cognitive psychologists make a distinction between two general kinds of knowledge in long-term memory: declarative and procedural. **Declarative knowledge** involves *knowing how things are, were, will be, or might be*: For example, roses are red, Christopher Columbus first sailed across the Atlantic in 1492, the 22nd century will begin on January 1, 2101 (nope, not 2100 – do the math), and medical researchers might eventually find ways to successfully cure all or most forms of cancer. Meanwhile, **procedural knowledge** is *knowing how to do things* – for instance, how to ride a bike, bake a cake, or send a text message. As you might guess, information encoded as language, numerical symbols, or images mostly falls into the declarative category, whereas much of our behavioral knowl-edge is procedural. Procedural knowledge often includes knowledge about how to behave differently under different circumstances, in which case it's also called **conditional knowledge**.

Once again recall how all those neurons and glial cells in the brain are interconnected in a gazillion ways. Okay, so *gazillion* isn't a real number, but there are so many interconnections in the brain that we might as well stop pretending that neuroscientists have pinned down anything close to a precise quantity. The point here is that information in long-term memory is interrelated and organized in countless ways. I mentioned a few possi-bilities in Chapter 3: concepts, schemas, scripts, personal theories, and worldviews. But if you think about it, virtually everything in long-term memory is probably somehow connected with everything else – albeit often by circuitous routes.

As an example of your own long-term memory's organization, try a little exercise. In a moment, I'm going to give you a word. Write down whatever other word most immediately comes to mind. Then write the word that the second word calls to mind, and afterward write the *next* word you think of, and so on until you have a string of at least 10 words, each of which has some mental association with the words preceding and following it. If a word in your train of thought immediately evokes a two- or three-word phrase, you should include it and treat it as a single entry. So . . . here's the word:

pizza

What final word or phrase did you end up with? When I did the exercise myself, the 10th entry in my train-of-thought list was *Treasure Island*. To my recollection, pizza isn't mentioned anywhere in Robert Louis Stevenson's classic book of that title. Here is how I got from one place to the other:

pizza → pepperoni → hotdogs → baseball → Red Sox → Boston → Charles River → sailboats → pirates → treasure → *Treasure Island*

Reflecting on this sequence a bit, I've been able to identify a few of the associations I have in my long-term memory; the diagram in Figure 4.4 gives you a glimpse of them.

Your list was almost certainly quite different from mine. For instance, perhaps *pizza* reminded you of tomatoes, parties, or Italy; with any of these associations, you would have mentally "traveled" in an entirely different direction than I did. But had we both traveled long enough, we might have eventually "arrived" at the same place – say, at "Sicily," "catfish," or "Johnny Depp."

How long does information in long-term memory last? Here we have yet another misconception:

Misconception #15: That all information stored in long-term memory stays there until we die

In the 1970s, many psychologists believed that such is the case – that once information is stored in long-term memory, it remains there permanently in some form. Thus, if we have trouble remembering it, these psychologists thought, it's only because we can't find, or *retrieve*, it.[19] And some kinds of information do seem to stick around for quite a long time after we've learned them, even if we haven't used them in the interim.[20] But many other things do seem to fade away over time, as you'll discover in Chapter 6. And

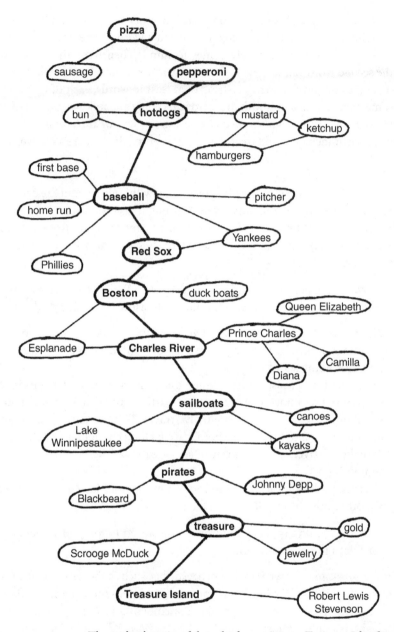

FIGURE 4.4. The author's train of thought from *pizza* to *Treasure Island*

ultimately, there's probably no way to show conclusively that *all* information stored in long-term memory remains there permanently.

THE CENTRAL EXECUTIVE: THE GENERAL SUPERVISOR OF COGNITION AND MEMORY

If you look yet again at Figure 4.1, you should notice that working memory has a subcomponent with two arrows going outward and then down from it. Many psychologists have suggested that our memory system must have some sort of **central executive** that focuses our attention on important environmental input, sets priorities in our sense-making efforts, selects and controls complex voluntary behaviors, and inhibits counterproductive thoughts and actions. Such processes – collectively known as **executive functions** – can greatly enhance our ability to think and learn both in formal instructional settings and in our informal, everyday experiences.[21]

The mental processes associated with the central executive appear to take place primarily in the prefrontal cortex – the part of the brain located right behind the forehead. As you should recall from Chapter 2, the prefrontal cortex continues to mature over the course of childhood, adolescence, and early adulthood; thus, we become increasingly able to regulate our thoughts and actions well into our twenties.[22] Even so, some of us are better self-regulators than others, as you'll learn in the discussion of *effortful control* in Chapter 9.

IMPLICIT LEARNING: A BYPASS ROUTE TO LONG-TERM MEMORY

Up to this point, I've been treating working memory as a necessary step on the way to long-term memory. In other words, I've been suggesting that we humans can remember information for the long run only if we actively, consciously think about it for at least a few seconds. But in fact, after capturing a little bit of our attention, some environmental stimuli and events seem to travel almost immediately from the sensory register to long-term memory, as indicated by the broken arrow going across the top of Figure 4.1.[23] For example, consider these questions:

> Which of these words occurs more frequently in English – *apple* or *apricot*?
> Where are you more likely to see a horse – in a field or in a shopping mall?

You probably had no trouble correctly answering these questions. *Apple* occurs more often than *apricot*, and horses are more often seen in fields than in shopping malls. We humans can easily answer many questions about frequency and location even if we've never consciously thought about such matters.[24]

It's possible that our brains acquire and retain information in two distinctly different ways.[25] One is a conscious, active-thinking route that travels through working memory. The other is a more basic, "thoughtless" route – **implicit learning** – that involves automatic detection and use of regular relationships and patterns in our physical and social environments.[26] Remember a point I made in Chapter 1: We humans seem to be naturally inclined to find patterns in our world, even if we don't intentionally look for them.

Within this context, it's helpful to make another distinction, this one regarding the *forms* that information can take in long-term memory. More specifically, some of what we have learned is **explicit knowledge**, in that we can easily recall and explain it. But long-term memory also contains **implicit knowledge**, which can affect our thoughts and behaviors even though we're not consciously aware of it. For example, I'm hoping that you now have some explicit knowledge about the concepts *sensory register, working memory*, and *long-term memory*, such that you should be able to write an informed paragraph about each one of them. But you probably had only implicit knowledge about the relative frequencies of apples, apricots, and horse locations until I asked you about them just now. My questions presumably made you *think* about what you knew, thereby bringing your knowledge into conscious awareness and converting it into explicit knowledge.

It's important to keep in mind that the "knowledge" we're talking about here includes not only facts but also *beliefs* that aren't necessarily grounded in reality. Let's return to a point I made about personal theories and worldviews in Chapter 3: They're often such an integral part of our thinking that we take them for granted and aren't consciously aware of them. In other words, personal theories and worldviews can take the form of *implicit knowledge*. When such below-the-surface "knowledge" flies in the face of scientific facts or other well-established truisms, it can wreak havoc with our thinking and future learning – a topic I'll return to in Chapter 8.

The Special Case of Infantile Amnesia: Why We Don't Remember Our Infancy and Toddler Years

Most of us remember little or nothing about the first three or four years of our lives. I, for one, can recall only one occasion, in which I was sitting on my Nana's cozy lap as she sat in her flower garden. I was quite content there, but then along came one of my father's sisters, who leaned down with outstretched arms and obviously wanted to pick me up and hold me. Seeing this woman's huge grin, black horn-rimmed glasses, and bright red hair and lipstick, I began to scream, frightened almost to death about the prospect of being transferred from an angel's care to that of a voracious harpy. I still remember the scene quite vividly, although who knows? I've revisited and described it so many times that my recollection might be far removed from what actually happened, and conceivably it never happened at all.

So, back to my point: We remember very little of our infancy and toddlerhood. Theorists have offered at least two plausible explanations for this **infantile amnesia**. For one thing, our infant brains are still developing, and those brain structures that are actively involved in forming explicit memories (e.g., the hippocampus and frontal cortex) still have quite a way to go in their development.[27] Also, although we're implicitly learning aspects of our native language almost from Day 1,[28] to the extent that we can't yet *talk* about our experiences, we have a harder time encoding them in ways that enable meaningful learning.[29]

AN ALTERNATIVE TO THE THREE-COMPONENT MODEL: MAYBE IT'S ALL JUST A MATTER OF ACTIVATION

As I warned you at the beginning of the chapter, the model of memory presented in Figure 4.1 oversimplifies – and also overcompartmentalizes – the nature of human memory. For example, in my earlier discussion of working memory, I mentioned that this component of memory seems to include an auditory playback mechanism that holds something we've just heard or said; it probably also has a computer-screen-like mechanism on which we can display visual information. At least for auditory and visual input, then, the sensory register and working memory probably rely on some of the same modality-specific areas of the brain. Also, you should recall a comment I made earlier about attention: Some theorists maintain that rather than being a process through which information moves on to working memory, attention is actually an integral *part* of working memory.

In addition, psychologists and neuroscientists disagree about whether working memory and long-term memory are distinctly different entities. An alternative view is that these two components simply reflect different levels of **activation** within a single memory system.[30] From this perspective, all of the knowledge and beliefs stored in our memory are in either an active or an inactive state. Active information is whatever we're currently attending to and thinking about; this is information that would be in working memory in the three-component model. As we shift our attention elsewhere, we activate other things, and the previously activated stuff fades into inactivity. For example, look back at the list of items that the word *pizza* led you to generate. As you free-associated from *pizza* and beyond, you sequentially activated a variety of words/phrases, and then, as you continued, you left the previous items behind in your mental dust. At any one time, the vast majority of the knowledge and ideas we've acquired over the years are inactive, such that we aren't currently thinking about them; in the three-component model, these would be in long-term memory.

I need to add one further complication to the mix here. Some research indicates that thinking itself can occasionally occur outside the confines of active, working memory. For example, we can sometimes tackle a complex problem more effectively when we don't actively think about it for a period of time.[31] Even though our minds might be focused on other matters altogether, in the "darker corners" of our minds we might be subconsciously mulling over the problem, perhaps identifying especially important aspects, imprecisely estimating certain quantities, or integrating problem-relevant information. The products of such nonconscious thinking are often hard to put an explicit finger on; we might simply describe them as "intuition" or "gut feelings."[32]

In sum, then, the three-component model doesn't give us a completely accurate story – and certainly not the *whole* story – about how memory works. Nevertheless, it can help you remember a few very important characteristics of the human memory system. For example, the model highlights the importance of *attention* in learning, the *limited capacity* of both attention and working memory, and the *interconnectedness* of the knowledge and beliefs we acquire and then remember over time. Such ideas are reflected in some of the self-strategies and instructional strategies I present now.

BEING STRATEGIC

As you strive to help both yourself and others learn and remember things more effectively and efficiently, you should build on the strengths of the human memory system – for instance, its ability to integrate new information with older stuff. But you must also be aware of human memory's limitations – for example, working memory's small capacity and short duration. With such points in mind, I offer the following recommendations.

Enhancing Your Own Thinking and Learning
in Everyday Life

- **Self-Strategy 4.1: Prioritize the must-knows over the would-be-nice-to-knows.** You can't possibly remember all the information you encounter every day. As you go along, then, try to identify the things that will be most useful to you. If you're not sure – as, unfortunately, can sometimes be the case in college classes – ask someone who can help you make good choices.
- **Self-Strategy 4.2: Pay attention during important learning and performance tasks.** We humans seem to be naturally inclined to mentally wander and daydream once in a while.[33] Perhaps something we see or hear reminds us of something else in long-term memory, which reminds us of yet another thing, and so on – much as your mind traveled from one word to a very different word in the pizza exercise – to the point that we're oblivious to what's going on around us. Given the nature of human memory, I can't tell you to keep your mind on what's in front of you every second of the day. But I *can* tell you to be alert to and minimize any potential lapses in attention when you're trying to learn and remember important information. Maybe a hot cup of coffee would help you focus your attention, or maybe some chewing gum would do the trick. Personally, I've found that a small bag of peanut M&Ms helps me get through a task that most college professors find quite dull and boring: grading a large stack of papers or essay exams.
- **Self-Strategy 4.3: Minimize outside distractions if you really need to concentrate.** For example, find a quiet place in a library or a coffee shop. Don't pretend that you can concentrate on a challenging, thought-intensive task when your television is on or when some of your friends are exchanging juicy gossip a few feet away from you. You can't do it!
- **Self-Strategy 4.4: Use paper or a computer to help you think about many things at once.** Virtually any task or problem requires your working memory to juggle several things at once. You have some information in there to start with, you have more information coming at you (perhaps because your own actions are creating it), and you need to mentally do one or more things with it all. Taken together, these things impose a certain **cognitive load** on your working memory. When the cognitive load exceeds what your limited working memory can

handle, you're out of luck until you figure out a way to offload part of this mental burden onto something else.[34]

Many centuries ago, our ancestors would scratch pictures and diagrams in the dirt. Then along came papyrus, ink, and paper, which weren't as messy and could be used indoors as well as outdoors. And now we have computer screens to supplement our limited working memory capacities as we work. For example, as I write this book, I have little notes-to-self all over my screen that help me remember the points I want to make in my discussion of strategies here. Throughout history, the most successful members of our species have rarely tried to rely exclusively on their inner mental hardware; in one way or another, they've written things down.

- **Self-Strategy 4.5: Don't assume that immediate recall of information will translate into recall at a later time**. Let's say that you're in your kitchen making a mental list of five things you need to get at the grocery store: milk, chicken soup, a loaf of bread, a can of tuna fish, and some green onions. You repeat this list over and over to yourself a few times: "Milk, soup, bread, tuna, onions ... milk, soup, bread, tuna, onions ... milk, soup, bread, tuna, onions." Okay, you've got it, you think. But when you get to the store, suddenly the list is "milk, soup ... milk, soup ..." What you had *really* done when you were in your kitchen was either (a) engage in maintenance rehearsal (in which case the list was only in your working memory) or (b) store the five items in your long-term memory without trying to connect them together (in which case remembering one item wouldn't necessarily help you activate and retrieve the other items). So here's a second reason to write things down: Memory is notoriously unreliable for miscellaneous tidbits that have few or no logical connections among them.

- **Self-Strategy 4.6: Actively create connections between the new and the old**. Sometimes you can easily identify logical connections between new information and things you already know, but in other cases you might have to artificially impose these links. For example, one way to remember milk, chicken soup, a loaf of bread, tuna fish, and green onions would be to connect them to a familiar song or poem. Perhaps you could sing the following lyrics to the tune of "Row, Row, Row Your Boat":

> Milk, milk, milk, and soup
> And a can of tuna,
> Green onions, yes, green onions,
> And a loaf of bread.

My little ditty here is an example of a *mnemonic* – an artificial memory aid that can help you remember a small amount of miscellaneous and seemingly unconnected information. Unless you have a lot of mental time on your hands, however, I don't recommend creating mnemonics for simple shopping lists you could easily write down. In Chapter 5, I'll describe a variety of strategies – some logical, some contrived – for connecting the new with the old.

Enhancing Other People's Thinking and Learning in Instructional Settings

- **Instructional Strategy 4.1: Direct students' attention to the things that are most important for them to notice and learn.** When people begin to study a new topic, they often don't know what things they should focus their attention on. For example, when reading their textbooks, many high school and college students are so concerned about remembering specific, isolated facts that they lose sight of a chapter's main ideas.[35] And when first learning a new sport – say, tennis, softball, or basketball – people may be so overwhelmed by all the action on the court or playing field that they fail to see the behavioral subtleties that make highly skilled individuals successful. Following are just three of the many ways in which you might help novices zero in on what they most need to learn and remember:
  - Describe what people should be able to do at the end of instruction, ideally in the form of specific goals, objectives, or evaluation criteria.[36]
  - Provide a few questions that people should try to answer as they read a textbook or listen to a lecture.
  - If you're demonstrating a new athletic skill, perform it in slow motion while drawing attention to especially important components of the skill (e.g., how to grip the racket or bat and how best to shift one's weight during execution of the skill).
- **Instructional Strategy 4.2: Keep instruction interesting and engaging enough that students *want* to pay attention.** In formal educational settings, successfully teaching any complex topic or skill requires not only that you *get* students' attention but also that you *keep* it for a while. Following are strategies you might use to keep students mentally attentive for extended periods of time:
  - Relate your subject matter to students' personal lives and interests.

- ○ Vary your instructional methods – for instance, by combining one or more short explanations, hands-on experiences, small-group assignments, and whole-class discussions into a single lesson.
- ○ Ask a lot of questions, and create a mechanism through which everyone can simultaneously respond to them, perhaps by requesting a show of hands or perhaps by using handwritten or preprinted cards with which they can "vote" on a limited number of possible answers.
- ○ Occasionally incorporate humor, fantasy, mystery, and/or gamelike activities into lessons.[37]

○ **Instructional Strategy 4.3: Encourage note taking**. One obvious advantage of taking notes is that it enables students to go back and review something they've previously heard or read. But research studies have shown that note taking has other benefits as well: (a) It helps students keep their attention on the content of a lesson; (b) it requires students to *encode* new information into written form, graphic form, or both; and (c) it encourages students to make sense of the information in some way – at a minimum by translating ideas into their own words and perhaps also by spurring them to draw self-constructed conclusions and implications.[38] Keep in mind, however, that the effectiveness of notes depends on their quality; ideally, notes are not only accurate but also fairly detailed and organized.[39] Even at the college level, many students need guidance in their note-taking efforts. For example, you might:

- ○ Provide a general organizational framework or worksheet for taking notes.
- ○ Write key concepts, definitions, and ideas on the board.
- ○ Explicitly identify important information (e.g., "This is a major point, so be sure to include it in your notes").[40]

○ **Instructional Strategy 4.4: Simplify activities and assignments sufficiently that they don't overload students' working memories**. Here's the *cognitive load* issue again. For example, if you're asking students in a high school physics lab to separate and control variables as they experiment with, say, a swinging pendulum or balls rolling down an inclined plane, you should limit the number of variables they need to consider at once (e.g., you might ask them to vary only the weight of the balls and the length of the pendulum or incline, while keeping other potentially influential variables constant). Likewise, if you're teaching beginning music students how to play the trumpet, you shouldn't expect them to simultaneously think about how to (a) place their fingers on the right valves for each note, (b) correctly blow into the mouthpiece, and (c) make logical sense of the sheet music for "Uptown Funk." Eventually your trumpet students should be able to do all of these things at once, but only after they've had quite a bit of practice with their fingering and blowing techniques.

○ **Instructional Strategy 4.5: Set realistic goals about what students should try to learn and remember from any single learning activity.** To some degree, setting high expectations for students' learning and achievement is a good thing, because high expectations communicate the optimistic message that everyone can and should do well. But – and this is a very important *but* – it's entirely too easy to go overboard and expect the impossible. As you now know well, we human beings can mentally process only so much information at a time, and we can process it only so fast.

Being realistic in your goals for students' learning involves two things. First, you must be realistic about the *scope* of what can be accomplished within a limited time period; it would be impossible for students to remember everything you tell them. And second, you must be realistic about the *pacing* of your instruction. I'm not saying that you should ... speak ... as ... if ... you ... had ... marbles ... in ... your ... mouth. Instead, good pacing might involve repeating important ideas several times and in several different ways (e.g., through both words and graphics), interspersing those ideas with examples and potential applications, and occasionally reminding students of related ideas they already have in their long-term memories.

○ **Instructional Strategy 4.6: Focus any assessments on what students most need to know and be able to do.** As I mentioned at the end of Chapter 1, teachers teach not only through the lessons they conduct but also through the ways in which they assess students' learning. I'm basically making the same point here, because it needs repeating. If you tell students that they should focus on major ideas and themes but then create multiple-choice or true-false tests that require them to recall trivial details ... well, think about it, what are you doing? Not only are you encouraging students to focus on the tiny "trees" of information instead of on the overall, interrelated "forest" of ideas, but you're also being a hypocrite: Students learn that they can't trust you to mean what you say.

NOTES

1. R. C. Atkinson & Shiffrin, 1968; for a similar but much earlier model, see James, 1890.
2. For good discussions of how a computer analogy falls short, see Hacker, Dunlosky, & Graesser, 2009a; Marcus, 2008; Minsky, 2006; Rubin, 2006.
3. There is no consensus on what this aspect of memory is called. Other commonly used terms are *sensory memory, sensory buffer, brief sensory store, iconic memory* (for vision), and *echoic memory* (for hearing).
4. Baddeley, Eysenck, & Anderson, 2009; Breitmeyer & Ganz, 1976; Lu & Sperling, 2003; Sligte, Sholte, & Lamme, 2009.
5. Gold, Murray, Sekuler, Bennett, & Sekuler, 2005; Sligte et al., 2009.
6. Baldwin, 2007; Cowan, Nugent, Elliott, & Saults, 2000; Lu, Williamson, & Kaufman, 1992.
7. Kuhbandner, Spitzer, & Pekrun, 2011; Mather & Sutherland, 2011; Ristic & Enns, 2015; Rothbart, 2011.
8. Barkley, 1996; Craik, 2006; Kaplan & Berman, 2010.
9. Cowan, 2007; Pashler, 1992; Sergeant, 1996.
10. For example, see Paller et al., 2009; Reznick, 2007; Siegel, 2012.
11. Baddeley, 2001, 2007; Logie, 2011; Shah & Miyake, 1996; Smith, 2000.
12. Baddeley (e.g., 2001; Baddeley et al., 2009) calls these three components the *phonological loop, visuospatial sketchpad*, and *episodic buffer*, respectively.
13. G. A. Miller, 1956.
14. Cowan, 2010; readers who are Beatles fans might recognize the *magical mystery four* as being a play on the album title *Magical Mystery Tour*. We psychologists like to think that we have a good sense of humor.
15. For example, see Cowan, 2007; Kiyonaga & Egner, 2014; Oberauer & Hein, 2012.
16. Barrouillet & Camos, 2012; Cowan, Wood, Nugent, & Treisman, 1997; L. R. Peterson & Peterson, 1959; Zhang & Luck, 2009.
17. Some models of memory include *both* short-term memory and working memory as separate entities, with the former serving only as a temporary holding bin and the latter enabling manipulation of information (e.g., see Baddeley et al., 2009).
18. Baddeley, 2001.
19. Loftus & Loftus, 1980.
20. Bahrick, 1984; Bowers, Mattys, & Gage, 2009; Mitchell, 2006; Semb & Ellis, 1994.
21. Baddeley, 2001; Banich, 2009; Logie, 2011; Masten et al., 2012; Meltzer, 2007.
22. Atkins, Bunting, Bolger, & Dougherty, 2012; Best & Miller, 2010; Luciana, Conklin, Hooper, & Yarger, 2005; E. Peterson & Welsh, 2014; Zelazo, Müller, Frye, & Marcovitch, 2003.
23. Frensch & Rünger, 2003; Hintzman, 2011; Zacks, Hasher, & Hock, 1986.

24. Hasher & Zacks, 1984.
25. Bachevalier, Malkova, & Beauregard, 1996; Frensch & Rünger, 2003; Pelucchi, Hay, & Saffran, 2009; Siegel, 2012.
26. If you have a background in psychology, it may help you to note that much of what we learn through classical (Pavlovian) conditioning probably takes the form of implicit, below-the-surface-of-consciousness knowledge (e.g., see Kim, Lim, & Bhargava, 1998; Olson & Fazio, 2001).
27. C. A. Nelson et al., 2006; Newcombe, Drummey, Fox, Lie, & Ottinger-Albergs, 2000; Oakes & Bauer, 2007;
28. For example, see McDevitt & Ormrod, 2016, chapter 9.
29. Fivush, Haden, & Reese, 2006; McGuigan & Salmon, 2004; K. Nelson, 1996.
30. J. R. Anderson, 2005; Campo et al., 2005; Collins & Loftus, 1975; Nee, Berman, Moore, & Jonides, 2008; Öztekin, Davachi, & McElree, 2010.
31. Dijksterhuis & Strick, 2016; Hassin, 2013.
32. Bargh & Morsella, 2008; Dijksterhuis & Nordgren, 2006.
33. Delaney, Sahakyan, Kelley, & Zimmerman, 2010; Immordino-Yang, Christodoulou, & Singh, 2012; Kane et al., 2007.
34. Plass, Moreno, & Brünken, 2010; Sweller, 1988, 2008.
35. Alexander & Jetton, 1996; Dole, Duffy, Roehler, & Pearson, 1991; Reynolds & Shirey, 1988.
36. Educators use a variety of terms for such specifications of the desired end results of instruction; common ones are *goals, objectives, outcomes, competencies, benchmarks,* and *standards.*
37. Grabe, 1986; Hidi & Renninger, 2006; Krapp, Hidi, & Renninger, 1992; Marmolejo, Wilder, & Bradley, 2004; Pellegrini & Bjorklund, 1997; Urdan & Turner, 2005.
38. Benton, Kiewra, Whitfill, & Dennison, 1993; Di Vesta & Gray, 1972; J. Lee & Shute, 2010; Peverly, Brobst, Graham, & Shaw, 2003.
39. Benton et al., 1993; Cohn, Hult, & Engle, 1990; Jackson, Ormrod, & Salih, 1999; Kiewra, 1989.
40. Benton et al., 1993; Kiewra, 1989; Meltzer, Pollica, & Barzillai, 2007; Ormrod, 2016a; Pressley, Yokoi, Van Meter, Van Etten, & Freebern, 1997.

5

In-Depth Cognitive Processing: Maximizing the "Long-Term" in Long-Term Memory

As you've learned, saving new information and skills for any significant length of time requires considerable mental activity. Some of this activity lies below our conscious awareness, in the form of the neurological consolidation processes described in Chapter 2. But a good deal of it must involve *deliberate, conscious thinking* about what we've just seen, heard, or done. In most cases, in-depth processing entails connecting new knowledge and skills to the things we already know so that we can *find meaning* in the new stuff. Hence, such connection making is often called **meaningful learning**.[1]

Sometimes meaningful learning occurs without our having to think very much about new stimuli. For example, when you see a cylinder-like object with an upside-down-sock-shaped lump sticking up at one end, some stringy stuff hanging down in a clump at the other end, and four spindly things on the underside moving the whole contraption rather quickly across a large grassy area, you might almost immediately think, "There's a horse running across a field." But in other circumstances, we might have to do a bit of mental work to make sense out of something we want to remember. To see what I mean, read the following sentence:

> By the time babies are 4 months old, some of them spend a longer-than-average amount of time looking at situations in which basic principles of nature are seemingly violated – for instance, situations in which one object (e.g., a toy car) appears to travel through a space already occupied by another object (e.g., a toy mouse) without bumping into or displacing that second object.[2]

To make genuine sense of this sentence, you must stop and think about its various bits and pieces. Why might an infant look longer at situations in which one solid object appears to pass directly through another one? What

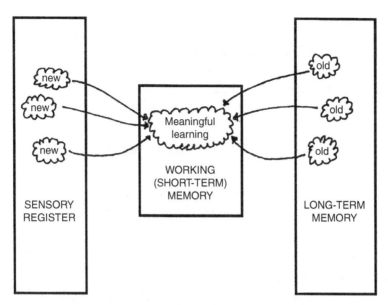

FIGURE 5.1. From the perspective of the three-component model of memory, meaningful learning occurs primarily in working memory, but it requires input from both the sensory register and long-term memory to do its work.

might this longer-than-average looking time suggest about what the infant is thinking or feeling? And what relevance might this research finding have for our understanding of infants' cognitive development and perhaps for human cognition in general? Only if you mentally ask yourself and then answer questions such as these are you likely to remember the content of the sentence for any length of time.

If we look at such situations from the perspective of the three-component model of memory presented in Chapter 4, we realize that the connection-making process must take place in working memory, with the new information coming in from the sensory register and the information we've previously learned being retrieved back into working memory from long-term memory. For us to make successful connections, both the "new" and the "old" must be in working memory at the same time (see Figure 5.1).[3]

But remember: Working memory has only a relatively small amount of "space" for holding and thinking about information. Although working memory's limited capacity can often make thinking and learning a bit challenging for us, it does have a silver lining. More specifically, it encourages us – might I say, it *forces* us – to condense and integrate the new things we learn. And the fact is, we usually don't need to remember all the nitty-gritty details we encounter in our everyday experiences.

With the concept of meaningful learning in mind, we now examine a variety of strategies that might or might not be effective in helping us store and keep new facts, ideas, and skills in long-term memory.

STRATEGIES THAT TEND NOT TO HELP VERY MUCH

Historically, some educators have advocated practices that do little, if anything, to help people learn and remember new things. The first three strategies I describe here fall into this not-terribly-helpful category.

Rehearsal: Saying Something Over and Over and Over Again

Perhaps you've had teachers who've encouraged you to repeat something over and over as a way of helping you remember it. If so, they – and you – have been victims of another common misconception:

> Misconception #16: That the best way to remember something is to repeat it over and over in a short period of time

Such **rehearsal** can definitely help you keep a small amount of verbal information in working memory indefinitely, as you discovered in the discussion of *maintenance rehearsal* in Chapter 4. But mindless – *thought-less* – repetition of information within, say, a 1-minute or 2-minute time interval usually doesn't work very well for the long run. Here I'm talking about **rote learning** – trying to learn something new in isolation from anything that's been learned in the past.

By and large, rehearsing new information within a *very short time span* is effective only if, at the same time, we also begin to associate it with information and ideas we've previously acquired – in other words, when meaningful learning comes into the picture.[4] In contrast, however, occasional repetition over the course of several weeks, months, or years has definite benefits, as you'll see in the discussion of *automaticity* later in the chapter.

Memorization Practice: Learning by Heart

When I was a child in the 1950s and 1960s, it was common practice for teachers to require students to learn certain poems and historically significant documents and speeches word for word, or "by heart." I specifically recall having to recite Robert Frost's poem "Stopping by Woods on a Snowy Evening" and Abraham Lincoln's Gettysburg Address ("Four score and seven years ago . . ."). It certainly makes sense to study such works. For instance, Frost's "Stopping by Woods" can both help students acquire an appreciation of well-written poetry and encourage them to occasionally pause to admire their natural surroundings. And with its embrace of "the proposition that all men are created equal," Lincoln's Gettysburg Address was an important step in my home country's efforts to abolish slavery.

Yet effectively studying something doesn't necessarily require *memorizing* it. The major misconception underlying frequently assigned memorization tasks is this one:

Misconception #17: That regular practice in memorizing verbal materials is a good way to strengthen our minds for other, unrelated purposes

This misconception was debunked more than 100 years ago when noted psychologist William James tried to memorize a new poem each day over the course of several weeks. His poem-learning ability didn't improve at all. If anything, so he reported, he learned his later poems more *slowly* than he had learned his early ones.[5] By and large, our brains aren't "muscles" that benefit from meaning*less* drill-and-practice exercise.

Studying "Mind-Strengthening" Subject Matter: *Cogito, Cogitas, Cogitat, Cogitamus, Cogitatus, Cogitant*

Another common practice in the early days of formal education, especially in the 1800s and early 1900s, was to intensively study topics such as Latin, ancient Greek, and formal logic, all of which require very rigorous, precise thinking. For example, in Latin, many nouns have 10 or more different forms, depending on whether the nouns are singular or plural and on what grammatical function they serve in a sentence. Latin is also quite picky about the appropriate ending for a verb, depending on what tense the verb is and on who or what is/are the agent(s) or passive recipient(s) of the "doing." For example, the Latin verb *cogitare* – meaning "to think" – has six forms in its present tense and active voice alone: *cogito* (for "I"), *cogitas* (for singular "you"), *cogitat* (for "he," "she," or "it"), *cogitamus* (for "we"), *cogitatus* (for plural "you"), and *cogitant* (for "they"). And you would need to use still other forms if you wanted to use a different tense or the passive voice.

Some academic content domains do indeed require considerable precision of thought; mathematics, chemistry, and physics are three good examples. But teaching a topic *only* because of its precision reflects this misconception:

Misconception #18: That studying any subject area that requires precise, rigorous thinking is another good way to strengthen our minds

Once again we're talking about general mental exercise here. Studying rigorous subject matter is quite appropriate *if* we want to learn about that specific topic. But if, instead, we study it only as a way of enhancing our ability to learn other, unrelated topics, we're better off just going straight to those other topics.[6] Yes, it's true that learning Latin or ancient Greek familiarizes us with the precursors to many vocabulary words in modern Western European languages; for instance, the Latin word *locus* (meaning "place") gave us such English words as *locate* and *local*, and the Greek terms *biblios* and *graphos* (meaning "book" and "something written," respectively) gave us *bibliography*. However, I argue (as have many others) that the time might be better spent simply learning the meanings of a wide range of English words. I speak from experience here: I studied Latin for three years in high school and one semester in college. I would have benefited much more from three-and-a-half years of Spanish, German, or Swahili – languages that would enable me to communicate more effectively with some of my fellow human beings in this 21st century.

Another rigorous topic that's quite appropriate to study for its own sake is computer programming, which requires very exact, detailed thinking about logical sequences of events. If we learn how to program in one computer language, we can subsequently learn another one much easier than we would otherwise because the logical reasoning processes tend to be quite similar. For example, virtually all computer programming languages include ways to specify steps such as *if-this-happens-then-do-that* and *do-this-for-a-certain-number-of-times*. But – again there's a big *but* here – experience in computer programming tends to have little or no impact on logical thinking in areas unrelated to computer use.[7]

Backpedaling a Bit: Some Forms of General Mental Exercise
Do Have Benefits

Despite what I've just said about the limitations of memorization practice and the study of rigorous subject matter, regularly exercising our brains with reasonably challenging tasks can enhance our daily functioning, especially in our later adult years. For example, in a study reported in 2014, healthy adults ages 65 and older participated in eighteen 60- to 75-minute training sessions in which they learned and practiced tasks involving (a) memory, (b) logical reasoning, or (c) fast reaction times. The first 10 of these sessions were given within a five- to six-week period; participants were then given four-session "boosters" one and three years later. In a follow-up 10 years after that, the people who had gotten the training and practice in either logical reasoning or fast reaction times were functioning at levels well above those who had gotten either the memory training or no training at all.[8]

Even as we approach our senior years, however, it's probably more productive to study new topics that have a practical purpose in our everyday lives – perhaps studying a new language (enabling us to travel to a country where we can use it), learning how to play bridge (providing a mechanism through which we can socialize more regularly with bridge-playing friends), or studying music theory (which might help us read music and play a musical instrument more meaningfully). Music theory is a precise, rigorous subject area indeed; I've recently had a few lessons on some of its intricacies. It's going to take a good deal of brainpower to totally wrap my head around it, but so what? I'm already making use of it.

STRATEGIES THAT CAN DEFINITELY ENHANCE LONG-TERM MEMORY: CONNECTING THE NEW WITH THE OLD

In one way or another, cognitive processes that effectively put and keep newly learned information and skills in long-term memory involve some form of meaningful learning. Following are several possible ways in which we might do this.

Elaboration: Using the Old to Embellish on the New

In Chapter 3, I asked you to read a passage about a possible robbery at a convenience store. In your efforts to make sense of the passage, you almost certainly added some things to the information actually presented on the page. Thus, you were engaging in **elaboration** – you were embellishing on the new information based on your current knowledge and beliefs about the world.

Probably because we humans are so eager to find meanings in our experiences, we often elaborate on the information we encounter in our day-to-day lives. "Joanne said *what*!!?? Are you kidding me!!?? She is *such* a jerk!" Joanne might have actually said what you think she said. But your conclusion that she's a jerk is your interpretation of her statement – you've just elaborated on the actual facts of the situation.

To be effective learners in formal instructional settings, we need to engage in elaboration as much as we reasonably – and *accurately* – can. Unfortunately, many students of all ages seem to be so concerned about learning academic subject matter exactly as it's presented to them that they neglect to draw from their prior knowledge and experiences to make reasonable sense of it.[9]

One way in which we might elaborate on new information is to *organize* it in some way. As a simple illustration, read the following twelve words. After you've read them, cover the page and try to recall as many of them as you can.

oak
mountain
daffodil
valley
tulip
daisy
cliff
maple
hill
rose
pine
elm

Could you remember all 12? Most people don't, at least not after a single reading. And did you recall them in the same order that you read them? Probably not. There's a good chance that you recalled them category by category – perhaps flowers, then trees, and then landforms. In general, we can learn and remember a body of new information more easily when we pull it together into some sort of logical organizational structure.[10] For example, we might identify cause-and-effect relationships and other inter-relations among the various tidbits we're studying. Or we might try to summarize it all, identifying main ideas and storing only the general meaning, or gist, of what we're reading or hearing.

Sometimes we don't have sufficient prior knowledge to productively elaborate on new information. As an illustration, following is the beginning of an abstract in an article recently published in the journal *Neuropsychology*:

> Objective: To better understand what influences interindividual differences in ability to navigate in the wilderness, we hypothesized that better performance would be seen in (a) BDNF (rs6265) Val/Val homozygotes' increased use of a spatial strategy, (b) KIBRA rs17070145 T/T homozygotes' superior episodic memory, (c) CHRNA4 (rs1044396) T allele carriers' better ability to focus visuospatial attention.[11]

Unless you have considerable knowledge of neuropsychology, you can't make much sense of this statement. The words "ability to navigate in the wilderness," "spatial," and "visuospatial attention" might give you a few clues regarding what the authors are talking about, but I haven't talked about episodic memory yet (that will come in Chapter 6), and I'm guessing that you have absolutely no idea what BDNF, KIBRA, and CHRNA4 are. If for some reason you had to remember this research objective, you would have little choice but to resort to rehearsal and memorization – rote learning – in an effort to try to make it stick in your long-term memory. And there's no way that it would last very long.

Another problem is that we sometimes elaborate on new information in counterproductive ways. For instance, we might relate it to our currently erroneous beliefs about a topic – perhaps thinking that reports of rapidly shrinking glaciers and ice caps near the North and South Poles can't possibly be true because "this whole climate change thing is a hoax." Or, instead, we might draw on correct beliefs that don't apply to the new information. Remember that 4-year-old in Chapter 3 who concluded that dinosaurs went extinct because they couldn't put on their sweaters? He was certainly right in thinking that sweaters can help keep people and certain domesticated animals warm on a cold day. But even those dinosaur species that might have been warm-blooded didn't have either the wherewithal or the inclination to knit sweaters.

Obviously, then, we need to be vigilant whenever we intentionally elaborate on new information – something that's often easier said than done. I'll pursue this point in greater depth a bit later.

Forming Images: Calling on Our Internal Artistic Talents

In Chapter 3, I mentioned *imagery* as one of the forms in which we encode new information. For example, what do Queen Elizabeth and

Leonardo DiCaprio look like? I'm predicting that images of both individuals come readily to mind. You probably didn't have to do much of anything (mentally) to store these images in your long-term memory. Now what does a violin sound like? What does dog poop smell like? And how does velvet feel when you rub your fingers across it? Your long-term memory contains many visual, auditory, olfactory (smell), and tactile images.

But right now I'm talking about *intentionally* forming images to help you learn and remember something. The bulk of the research on this topic has focused on **visual imagery** – forming a mental picture that captures how one or more objects or events might look. To see visual imagery at work in your own head, try conjuring up images of each of the following scenarios:

- A dog riding cowboy-style on a pig
- A yellow sailboat with a red sail gliding across a lake
- Leonardo DiCaprio wearing a grass skirt and doing the hula

Some of my readers should have an easy time doing this exercise; others might struggle with the task. People of all ages differ considerably in their ability to create visual images.[12]

It's unlikely that you'd ever *really* need to imagine Leonardo DiCaprio in a grass skirt. But visual imagery can come in quite handy if you're trying to learn and remember certain kinds of information – say, how you might use one or more pulleys and a sturdy rope to reduce the amount of effort needed to lift a heavy object or how you might use various colors to paint an aesthetically pleasing watercolor landscape. Visual imagery can also enhance your understanding of and appreciation for good literature. For example, in his classic novel *The Scarlet Letter* (set in the Massachusetts Bay Colony in the 1600s), Nathaniel Hawthorne described one character, the Reverend Arthur Dimmesdale, like so:

> He was a person of very striking aspect, with a white, lofty, and impend-ing brow, large, brown, melancholy eyes, and a mouth which, unless when he forcibly compressed it, was apt to be tremulous, expressing both nervous sensibility and a vast power of self-restraint. Notwithstanding his high native gifts and scholar-like attainments, there was an air about this young minister, – an apprehensive, a startled, a half-frightened look, – as of a being who felt himself quite astray and at a loss in the pathway of human existence, and could only be at ease in some seclusion of his own.

Can you picture such an individual? Doing so might give you an inkling that something wasn't right with this presumably pious preacher. Something definitely wasn't: He had fathered an illegitimate child but wouldn't own up to the fact even when the child's mother was being punished for her alleged sinfulness.

Visual imagery can be a highly effective means of remembering the kinds of information that easily lend themselves to visualization.[13] In fact, we can often better remember something if we encode it in *both* verbal and visual forms, providing that doing so doesn't overburden our limited working memory capacity.[14] As an illustration of this point, Figure 5.2 shows four simple line drawings with verbal labels that can help you remember them. Chances are that the labels are making the drawings more memorable for you. In Chapter 6, I'll ask you to test your memory of them.

Although auditory imagery hasn't been studied in the depth that visual imagery has, some people are obviously quite adept at mentally "hearing" sounds in combinations that they haven't specifically heard in their outside environments. For example, as great musical composers do their work, they're able to conjure up many auditory images of how certain sequences of chords would sound, and they can envision how various musical instruments might contribute to an elegant symphony.[15] And in my own informal observations, I've found that many good writers mentally "listen" to the underlying rhythm and overall flow of their sentences and then rework the words and phrasing until they "hear" something that "sounds" good.

The intentional formation of visual and auditory images seems to rely on some of the same brain regions that we use in visual perception and auditory perception, respectively.[16] And because intentional imagery requires us to draw on our existing knowledge of how certain aspects of the world look or sound, it's definitely a form of meaningful learning.

FIGURE 5.2. See if you can remember these labeled drawings. A test of your memory for them will come in Chapter 6.

Source: Adapted from "An Experimental Study of the Effect of Language on the Reproduction of Visually Perceived Form" by L. Carmichael, H. P. Hogan, and A. A. Walters, 1932, *Journal of Experimental Psychology, 15*, p. 80.

Using Mnemonics: Finding Meaning Where There Really Isn't Any

Sometimes we need to remember information that we simply *can't* find meaning in, perhaps because we don't have sufficient background knowledge to understand it or perhaps because there really isn't any rhyme or reason to it. For example, how do you spell the chief administrator of an elementary or secondary school? Is that individual a *principle* or a *principal*? Why is Augusta the capital of the state of Maine, rather than, say, Bangor or Portland? What are the names of the five Great Lakes of North America? And as someone who has only begun to study music theory, for the life of me I don't understand why all major scales have the same structure: whole-step, whole-step, half-step, then three more wholes, and finally a half (W-W-H-W-W-W-H).

For such situations, **mnemonics** – artificial memory aids or tricks – can make new information and skills quite memorable.[17] Consider this fairly exotic example: Lying just outside of Cusco, Peru, are some well-preserved ruins of a hilltop complex skillfully crafted many centuries ago by the Killke and Incan peoples. How might an English speaker remember "Saqsaywaman," the Quechan name for this complex? Local guides suggest that visitors pronounce its English sound-alike "sexy woman."

Some mnemonics take the form of **verbal mediation**, in which a word or phrase forms a mental "bridge" between two ideas that we need to connect in long-term memory. For instance, a widely recommended mnemonic for remembering the correct spelling of that chief school administrator – a *principal* – is to learn that "The *principal* is my *pal*." Verbal mediators can be quite helpful in remembering the meanings of foreign vocabulary words. For example, to remember that the German word for *dog* is *Hund*, think "hound." And to remember that the Spanish word for *snake* is *serpiente*, an obvious mediator is "serpent."

Alternatively, a mnemonic might involve the creation of visual images. For example, to remember that the Mandarin Chinese word for *house* is *fáng*, picture a house with *fangs* jutting out from its roof and walls, and to remember that Mandarin for *door* is *mén*, picture a restroom door with the word *MEN* printed on it.

Certain other mnemonics combine verbal mediation with visual imagery, in a technique known as the **keyword method**. This approach involves two steps. First, we need to convert one or both of the to-be-associated ideas into related words or phrases (*keywords*) that are easy to visualize. Second, we form a visual image that combines the two ideas or keywords. For example, to remember that the capital of Maine is Augusta,

FIGURE 5.3. Using the keyword method to remember that Augusta is the capital of the state of Maine

you might picture *a gust of* wind blowing through a lion's *mane* (see Figure 5.3). To remember that the Spanish word for *love* is *amor*, you might picture a suit of *armor* with a *heart* (symbolizing "love") painted on its chest.

Finally, when we want to remember a seemingly arbitrary list of things, an especially handy technique is a **superimposed meaningful structure** – a mnemonic in which we organize information into an acronym, sentence, poem, familiar shape, or other memorable entity. For example, you can remember the five Great Lakes (Huron, Ontario, Michigan, Erie, Superior) using the word HOMES. You can easily find Italy on a map of Europe by thinking "boot." The sentence "While watching hippos, wear waterproof white hats" (for W-W-H-W-W-W-H) can help you remember the structure of a major scale in music.[18] And I've always loved the creative poem that some students in the United Kingdom use to help them remember the sequence of English kings and queens, beginning with the first King William. Internet websites provides several versions; here's one that many sites offer:

> Willie, Willie, Harry, Steve,
> Harry, Dick, John, Harry three.
> Edward one, two, three, Dick two,
> Harrys four five six, then who?
> Edwards four, five, Dick the Bad,

Harrys twain and Ned the lad.
Mary, Bessie, James the vain,
Charlie, Charlie, James again.
William and Mary, Anna Gloria,
Georges four, William, Victoria.
Edward seven, Georgie five,
Edward, George, and Liz (alive).

This poem might be sung to a catchy tune, such as "Good King Wenceslas." But even in its nonmusical version, its overall rhythm gives the list some structure. Personally, I don't have any reason to remember all the English monarchs in order, but for people who do, the poem or song is a relatively painless alternative to rote memorization – and a much more effective one.

Review and Practice: Use It or Possibly Lose It

Earlier I stated that rehearsal – mindless repetition within a short time period – isn't terribly effective as a means of storing new ideas and skills in long-term memory. But once we've already put them in long-term memory – ideally by making meaningful sense of them – occasional repetition and practice can help us keep them there.[19]

Regularly reviewing and practicing the things we've learned has several potential advantages. For one thing, we're likely to think about these things in new ways or in greater depth; that is, we'll continue to elaborate on them and thus understand them even better than we did before. A second, related benefit is that, especially if we're reviewing the relatively new material in somewhat different contexts than we did before, we're apt to make additional connections with knowledge we've previously acquired, and as a result we're more likely to recall it in future situations where it might be relevant and useful.[20]

A third benefit is that by occasionally reviewing and practicing new knowledge and skills, we can eventually learn them to a level of **automaticity** – that is, we become increasingly able to recall them quickly, skillfully, and with little or no mental effort.[21] Automatically retrieved information and skills take up very little "space" in working memory, thereby allowing us to apply them to complex new tasks and problems.[22] For example, we can successfully read and understand textbooks and classic works of literature only if we immediately recognize almost every word on the page. We can write a good composition only if we don't have to stop and think about how to spell our words or about where periods, commas, and apostrophes should go. We can solve simple math problems in our heads only if we can automatically retrieve such basic number facts as $2 + 7 = 9$ and $3 \times 6 = 18$. And we can use computers and other digital technologies more effectively if we've had extensive practice with "opening" and "closing" files and with "copying" and "pasting" text and graphics.

Keep in mind, however, that automaticity has a downside. More specifically, it increases the probability that we'll recall often-used perspectives and procedures when other, less frequently used ones might be more helpful.[23] We can be more flexible and creative in addressing challenging situations and problems when we don't zero in too quickly on the seemingly most obvious answers. This last point brings us to our next topic – *transfer*.

MAXIMIZING TRANSFER: APPLYING WHAT YOU HAVE LEARNED TO NEW SITUATIONS AND CONTEXTS

So, then, you've acquired many new ideas and skills. When, where, and how might you use them? And how often are you likely to use them? Although there's nothing wrong with having a gazillion bits of information scattered about in your head for no particular purpose, Mother Nature didn't equip us with sophisticated mental hardware simply so that we could be know-it-alls. Instead, she wanted us to *use* what we learn to adapt to the many challenging circumstances that will inevitably come our way as we meander through life.

When we apply something we've learned at one time to a future situation or problem, we're engaging in what psychologists call **transfer**. In our everyday lives, we regularly transfer our knowledge and skills to new situations. For example, when we talk, we're constantly combining words in ways we've never combined them before. When we're filling out an application for, say, a new job or credit card, we know what kinds of information we need to put in various spots on the form. And when we purchase new, ever-fancier cell phones, most of us immediately know how to use them to make a phone call or send a text message.

The examples I've just given you are all forms of *positive transfer* – that is, what we've learned before *helps* us in a new situation. But as I alluded to in my previous discussions of elaboration and automaticity, our existing knowledge can sometimes lead us astray – a phenomenon known as *negative transfer*. For example, when given a problem such as this one

$$24 \div 0.3 = ?$$

many children and an appalling number of adults incorrectly apply a principle they've learned about whole numbers: Division always leads to a smaller number.[24] The correct answer to the problem is 80 – a number much larger than 24.

So far I've been presenting examples of *specific transfer*, in which what we need to do in a new situation is similar to what we've previously learned how to do. Psychologists contrast it with *general transfer*, in which earlier experience helps us with a future one even though the two don't have much in common. General transfer occurs far less frequently than specific transfer does. For instance, as noted earlier, memorization practice usually doesn't help us become better memorizers.[25] And although knowledge of Latin and ancient Greek can help us make sense of scientific names for various living species (e.g., *tyrannosaurus rex* and *narcissus pseudonarcissus*), for the most part it doesn't help us become better scientists, mathematicians, journalists, or artists. This isn't to say that general transfer never occurs, because it does. For example, the kinds of strategies I'm including in the "Being Strategic" sections in this book can be applied to a wide range of situations. Certain general dispositions and attributions are also widely applicable, as you'll discover in Chapter 9.

So now let's return to the main point of this chapter – to emphasize the importance of in-depth processing as the most effective way to store and keep new knowledge and skills in long-term memory – and more specifically let's return to the process of elaboration. When we elaborate on new information – especially in formal instructional settings – we should be constantly asking ourselves and then trying to answer questions such as these: *What implications does this stuff have? In what situations might it be useful? Might it help me do something better? Or might it help me better understand certain phenomena in my physical or social environment? And in what ways might it help me make meaningful contributions to my society or cultural group?* Mentally answering these types of questions encourages us to make the kinds of connections in long-term memory that will spur us to retrieve and apply the new information when we need it.

CRITICAL THINKING: EVALUATING AS WELL AS ELABORATING ON NEW INFORMATION

Not only must we be careful about elaborating accurately rather than inappropriately on new information, but we must also ascertain whether the new information is *itself* accurate. Generally speaking, **critical thinking** involves evaluating the accuracy, credibility, and worth of information and lines of reasoning. As illustrations, use what you already know about the world to evaluate the following three tidbits of information:

- In 1492, Christopher Columbus became the first European to sail across the Atlantic to North America.
- People who eat a lot of carrots are less likely to be overweight than people who don't eat carrots, so if you want to lose weight, you should eat a lot of carrots.
- Each time you roll a pair of dice, chances are 1 in 6 that you'll roll a 7 (which you might get with 1 + 6, 2 + 5, 3 + 4, 4 + 3, 5 + 2, or 6 + 1). But if you haven't rolled a single 7 in the last 10 rolls, then your chances of rolling a 7 on the next roll are greater than 50%.

Wrong, wrong, and wrong – none of these statements is completely true. Although Columbus did indeed sail across the Atlantic, he was hardly the first guy to do so; the Vikings of Scandinavia made the crossing long before he did, as did many Portuguese fishermen.[26] And although it might be true that carrot eaters weigh less, on average, than noncarrot eaters (I have no information about this point one way or the other), all we have is a *correlation* here. As many of my readers have probably learned in some of their coursework, *correlation does not necessarily indicate causation*. For example, I suspect that carrot eaters are more likely than noncarrot eaters to eat other vegetables as well, and perhaps they're less likely to eat high-calorie snacks and French fries. Furthermore, maybe carrot eaters get more physical exercise than noncarrot eaters do. I don't know, but any one of these differences – as well as differences we haven't thought of just now – might explain the average difference in body weight.

What about those stubborn dice that haven't rolled a 7 in the last 10 rolls? The chance of rolling a 7 on the 11th roll is, again, only 1 in 6. If you thought that a 7 was long overdue and thus more likely to appear at this point, you fell victim to a logical error known as the *gambler's fallacy*.

Critical thinking isn't a single skill that people either have or don't have. Rather, as you may have deduced from the preceding three examples, it takes different forms in different situations. For example, in science, it involves scrutinizing research reports to determine both (a) whether methodologies and statistical analyses have been systematic and appropriate for the question at hand and (b) whether implications, applications, and other conclusions are justifiable based on the data presented. In history, critical thinking involves carefully inspecting both primary sources (e.g., original historical documents such as census reports and personal diaries) and secondary sources (e.g., history textbooks) to determine whether the information and data contained within them are completely factual and valid, on the one hand, or misrepresented as a result of personal, social, or cultural biases, on the other. And in reading and listening to virtually *anything* – whether it be in textbooks, in classroom lectures, or on the Internet – critical thinking is *critical* in our ever-expanding access to new information and *mis*information that other people have either gathered or self-constructed.

We humans become increasingly capable of critical thinking as we move through childhood and adolescence and then on to adulthood.[27] Yet (I'm gritting my teeth as I write this) many well-educated adults are entirely too willing to take what they read and hear at face value.[28] To some extent, our tendencies to inspect new information with a critical eye or, instead, a very gullible one depend on certain personality characteristics. For instance, on average, critical thinkers enjoy intellectual arguments and challenges, and they're comfortable with the fact that they might occasionally be wrong about a topic they hold near and dear to their hearts.[29] We're also more inclined to evaluate new information regarding its accuracy and credibility if we believe that any human-created "knowledge" about a topic is an inevitably dynamic entity that can change as new data arrive on the scene. In this case, I'm talking about the nature of our *epistemic beliefs*, which I'll describe in greater detail in Chapter 7.

BEING STRATEGIC

I can't stress enough the importance of in-depth cognitive processing for information and skills you want to keep and use over the long run. Accordingly, I offer the following recommendations. Some of them may give you a sense of déjà vu from preceding chapters, but at this point I'm trying to be more specific about what you might do both for yourself and for others.

Enhancing Your Own Thinking and Learning in Everyday Life

- **Self-Strategy 5.1: Elaborate on what you're learning**. For example, identify interrelationships among ideas. Draw reasonable conclusions. Generate new examples and implications. Speculate about possible applications.

- **Self-Strategy 5.2: Be open to your skeptical side**. Remember that the things other people say and write reflect their own self-constructed meanings and thus aren't necessarily accurate depictions of reality. This can be the case even if those people are supposedly "experts" or "authorities." So look or ask for irrefutable evidence that can back up various claims. Actively seek out *counter*evidence for claims. Check the logic underlying someone's reasoning: Can you actually say that if one such-and-such is true, then another such-and-such must also be true? And definitely don't mistake correlation for causation. A joke that a friend once sent me comes to mind here:

  > I don't trust joggers. They're always the ones that find the dead bodies. I'm no detective . . . just sayin'.

  I'm sure I don't need to tell you that correlation does *not* reflect causation here.

- **Self-Strategy 5.3: In addition to critically evaluating other people's claims, turn your critical thinking inward to evaluate your own beliefs**. You might be tired of me saying this by now, but I'll say it again anyway: Your own self-constructed meanings aren't necessarily any more accurate than those of others. Such self-reflection can be quite difficult – many people don't seem to do it at all[30] – but ultimately it's the only way that as a society we can live cooperatively and productively with one another. I'll offer more specific strategies in my discussion of conceptual change in Chapter 8.

- **Self-Strategy 5.4: Identify or invent mnemonics for important things that are hard to make logical sense of**. In other words, create verbal or imagery-based connections between two ideas you need to associate. For example, to remember that "cow" is *vaca* ("vah-cah") in both Spanish and Portuguese, picture a cow dancing on its two hind legs and holding a margarita in one of its front hooves – this cow is taking a *vaca*tion. (So, okay, maybe the pronunciations of *vaca* and *vacation* don't match, but the image can get you thinking in the right direction.) And identify easily memorable structures to help you recall lists and procedures. For example, a popular mnemonic for remembering which way to turn screws to either tighten or loosen them is this rhythmic expression "Righty, tighty, lefty, loosey." I use it pretty regularly when I'm puttering around the house.

- **Self-Strategy 5.5: Review and practice, review and practice**. The best approach is to space your reviewing and practicing over a lengthy period rather than doing it all at once; in other words, *distributed* practice is usually more effective than *massed* practice.[31] Ideally, too, you should mix up your review of one thing with your review of one or more other, related topics or skills – an approach that some psychologists call *interleaved* practice.[32]

Enhancing Other People's Thinking and Learning in Instructional Settings

○ **Instructional Strategies 5.1: Stress the importance of meaningful learning rather than rote learning**. This should be true not only in what you say but also in what you do. For instance, if you're a teacher, the final outcomes you tell students you want them to achieve in any lesson should focus on understanding and application – *not* on memorization and recall of discrete, trivial facts. And your assignments and assessment methods should reflect these desired outcomes. If you tell students that you want them to "understand" the material you're teaching but then hold them accountable for, say, *what-are-the-major-rivers-in-each-continent* in a geography class or *who-did-what-and-when* in a history class . . . well, your actions will speak much louder than your words.

○ **Instructional Strategy 5.2: Introduce new material at a level that makes meaningful learning possible**. Let's return (mentally) to that brief excerpt from the journal *Neuropsychology* that you read earlier in the chapter. One key reason you couldn't make much sense of it was that you didn't know what BDNF, KIBRA, and CHRNA4 are. You can certainly find information about these things using Google or some other search engine (e.g., BDNF is an acronym for the protein *brain-derived neurotrophic factor*), but unless you already know a great deal about brain functioning, the websites you find aren't going to help you very much.

So now let's put you in the driver's seat in an instructional situation: You're the teacher, and your students are relative novices about a topic that *you* know quite well. Your students are apt to have the same kind of roadblock to meaningful learning that you had when you read the *Neuropsychology* excerpt: They'll have only limited knowledge on which they can draw as they try to make sense of what you're teaching them. You need to simplify the subject matter enough that they can build on what they *do* know. You shouldn't think of this strategy as "dumbing down" what you're teaching; rather, you should think of it as helping your students think *smartly*.

- **Instructional Strategy 5.3: Accompany verbal information with illustrative visual materials**. For example, provide diagrams, photographs, bar graphs, pie charts, videos, three-dimensional concrete models, live demonstrations – whatever is appropriate for the subject matter at hand. In doing so, you're helping others encode information both verbally and visually. Just as two heads are often better than one, most of the time two forms of encoding are better than just a single form.

- **Instructional Strategy 5.4: Scaffold students' meaning-making efforts**. In developmental and educational psychology, the word **scaffolding** means providing one or more support mechanisms that can help people more easily and successfully tackle challenging tasks.[33] For example, you might (a) initially present a simplified version of a task, (b) list elements of desired performance on a note card, (c) offer frequent suggestions and feedback, or (d) provide hardware or software that can assist students as they work toward task completion.

  Scaffolding can be especially helpful when students need to *organize* what they're learning. For example, you might provide outlines that students can use as they take notes. You might give students two-dimensional compare-and-contrast tables they can fill in as they learn about various kinds of rocks, clouds, chemical reactions, or forms of government. Alternatively, you might give students rudimentary *concept maps* to which they can add as they study a topic that includes many logical interconnections. As an illustration, Figure 5.4 provides the beginning of a concept map related to the contents of this chapter. As your "instructor" right now, I'm giving it to you, my "student," as a possible starting point for elaborating on what you've been learning about long-term memory storage processes.[34]

- **Instructional Strategy 5.5: Ask probing questions that require students to elaborate on, apply, or critically evaluate what they're studying**. Probing questions provide another means through which you might scaffold effective in-depth cognitive processing. Following are examples:
  - Why does _____ cause _____ to _____?
  - What's the difference between _____ and _____?
  - How might you use _____ to _____?
  - Who created this ___[document/website]?___ What motives or biases might the author have?
  - What key assumptions underlie the claims being made here?

FIGURE 5.4. A good concept map includes key concepts and their interrelations relative to a particular topic. After reading this chapter, how might you add to this concept map about long-term memory storage processes?

- What evidence or logic is the author using to support the claims? Can you think of evidence that might *contradict* one or more claims?
- Is the information presented here consistent with what you've learned from other sources? If not, how is it different? Is it possible to synthesize the varying perspectives in some coherent and logical way?[35]
- **Instructional Strategy 5.6: Teach specific mnemonics for important but hard-to-remember facts and lists.** Over time, many teachers amass a variety of mnemonics that they introduce when students can best use them. For example, a popular mnemonic in biology is "King Philip comes over for good spaghetti," which can help students remember the traditional classification hierarchy for plants and animals: *kingdom, phylum, class, order, family, genus,* and *species.* The word "FOIL" can

help middle school students simplify a mathematical expression of the form $(ax + b)(cx + d)$: Multiply the *first* terms in each set of parentheses, then the *outer* terms, the *inner* terms, and finally the *last* terms. Likewise, "Elvis's guitar broke down Friday" can help beginning music students remember the five lines on the treble clef: E G B D F. And for millions of young children over the years, the "Alphabet Song" – sung to the tune of "Twinkle, Twinkle, Little Star" – has provided the way through which they've learned the correct sequence of the 26 letters in the English alphabet.

o **Instructional Strategy 5.7: Facilitate transfer through authentic activities and interactive simulations**. We're more likely to apply what we've learned to new tasks and problems if certain elements of those tasks and problems remind us of potentially relevant knowledge. One really good way to help other people make those all-important connections in long-term memory is to have them learn and practice new material in real-world-like situations that require it – that is, to have them engage in **authentic activities** during the learning process.[36] For example, depending on the subject matter you're teaching, you might have people plan a camping trip, fix a malfunctioning engine, design an energy-efficient building, or work on projects that contribute to the local community's general welfare.[37]

Technology-based simulations of real-world tasks are also a possibility. For example, elementary school children might learn how to use and apply fractions by working with virtual "manipulatives" on a computer screen, and high school students might practice their scientific experimentation skills in computer-simulated "experiments." One particular advantage of computer simulations is that their creators can design them in such a way that students' cognitive loads are manageable ones, with appropriate scaffolding provided as needed.[38]

o **Instructional Strategy 5.8: Create frequent opportunities for review and practice**. Once again, distributed practice is better than massed practice, and mixed practice with multiple (albeit related) tasks is better than practicing only one task at a time. And if such review and practice opportunities can occur within real-world or pseudo-real-world situations . . . all the better!

NOTES

1. For a classic discussion of this idea, see Ausubel, 1963.
2. For example, see Baillargeon & DeVos, 1991.

3. Daneman, 1987; Nuthall, 2000; Plass et al., 2010.
4. Baddeley, Eysenck, & Anderson, 2009; Craik & Watkins, 1973; Watkins & Watkins, 1974.
5. James, 1890.
6. For a classic research article regarding this point, see Thorndike, 1924.
7. Mayer & Wittrock, 1996; Perkins & Salomon, 1989.
8. Rebok et al., 2014.
9. Flavell, Miller, & Miller, 2002; Hall, Hladkyj, Perry, & Ruthig, 2004; Kail, 1990; Schneider & Pressley, 1989.
10. Nesbit & Adesope, 2006; Novak, 1998; Robinson & Kiewra, 1995.
11. Rovira et al., 2016, p. 709.
12. Behrmann, 2000; J. M. Clark & Paivio, 1991; Kosslyn, 1985.
13. Cothern, Konopak, & Willis, 1990; Dewhurst & Conway, 1994; Leopold & Mayer, 2015; Sadoski & Paivio, 2001; Sweller, 2008.
14. Mayer, 2011; Sadoski & Paivio, 2001.
15. For example, see Zatorre & Halpern, 2005.
16. Behrmann, 2000; Kosslyn, 1994; Speer, Reynolds, Swallow, & Zacks, 2009; Zatorre & Halpern, 2005.
17. For example, see R. K. Atkinson et al., 1999; Jones, Levin, Levin, & Beitzel, 2000; Pressley, Levin, & Delaney, 1982; Soemer & Schwan, 2012.
18. I thank my former student Lee Boissonneault for creating this mnemonic.
19. Dunlosky, Rawson, Marsh, Nathan, & Willingham, 2013; Proctor & Dutta, 1995; Rohrer & Pashler, 2010; Rovee-Collier, 1993; Soderstrom, Kerr, & Bjork, 2016.
20. Calfee, 1981; Karpicke, 2012; McDaniel & Masson, 1985; Vaughn & Rawson, 2011.
21. J. R. Anderson, 2005; Beilock & Carr, 2004; Cheng, 1985; Ericsson, 1996.
22. De La Paz & McCutchen, 2011; Fuchs et al., 2013; Klauda & Guthrie, 2008; Lervåg & Hulme, 2009; Mayer & Wittrock, 2006.
23. Killeen, 2001; Langer, 2000; LeFevre, Bisanz, & Mrkonjic, 1988.
24. Karl & Varma, 2010; Ni & Zhou, 2005; Tirosh & Graeber, 1990.
25. For exceptions, see Foer, 2011, but note that the astounding feats of memory described in that book require extensive and well-practiced use of mnemonics.
26. For a good read about Portuguese fishermen in pre-Columbian days, I recommend Mark Kurlansky's *Cod: A Biography of the Fish That Changed the World* (1997).
27. Amsterlaw, 2006; Kuhn & Franklin, 2006; Pillow, 2002.
28. Kuhn, 2009; Marcus, 2008; Metzger, Flanagin, & Zwarun, 2003; Sinatra, Kienhues, & Hofer, 2014.
29. Halpern, 2008; Moon, 2008; Schraw, McCrudden, Lehman, & Hoffman, 2011.

30. Colbert & Peters, 2002; Roets & Van Hiel, 2011; Van Hiel, Pandelaere, & Duriez, 2004.
31. Dunlosky et al., 2013; Kornell, Castell, Eich, & Bjork, 2010; Pashler, Rohrer, Cepeda, & Carpenter, 2007.
32. Dunlosky et al., 2013; Rohrer, Dedrick, & Stershic, 2015.
33. Collins, 2006; Gallimore & Tharp, 1990; Rogoff, 1990; D. Wood, Bruner, & Ross, 1976.
34. For a classic discussion of concept maps, see Novak, 1998. Also, some instructional software programs teach students how to create good concept maps. A good example is *Betty's Brain* (e.g., Leelawong & Biswas, 2008; Segedy, Kinnebrew, & Biswas, 2013); as this book goes to press, you can see *Betty's Brain* in action at teachableagents.org.
35. Questions based on suggestions by De La Paz & Felton, 2010; Halpern, 1998; A. King, 1999; Stahl & Shanahan, 2004; Wiley et al., 2009.
36. Barab & Dodge, 2008; Edelson & Reiser, 2006; Greeno, Collins, & Resnick, 1996.
37. Bransford, Franks, Vye, & Sherwood, 1989; Kahne & Sporte, 2008; Linn, 2008; Mayer, 2010; Walkington, Sherman, & Petrosino, 2012.
38. Baroody, Eiland, Purpura, & Reid, 2013; de Jong, 2011; Kuhn & Pease, 2010; Sarama & Clements, 2009.

6

Remembering, Forgetting, and Misremembering: Why Long-Term Memory Isn't Always Dependable

In your many experiences as a human learner, you've undoubtedly discovered that you can remember some information and skills quite easily, whereas other things can be quite difficult to recall. The following five questions can put your retrieval skills to work. Take your time with the questions, and as you do so, look inward and reflect on what your mind seems to be doing in your efforts to answer each one.

1. What is your name?
2. What is your phone number?
3. What is the capital of Italy?
4. The discussion of the brain in Chapter 2 mentions a large bundle of axons that connects the left and right hemispheres and enables constant communication between the two. What is that structure called?
5. What did you have for dinner on this date three years ago?

Question 1 (your name) was almost certainly the easiest one to answer. You might have had to think for a few seconds before you could answer Question 2 (your phone number); some people have to look at their cell phones to know for sure. Likewise, you might have struggled a bit with Question 3 (the capital of Italy). If Rome didn't immediately spring to mind, perhaps you found yourself mentally "wandering around" in your head in search of a logical Italian city to be the capital; maybe you even toyed with the possibility that some other city – say, Florence or Venice – might be the correct answer. As for

Question 4 (that connective brain structure), did you remember the term *corpus callosum* either from Chapter 2 or from your previous knowledge about the brain? If you couldn't recall the term despite thinking about the matter for a while, does it at least look familiar now that you're seeing it again? And regarding Question 5 (your dinner menu three years ago), maybe you thought about where you probably were that day and whom you might have been with – things that could conceivably have helped you guess what you would have eaten. Nevertheless, chances are pretty good that you have absolutely no clue what you actually ate that night.

As you learned in Chapter 5, the ways in which we cognitively process new information – and also how much we process it – influence how memorable that information becomes. Yet despite cognitively processing new material in considerable depth, we don't always remember it when we'd like to. In this chapter, we look more closely at the nature of finding – or not finding – the things we've previously stored in long-term memory.

THE NATURE OF RETRIEVAL: LOCATING DESIRED INFORMATION IN LONG-TERM MEMORY

Metaphorically speaking, long-term memory is gigantic, enormous – *ginormous* – in size and scope. Its contents are so voluminous that we can't possibly "look" at them (mentally) all at once. Instead, we must rummage around a bit, looking here and then there and then somewhere else until, maybe, we stumble on what we need. As two psychologists once suggested, trying to retrieve a desired piece of information from long-term memory is like looking for something in a large, dark room with only a small flashlight.[1] Sometimes our flashlight eventually focuses on the desired spot, but sometimes it doesn't; thus, we don't always remember the things we're pretty sure are in our heads somewhere. The *activation* model of memory I introduced in Chapter 4 is relevant here: The flashlight's illuminated focus is the part of long-term memory that's currently activated; as we gradually shift our mental attention (our "flashlight") elsewhere, other contents in long-term memory become activated.[2] We can shine the light on only a small area at any one time – that *limited-capacity* issue rearing its head once again.

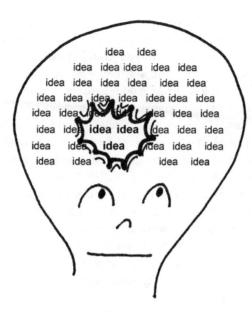

At any one time, we can mentally "look" at only a tiny fraction of the gazillion things we've stored in long-term memory.

And yet we often *do* find what we need, in large part thanks to the countless interconnections among the tidbits of knowledge we've accumulated over the years. Here's how many psychologists think retrieval might work. Any retrieval effort needs to start somewhere, and that "location" is typically triggered either by something in your environment or by something you're already thinking about; in one way or another, this trigger is in working memory when you begin your search. For example, the question "What is your name?" should immediately send you to wherever your name "is" in your long-term memory. (Once again, I'm speaking metaphorically, because virtually any bit of knowledge is distributed across many parts of the brain.) Likewise, "What is the capital of Italy?" should send you to Italy, or maybe to a geography class you took in middle school. From your starting point, you mentally travel along (i.e., activate) one or more of the interconnections to other, related tidbits and then, if necessary, travel even farther until eventually (maybe) you reach your desired destination.

Whether or not you find what you're looking for depends on the route you travel while you're searching. For example, when you thought about Question 3, if you traveled from "Italy" to "Venice" but never to "Rome," you wouldn't have retrieved the correct answer. Likewise, when you turned to Question 4, if your search of your knowledge about the brain never led you to "corpus callosum," you would have come up with a blank. Earlier I asked you if the term *corpus callosum* looked familiar to you once you saw it. This question would have *started* your retrieval process with "corpus callosum" rather than with "brain," so you were already where you needed to be. (If the term *didn't* look familiar to you at that point, you probably didn't really read Chapter 2; perhaps your mind was somewhere else altogether as your eyes were moving down the pages.)

Let's return to the concept of *automaticity* – that ability to recall some things quickly and with little or no effort. As we practice using certain information or skills over and over, we strengthen the pathways that lead from one thing to another. For instance, you've been asked what your name is so many times in your life that your path to the answer is a superhighway. The same might be true for your phone number. As for your path to "corpus callosum," it's probably only a dirt road at best, or maybe just a small hiking trail through dense woods – a trail on which it's easy to wander off and get lost. And as for your dinner menu three years ago, you can't find something that may not be there at all (more about this point shortly).

Now is a good time to try to recall those four labeled drawings that I asked you to study and remember in Chapter 5. No peeking!! This is a memory test, not a test of your copying skills. Following are the four labels I gave you at the time:

bottle sun broom dumbbells

I'm hoping that the labels get you started in the right directions as you "look" for the images in your long-term memory. We'll analyze your drawings later in the chapter.

Importance of Context: It Helps to Be in the Right Place
at the Right Time

Stop for a moment to conjure up the smell of one of your favorite foods – perhaps chocolate chip cookies or a ripe pineapple. Does this smell remind you of something – say, your mother's kitchen or a recent tropical vacation? And how about the smells of roses, a particular cologne or after-shave lotion, and the ocean? Do these smells conjure up certain visual images, friends or relatives, or the beach?

Now bring to mind some of your favorite musical pieces – maybe songs that were often on the radio when you were in high school or songs that you used to sing in your school choir, at church, or around a campfire. Like your favorite smells, these songs probably evoke some memories. For example, virtually any Motown song from the late 1960s reminds me of one of my college boyfriends, and a few other songs from the same era remind me of a summer waitressing job I had at the time – mainly because people were constantly playing those songs on the restaurant's juke box. I swear, every time I hear Sam the Sham & the Pharaohs' 1966 hit "Li'l Red Riding Hood," I immediately imagine myself carrying a large metal tray loaded with burgers, milkshakes, or ice cream sundaes.

The environmental context in which we find ourselves at any given moment is apt to provide a variety of stimuli that can trigger a voluntary or involuntary trip along Memory Lane.[3] Some of these **retrieval cues** are simply integral parts of whatever we happen to be experiencing at the moment. Such is the case when we return to a city or town we haven't visited in many years or when we hear certain "oldies" playing on the radio or someone's smartphone playlist. Other retrieval cues come from things people say and do within those contexts – perhaps when they ask us what our names are, remind us to "keep your eye on the ball" during sports practice, or put their fingers to their lips during activities in which we're supposed to keep our voices down. The most effective retrieval cues are those that send us in the right directions in our travels through long-term memory's highways and byways.

In my discussion of transfer in Chapter 5, I suggested that you regularly ask yourself certain questions as you study new material – for instance, *In what situations might it be useful? Might it help me do something better? Or might it help me better understand certain phenomena in my physical or social environment?* Mentally answering these kinds of questions encourages you to make meaningful connections between the new material and the contexts in which it might be relevant – connections that increase the probability that, later on, you'll spontaneously remember the material in contexts where it might come in handy.

WHY WE OFTEN FORGET – OR *THINK* WE'VE FORGOTTEN – WHAT WE'VE LEARNED

Sometimes we say we "forgot" something when we never really learned it in the first place. Maybe we didn't pay attention to what we were supposedly seeing or hearing, in which case it didn't get into working memory. Or maybe it *did* get into working memory, but we didn't ponder it long enough to store it effectively in long-term memory.

As an example, imagine yourself at some sort of social event. A friend approaches you with a companion and says, "I'd like you to meet my business associate, Lucy McGillicuddy." You smile, shake Lucy's hand, and exchange a few pleasantries about the weather and local events. An hour later, when you're chatting with another friend, Lucy approaches the two of you. It's clear that she doesn't know this second friend of yours; ideally, then, you should introduce them to each other. But you haven't a clue as to what your new acquaintance's name is. Jennifer? Maria? Candace? Elmira? Her last name might possibly have begun with a "Mac" or a "Mc," but you can't be sure. *Awkward!!* Quite possibly, when Friend #1 was introducing her to you, you never really listened – that is, you never paid attention. Even if you did pay attention, you might not have been able to connect "Lucy McGillicuddy" to anyone or anything else in your long-term memory. (For my readers who are fans of the old television show "I Love Lucy," you might recall that the title character, Lucy Ricardo, had been Lucy McGillicuddy before she married Ricky. If you knew this bit of trivia, then meaningful learning and effective long-term storage could have been quite easy.)

Yet even when we've paid attention and engaged in some degree of meaningful learning, we often forget things that we know we've previously learned. In the next few pages, I'll discuss several possible reasons why. I'll also explain why forgetting isn't necessarily a bad thing.

Failure to Retrieve: It's in There Somewhere, But We Can't Find It When We Need It

You're walking through a crowded shopping mall. You see a man who looks very familiar – you know you should know who he is – but your mind is coming up blank. Who *is* this guy? You rack your brain. Is he someone you know at work? Nope. Is he someone you recently met at a party? You don't think so. Maybe he's one of your classmates? No. Only much later does the answer come to you: The guy owns a local car dealership and is often on television advertising one of his "super-duper, impossible-to-beat discount sales events."

Sometimes we simply can't find something when we need it. **Failure to retrieve** occurs when we don't focus our mental flashlight on the part of long-term memory that holds the information we're looking for. Perhaps we initially stored the information within a very different context; for instance, we might have associated a particular guy's face with our knowledge about extremely annoying television commercials. Or maybe we initially stored the information in relative isolation from other, previously acquired bits of knowledge. In neither situation would we be likely to point our flashlight in the right direction.

Failure to retrieve occasionally involves forgetting to do something we really need to do – perhaps go to an important meeting, fill an almost-empty gas tank, or pick up a bottle of milk on the way home from work. Here we have a problem with **prospective memory**, remembering to do something at the time we need to do it.[4] As an illustration, I sometimes bring my outgoing mail with me when I drive to the local gym, because the post office is right along the way. I'll put the stamped envelopes beside me on the passenger seat, and yet I often arrive at the gym to find the mail still sitting there. Damn, I forgot to put it in the drive-up mailbox at the post office. Likewise, some friends of mine once forgot to put a full bag of garbage in the neighborhood dumpster as they drove to the airport. When they got to their car in the airport parking lot a week later ... well, not a happy experience.

One way to prevent ourselves from forgetting need-to-do behaviors is to keep the information active in working memory until we actually complete them. For example, if I find that I've forgotten to swing through the post office parking lot on the way to the gym, I have a foolproof strategy for making sure that I do so on the way home. As soon as I get in my car, I start singing the classic kids' song "Ninety-nine bottles of beer on the wall, ninety-nine bottle of beer, If one of those bottles should happen to fall ..." and then continue to sing the countdown until I reach the post office; usually I have about 40 bottles left when I get there. My song doesn't mention the mail, but it does keep my working memory alert to the fact that I need to do something on the way home before I can stop singing it.

Fortunately, there's also a second, less irritating way to prevent problems with prospective memory. In particular, we can use *external retrieval cues*, which I'll describe near the end of the chapter.

Interference: Sometimes We Get Confused

We now go back to Question 3: "What is the capital of Italy?" You can probably think of many Italian cities – not only Rome, Florence, and Venice but perhaps also Naples, Milan, Pisa, and Genoa. If your association between Italy and Venice is an especially strong one, you might have mentally voted for Venice over Rome. And what's the capital of Turkey?

Many people immediately retrieve "Istanbul" as the likely answer. But no, Turkey's capital is Ankara, a city that few non-Turks know much about. For most of us, then, the Turkey-Istanbul association is much stronger than the Turkey-Ankara one.

Interference occurs when a retrieval cue sends us down the wrong path in long-term memory. It's most likely to happen when our mental starting point has many interconnections – possibly including some well-paved highways – that can potentially lead us in counterproductive directions.[5] Once again, we haven't completely lost the information; it's just hard to find.

Decay: Some Stuff Probably Fades Away

Some information probably does fade away into nothingness, especially if we rarely or never use it. In other words, it undergoes **decay**.[6] What did you have for dinner on this date three years ago? I'm willing to bet that your menu isn't anywhere in your long-term memory; it's vanished, outta there, gone without a trace. We're apt to lose the precise details of a new stimulus or event fairly quickly; its general meaning or gist will probably last longer, although not necessarily forever.[7]

However, we do tend to remember the little stuff if it was surprising, personally significant, or in some other way worthy of remembering.[8] And for better or for worse, we're more likely to hold onto details that evoke strong emotions – for instance, details that we associate with excitement, horror, or extreme disgust.[9]

Inhibition: Sometimes We Consciously or Unconsciously *Try* to Forget

Following are four obscure English nouns and their meanings. Ponder them for a while – long enough that you might be able to define them correctly on a quiz I'll give you a bit later.

- *blistomorph:* an irregular but noncancerous growth on a finger or toe
- *mellicyte:* a small yellow flower found only in cold, mountainous areas
- *adiomic:* a nine-line poem with rhyming words at the ends of lines 3, 6, and 9
- *farumph:* a gaseous discharge emanating from the large intestine, typically as a result of eating beans or other legumes

I'm putting a row of asterisks following this sentence in an effort to discourage you from reading ahead until you've studied all four words for a while.

* *

Now that you supposedly know what the four words mean, I must confess that I defined them incorrectly. Actually, a blistomorph is a very large, sloppily dressed, and boisterous drunkard. A mellicyte is a certain kind of microscopic, one-celled, aquatic creature. An adiomic is a cologne with a smell similar to that of roses. A farumph is an old and usually ugly woman who possesses magical powers.

So, now, what's the first thing that comes to mind when you see the word *mellicyte*? And what's the first thing you think of when you see the word *adiomic*? How about *blistomorph*? *Farumph*? Are the first definitions – the ones you actively studied – coming to mind even though they're incorrect? It's quite possible that they are.[10]

All right, full disclosure here. None of the four new "words" I just defined for you actually exists in the English language. I made them all up; sorry. The point of the exercise was to show you how we sometimes *want* to forget things that we've learned incorrectly. More specifically, we may consciously try to **inhibit** or *suppress* certain neural pathways we've created.[11] One way of doing this is to intentionally try to retrieve other, contradictory information (such as remembering that a mellicyte is a microscopic critter rather than a yellow flower) and then to keep retrieving the correct information over and over, potentially weakening the path to the incorrect information. This phenomenon, called **retrieval-induced forgetting**, has been well documented in laboratory settings, although some previously learned misinformation can be stubbornly difficult to erase.[12]

Unconscious forces might conceivably be involved in inhibition as well. A century ago, Sigmund Freud proposed that some memories are so psychologically painful and distressing that we unconsciously push them to the far corners of our minds, where we're unlikely to stumble across them in our everyday retrieval activities. Freud called this phenomenon *repression*.[13] In recent years, however, psychologists have become increasingly skeptical about whether complete repression of a painful memory is really possible; much of the "evidence" for it comes in the form of people's "recall" of memories that can't be checked for accuracy.[14] In any case, it seems that most of us don't repress painful information as a matter of course.[15]

Why We Don't Want to Remember Everything We've Learned

As you've just seen, forgetting isn't necessarily a bad thing. Not only would we like to forget many of our most painful memories, but we also hope we can forget those past events in which we've felt even moderately sad or embarrassed.[16] Furthermore, many of the trivial details we encounter day after day will be of little or no use to us later on. In fact, if we saved every scrap of information we ever acquired, we'd have a terrible time wading through all the clutter to retrieve the stuff we really do need to remember.[17]

One distinction that's useful in this context is that between semantic memory and episodic memory, both of which reside in long-term memory.[18] **Semantic memory** is our general knowledge about the world – say, what the capital of Italy is or why most plants need a regular supply of water to keep them alive and growing. In contrast, **episodic memory** is our memory of personal experiences – say, what we had for dinner last night or what we did on a recent holiday or vacation. On average, things in our semantic memory stick with us much longer than do those in our episodic memory – with exceptions, obviously. And although the two types of memory regularly interact, to some degree they seem to involve different areas of the brain.[19]

Especially if events in our episodic memories inform us about key aspects of ourselves or the world around us, they can morph into semantic memories. Otherwise, we might not want them hanging around, as they could completely overwhelm us.[20] Consider the case of Jill Price, a middle-aged school administrator in California who remembers virtually everything that she's seen and heard since she was 14 years old; for example, she could almost certainly tell us what she had for dinner on this date three years ago.[21] She isn't especially gifted otherwise; intelligence tests have yielded IQ scores within an average range, and she has said that she didn't do especially well in school. But she can tell you precise details of what she did, learned, and felt on any particular day during the past 3 decades – details that can be verified either by external sources (e.g., newspaper accounts) or by her tens of thousands of personal journal pages she's written over the years. And she is continually revisiting these details in annoying, unstoppable trains of thought throughout each day. As Jill once told researchers, "I run my entire life through my head every day and it drives me crazy."[22] Scientists have yet to pin down the neurological basis for her extraordinary ability to remember her life events – or, we might instead say, her *dis*ability to forget them.[23]

MISREMEMBERING WHAT WE'VE LEARNED

It's now time to look at those drawings you made of the bottle, sun, broom, and dumbbells. Compare your drawings to the ones you previously saw in Chapter 5, which I now show you again in the leftmost column of Figure 6.1. Chances are pretty good that your bottle looks more like a real bottle than my original did. And probably your sun was more "sunny," your broom more "broomy," and your dumbbells more "dumbbellsy" than mine were. If so, the labels were clearly responsible for the distortions in what you remembered. But you can rest assured that you're in good company. Many years ago, when college students and professors were asked to recreate these and other drawings, their recollections were influenced by the labels, and in fact different labels led to different distortions.[24] For example, as illustrated in Figure 6.1, people who looked at a "stirrup" recreated drawings quite different from those who saw a "bottle." Likewise, those who looked at a "ship's wheel," a "gun," or "eye glasses" recreated drawings different from those who saw a "sun," "broom," or "dumbbells."

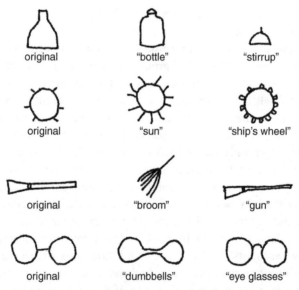

FIGURE 6.1. How people might "remember" the same drawings differently depending on how the drawings are labeled

Source: Adapted from "An Experimental Study of the Effect of Language on the Reproduction of Visually Perceived Form" by L. Carmichael, H. P. Hogan, and A. A. Walters, 1932, *Journal of Experimental Psychology, 15,* p. 80.

Not only do we impose our own constructions on information as we store it in long-term memory – often filling in gaps in the raw data as a way of making those data more meaningful – but we may also *reconstruct* our memories as we're retrieving them. Thanks (or *no* thanks) to the various processes that cause us to forget things (e.g., interference or decay), sometimes we can recall only bits and pieces of the stimuli and events we've witnessed. Given our general constructive, meaning-making nature, we try to mentally "complete" our memories based on what's logical or consistent with our existing knowledge and beliefs.[25]

With this point in mind, psychologists and other experts have become increasingly concerned about the use of eyewitness testimonies in courtroom settings. Within the past few decades, a significant body of research has revealed that many eyewitnesses have only partial memories of crimes they've witnessed. They're apt to fill in the holes based on (a) their prior beliefs about the individuals involved; (b) their assumptions about what "must have" happened; or (c) erroneous information, leading questions, or other deviations from reality that interrogators have presented after the event took place. Accordingly, eyewitness testimony isn't necessarily an accurate representation of what actually happened, even if the witness claims to be quite confident that such-and-such occurred.[26]

Reconstructing Our Memories: Remembering What We Remembered Before Instead of What Really Happened at the Time

Whenever we recall an event we've previously experienced – and especially if we verbally describe it and perhaps embellish on it in some way – we're revising our memory of the event, spurring us to *reconsolidate*, or firm it up anew, in the brain.[27] The result is that we tend to remember how we remembered the event before rather than how it actually happened. Author Marion Winik has captured this process well:

> Sometimes I think childhood memories are fabricated like pearls around a grain of sand. You know how it works: take one old photograph and the quick current of memory it sparks; add what you heard happened, what could have happened, what probably happened; then tell the story over and over until you get the details down. It doesn't take a degree in psychology to reverse-engineer your childhood based on the adult it produced.
>
> Even if I've made it all up, it doesn't matter. I'm stuck with the past I believe in, even if it's wrong.[28]

A good illustration of this recalling-what-you-previously-recalled phenomenon can be found in research regarding **flashbulb memories** – especially vivid memories of how we've learned about especially noteworthy
events. For example, I can recall quite clearly where I was and what I was
doing when I learned that President Kennedy had been assassinated (1963):
I was a high school student who was sick that day and not at school, and my
mother told me about it after she got a phone call from a friend. I also
remember how I learned that the Berlin Wall was coming down (1989):
My husband and I were in bed watching television that evening. I can
picture these two events quite clearly. But was I *really* home sick that day in
1963? And was I *really* in bed watching television that evening in 1989?
I know only what I remember.

With regard to flashbulb memories and our memories of life events in
general, we have another common misconception:

> Misconception #19: That if we can recall an event quite vividly and in
> considerable detail, then the event almost certainly happened the
> way we remember it happening

Not true: The vividness of our memories doesn't necessarily mean that
they're accurate.[29] In a study that began in 1996,[30] researchers in the United
States asked college students to describe where they were when they first
heard about an especially distressing news event that had occurred the day
before: the horrific explosion and crash of the U.S. space shuttle *Challenger*,
which immediately plunged into the ocean, killing the seven astronauts
aboard. One of the astronauts was Christa McAuliffe, a high school teacher
whose students had been watching the launch and witnessed the explosion
as it happened. Video footage of the tragedy made the national news and
quickly captured the hearts and minds of most U.S. citizens. Thus, many of
the participants in the study could describe in considerable and presumably accurate detail where they were and what they were doing at the time
they heard the news. Following is an example:

> I was in my religion class and some people walked in and started talking
> about [it]. I didn't know any details except that it had exploded and the
> schoolteacher's students had all been watching which I thought was so
> sad. Then after class I went to my room and watched the TV program
> talking about it and I got all the details from that.[31]

In a follow-up two-and-a-half years later, the students were asked a second
time to describe their whereabouts and activities at the time they heard the
tragic news. Some of them gave different answers than they had given before,

as reflected in the second response given by the student who had previously reported being in a religion class:

> When I first heard about the explosion I was sitting in my freshman dorm room with my roommate and we were watching TV. It came on a news flash and we were both totally shocked. I was really upset and I went upstairs to talk to a friend of mine and then I called my parents.[32]

Students were asked the question yet a third time three years after the crash, and thus six months after their previous recollection. Most of them basically repeated what they'd said the second time; that is, they remembered what they had previously remembered. If their second and third recollections were inaccurate ones, the researchers gave them hints about where they'd actually been and what they'd actually been doing at the time. But despite the hints, the students stuck with their reconsolidated versions, and they were quite surprised to read their first, day-after recollections.

A common expression comes to mind here: "That's my story and I'm sticking to it!" As you can see, the stories we stick to can sometimes be a fair distance from reality.

FALSE MEMORIES: "REMEMBERING" THINGS THAT NEVER HAPPENED AT ALL

Occasionally people have **false memories** – memories that have virtually no basis in fact.[33] In some research studies, such memories have their origins in stimuli that experimenters present (perhaps stories or photographs) to suggest that something *might* have happened. For instance, when people see photos of themselves apparently engaging in a particular activity – say, when they see a picture of themselves digitally imposed on a photo of one or more other people riding in a hot-air balloon – many of them confess that, yes, they did that.[34] Even when experimenters simply ask them to imagine a certain object or event, they might later recall that they actually saw it. Young children are especially susceptible to the power of such imagery-based suggestion.[35]

For older children and adults, the key to the formation of false memories is *plausibility* – whether the stimuli or events in question might reasonably or logically have been experienced.[36] A study involving adolescents with different religious backgrounds provides an example.[37] In this study, researchers asked high school students whether they had had certain experiences when they were eight years old. Some of the experiences presented were real ones, but among them were two religious occasions that the researchers had totally fabricated. One of these not-true experiences involved a common Jewish ritual; the other involved a common Catholic ritual. As you might suspect, Jewish students were more likely to "remember" the Jewish occasion, whereas Catholic students were more likely to "remember" the Catholic one. Furthermore, the students' general knowledge about their respective religious rituals enabled them to "recall" all kinds of details about these nonevents.

SOME MEMORIES LINGER EVEN WHEN WE CAN'T CONSCIOUSLY FIND THEM

In Chapter 4, I made a distinction between *explicit knowledge* (stuff that we can easily recall and explain) and *implicit knowledge* (stuff that lies below the surface of our conscious awareness but can influence our thoughts and behaviors nonetheless). Sometimes a new experience leads to both kinds of knowledge, with its implicit aspects staying with us much longer than its explicit aspects. For instance, people who seemingly can't recall anything they learned about a topic several weeks or years ago can more quickly learn it – *re*learn it, really – than people who haven't previously studied the topic.[38] And seemingly irrational emotional reactions to certain stimuli or events can stick around long after the circumstances that initially caused those reactions have completely disappeared.[39]

BEING STRATEGIC

We all have unpleasant memories that we wish we could forget. In general, however, we're far more likely to be in situations in which we *want* to remember something, and we can get quite frustrated when a search of long-term memory fails us. In both this chapter and the preceding one, I've mentioned a couple of things that are worth repeating once again:

- Review and practice, and then later, review and practice some more.
- Think about how you might apply (transfer) newly acquired knowledge and skills to additional contexts and situations. Better still, regularly *use* them in those contexts and situations.

Following are additional suggestions for helping you and other people retrieve things that need retrieving.

Enhancing Your Own Thinking and Learning
in Everyday Life

- **Self-Strategy 6.1: Create external retrieval cues regarding must-do future tasks.** Recall the concept of *prospective memory* – trying to remember something you need to do. Personally, I've found that the best way to prevent absent-mindedness about such matters is to create **external retrieval cues** – hard-to-miss stimuli that I won't be able to ignore as I go about my daily activities. I don't just put things on my calendar, because I know I might forget to look at it. Instead, I write "notes to self" (e.g., "Piano lesson at two o'clock," "Buy sunscreen") that I place in impossible-to-overlook spots on the floor between my desk and office door. I set the timer on my cell phone to alert me to take the chicken out of the oven 50 minutes after I've put it in there to cook. (My oven timer beeps only once and so is easy to ignore, but my phone keeps badgering me until I turn it off and presumably also deal with the chicken.) And I sing "Ninety-Nine Bottles of Beer on the Wall" until I stop at the post office on my way to or from the gym.
- **Self-Strategy 6.2: To find a misplaced item, mentally review your recent activities to see where you might have absent-mindedly left it.** Where did you put your car keys? your cell phone? your reading glasses? Perhaps you already use the strategy I describe here: You mentally go back in time, tracing your recent steps and identifying possible spots where you might have put something en route. Once last year I had to mentally travel quite a distance before finding my house keys. Here's the story: I went out to do a few errands and then, when I got home, discovered that I didn't have my house keys with me. Those keys were on a ring with many other indispensable keys (though obviously not my car key, as I had just been driving). I called the places where I had just been (a doctor's office, Home Depot, and Target), but no one had seen my keys. Geez Louise, replacing all those keys was going to be a real pain in the neck. But several hours later, after I'd managed to get in the house and fret quite a bit (were my keys still lurking on one of the shelves at Target?), I mentally reviewed what I had done the day before. Ah yes, midafternoon I had gone down the street to fetch the mail. I had had the key ring, including the mailbox key, in my jacket pocket – a *different* jacket than the one I had worn when I did my errands. Sure enough, my keys were still in that jacket's left pocket. My mental time travel saved me hours of needless aggravation.

- **Self-Strategy 6.3: Mentally incubate a situation or problem for a while**. Notice how it took me a few hours to figure out where I might have left my keys. One widely recommended strategy for solving a difficult problem is **incubation** – letting the problem mentally "percolate" while you're doing other things. You've initially searched through your long-term memory to find something that might be helpful in solving the problem, but nothing appropriate has come to mind, so you turn your attention to other activities. Even so, the problem is still lurking in your head, and as you search seemingly irrelevant parts of your long-term memory to accomplish your other tasks, you may eventually stumble on one or more tidbits that can truly help you with the problem. Some of these tidbits might even enable you to think outside the box about how you could possibly solve the problem.[40]
- **Self-Strategy 6.4: Keep in mind that even very vivid memories aren't necessarily accurate ones.** As I've said before in a variety of ways, never completely trust your long-term memory, no matter how convincingly it might "tell" you things.

Enhancing Other People's Thinking and Learning in Instructional Settings

- **Instructional Strategy 6.1: Give students time to think about how they might best answer your questions**. Given the challenges of retrieving needed knowledge from long-term memory, it's unreasonable to expect students to remember something at a moment's notice (unless, of course, you want them to learn certain information and skills to a level of automaticity). Instead, give them time to mentally look around a bit – a concept that educational psychologists refer to as **wait time**. For example, when teachers wait a few seconds after asking a question, students are more likely to give thoughtful answers, and they're more likely to support their answers with evidence and logic.[41]
- **Instructional Strategy 6.2: Have students brainstorm ideas in small groups**. In Chapter 3, I suggested that when it comes to meaning making, two or more heads are often better than one. The same is true for retrieval. More specifically, the long-term memories of several people collectively contain many more facts, ideas, and skills than can the long-term memory of any single individual – a concept that psychologists refer to as either *distributed knowledge or distributed intelligence*.[42] In **brainstorming**, a small group gets together to retrieve a wide variety of possible solutions to a challenging question or problem, initially

tossing virtually anything that springs to mind onto the pile of ideas. Some ideas might at first glance seem bizarre or outlandish, but so what? Only after generating a lengthy list do group members start to evaluate each possibility for its potential relevance and usefulness. By postponing evaluative judgments until after they've broadly searched their respective long-term memories, they increase the odds that, working together, they'll identify effective and creative approaches to the question or problem at hand.[43]

○ **Instructional Strategy 6.3: Teach seemingly absent-minded individuals how to create external retrieval cues.** People typically learn that their prospective memories are far from perfect only after they've forgotten entirely too many important errands and appointments; and even then, some of them don't know how to remediate the problem. Programmed alerts on smartphone timers or calendar apps, note-to-self reminders on backpacks or bathroom mirrors, repetitive self-instructions, and, yes, annoying self-songs such as "Ninety-Nine Bottles of Beer on the Wall" – all of these can be effective reminders of things that absolutely must be done by a certain time on a certain day.

○ **Instructional Strategy 6.4: Using age-appropriate language, help students understand that good memories come partly from effective learning strategies.** Not only must students acquire effective study strategies – many of which I've described in previous chapters – but they must also understand *why* such strategies are effective. Such knowledge falls into the category of *metacognition*, a topic we turn to in Chapter 7.

NOTES

1. Lindsay & Norman, 1977.
2. J. R. Anderson et al., 2004; Collins & Loftus, 1975; Siegel, 2012.
3. Balch, Bowman, & Mohler, 1992; Holland, Hendriks, & Aarts, 2005; Schab, 1990.
4. Einstein & McDaniel, 2005; Stokes, Pierroutsakos, & Einstein, 2007.
5. J. R. Anderson, 1983; J. R. Anderson et al., 2004; Healey, Campbell, Hasher, & Ossher, 2010.
6. Altmann & Gray, 2002; Byrnes, 2001; Loftus & Loftus, 1980; Schacter, 1999.
7. Brainerd & Reyna, 1992, 2002, 2005; G. Cohen, 2000.
8. Davachi & Dobbins, 2008; Hunt & Worthen, 2006; Pansky & Koriat, 2004.
9. Heuer and Reisberg, 1990; Kensinger, 2007; Talarico, LaBar, & Rubin, 2004; Talmi, 2013.
10. Hall, 1971; Osgood, 1949.

11. M. C. Anderson, 2009; M. C. Anderson & Levy, 2009; Nørby, 2015; Raaijmakers & Jakab, 2013.
12. Bäuml & Samenieh, 2010; M. D. MacLeod & Saunders, 2008; Román, Soriano, Gómez-Ariza, & Bajo, 2009; Storm, 2011.
13. Freud, 1922, 1915/1957; also see Arrigo & Pezdek, 1997; Nadel & Jacobs, 1998; Ray et al., 2006.
14. Geraerts et al., 2009; Loftus, 1993; McNally, 2003; Patihis, Ho, Tingen, Lilienfeld, & Loftus, 2014.
15. Berntsen, 2010; G. S. Goodman et al., 2003; Porter & Peace, 2007.
16. Howe, 2011; Nørby, 2015.
17. J. R. Anderson & Schooler, 1991; Ratey, 2001; Schacter, 1999.
18. For a classic book regarding this distinction, see Tulving, 1983.
19. Buckner & Petersen, 1996; Davachi & Dobbins, 2008; Prince, Tsukiura, & Cabeza, 2007.
20. Nørby, 2015.
21. E. S. Parker, Cahill, & McGaugh, 2006; Price, 2008.
22. E. S. Parker et al., 2006, p. 35.
23. For another example of an individual who had trouble forgetting the details of daily activities, see Luria, 1987.
24. Carmichael, Hogan, & Walter, 1932.
25. Bergman & Roediger, 1999; Brainerd & Reyna, 2005; Dooling & Christiaansen, 1977; Schacter, 2012.
26. Brainerd & Reyna, 2005; G. S. Goodman & Quas, 2008; Loftus, 1991, 1992; Perfect, 2002; Wells et al., 2002; Zaragoza, Payment, Ackil, Drivdahl, & Beck, 2001.
27. Chrobak & Zaragoza, 2012; Karpicke, 2012; Marsh, 2007; Seligman, Railton, Baumeister, & Sripada, 2013.
28. Winik, 1994, p. 40.
29. Hirst & Phelps, 2016; Talarico & Rubin, 2003; Winograd & Neisser, 1992.
30. Neisser & Harsch, 1992.
31. Neisser & Harsch, 1992, p. 9.
32. Neisser & Harsch, 1992, p. 9.
33. Brainerd & Reyna, 2005; Loftus, 2003, 2004.
34. Garry & Gerrie, 2005.
35. Foley, Harris, & Herman, 1994; Gonsalves et al., 2004; Mazzoni & Memon, 2003; J. Parker, 1995.
36. Bernstein & Loftus, 2009; Ghetti & Alexander, 2004; Pezdek, Finger, & Hodge, 1997.
37. Pezdek et al., 1997.
38. Bowers, Mattys, & Gage, 2009; C. M. MacLeod, 1988; T. O. Nelson, 1978.

39. Feinstein, Duff, & Tranel, 2010; Nadel & Jacobs, 1998; Zajonc, 2000; some of my readers might realize that classical conditioning can be at work in such instances.
40. Baird et al., 2012; Dijksterhuis & Strick, 2016; Kounios & Beeman, 2009; Topolinski & Reber, 2010; Zhong, Dijksterhuis, & Galinsky, 2008.
41. Moon, 2008; Rowe, 1974; Tobin, 1987.
42. Bromme, Kienhues, & Porsch, 2010; G. Fischer, 2009; Pea, 1993; Salomon, 1993.
43. Baer & Garrett, 2010; Runco & Chand, 1995; Sweller, 2009.

7

Metacognition: Thinking about Thinking

Our awareness, understanding, and control of our own thinking and learning processes are collectively known as **metacognition**. We aren't the only species with metacognitive skills – quite the contrary. Other primates, dolphins, and, yes, even laboratory rats have some ability to differentiate between what they know and don't know.[1] But we humans seem to have a much greater ability to *learn how to learn* than is true for our nonhuman companions on the planet.

By the time most of us reach school age, we've already begun to construct a personal theory about our own and other people's inner mental worlds. As we grow older, this **theory of mind** encompasses increasingly complex understandings of human thoughts, beliefs, feelings, motives, and intentions.[2] Yet even as adults, most of us really don't know very much about our mental hardware and software. Notice that I've already mentioned 19 common misconceptions about how people think and learn, and I'm not done yet.

METACOGNITIVE PROCESSES: EFFECTIVE LEARNING REQUIRES BOTH SELF-REFLECTION AND SELF-DIRECTION

Metacognition includes knowledge and skills such as these:

- Knowing what learning tasks we can reasonably accomplish within a certain timeframe
- Planning how we might best tackle a new learning task
- Knowing which learning strategies work well and which do not
- Tailoring learning strategies to the task at hand
- Self-reflecting on our present knowledge state – more specifically, determining whether or not we've successfully learned something

- Knowing effective strategies for retrieving information we've previously stored but can't presently recall

Thus, good metacognitive learners engage in both *self-reflection* ("looking" inward to see what is mentally going on) and *self-direction* (strategically controlling a learning activity).

Different learning tasks call for different cognitive skills. I'll give you three examples to illustrate the kinds of strategies that might be involved.

One Example: Reading for Learning

Reading a novel for fun is one thing; reading a book in order to gain new knowledge can be another thing altogether. Good readers – people who can effectively make sense of, remember, and make use of what they read – typically engage in many of the following cognitive processes:

- They clarify their reasons and goals for their reading and adjust their strategies accordingly.
- They focus their attention and learning efforts on the contents most important for their purposes.
- They draw on what they already know to make sense of and elaborate on the new material – for instance, by drawing inferences or envisioning possible applications.
- They critically analyze what they read in terms of its plausibility and credibility.
- They persist in their sense-making efforts when they encounter puzzling or ambiguous sections of text.
- They read with the mindset that the author might present ideas that conflict with their own beliefs, and they revise their existing beliefs when the author presents sufficiently convincing evidence and logic.[3]

In contrast, poor readers – those who don't seem to gain much from what they read – engage in few, if any, of these processes.

A Second Example: Learning from the Internet

How often do you use Google, Bing, or some other search engine to get your answers to questions you have about, say, current events, recent medical advances, or your favorite sports team's upcoming schedule? If you're like me, you search the Internet several times a day for one thing or another. In addition to good reading skills, effective learners also use strategies such as the following to make the most of their Internet searches:

- At the beginning of a search, they think creatively about potentially fruitful words and phrases to put in the search box.
- They scrutinize the various paths and hotlinks on a webpage to determine which ones might best help them accomplish their purposes.
- They self-monitor their progress toward their goals, and they may adjust their goals and strategies as new information comes to light.
- They critically evaluate the information and potential *mis*information they find on various websites.
- They analytically compare and try to synthesize the things they learn from two or more sources.[4]

Unfortunately, most adolescents and many adults don't effectively engage in these strategies, especially in cases where they know little or nothing about the topic in question. Furthermore, many naively assume that everything posted on the Internet must be "fact" and so take it at face value.[5] For instance, if you're a regular user of Facebook or another social media site, you may occasionally have been horrified – as I have – about some of the sites friends have "shared" with the rest of the world. Personally, if I were to take some of my friends' posted sites seriously, I would be an adamant climate change denier and, in national elections, would vote for individuals who almost certainly would *not* work in my country's best interests.

A Third Example: Learning How to Play the Piano Meaningfully

I've based the preceding two examples on research, but this one comes from my own experiences in relearning how to play the piano over the past year or so. When I was a child, I took five years of piano lessons, and I practiced my pieces for 30 minutes a day; well, no, that's not quite true – I actually practiced only on days when Mom nagged me to do so. The result was that I could "read" music, in the sense that I could translate many musical symbols into action and could find virtually any note on the keyboard. Could I make *sense* of what I was seeing on a page of sheet music? Not a bit. In fact, aside from knowing that written music visually captures a melodic tune, I didn't know there was *any* sense to be made of it.

Now, more than 50 years later, I've resumed my lessons – this time with a very different teacher and also with a very different goal in mind. (To be honest, I'm not sure that I *had* a goal during my childhood lessons.) I figure that if I can find meaning in each page – that is, if I can detect underlying patterns and principles in what I'm seeing – I can ultimately become a fairly decent piano player. Following are a few of the things my teacher has been encouraging me to do:

- Look at the keyboard as little as possible. Instead, I should focus my attention on the written music and rely on my increasing familiarity with how far apart various keys are on the keyboard.
- Analyze various chords and arpeggios with respect to the major and minor scales and possible inversions they represent. (Of course, I first had to learn what minor scales and inversions were; I didn't know these things until a few months ago.)
- Look ahead to see what notes will soon follow, and plan finger placements to maximize the smoothness of flow from one set of notes to the next. (In other words, I can't just focus on the moment; I need to plan ahead.)
- Practice, practice, practice playing the major and minor scales to the point where both their recognition and execution are learned to automaticity. (This way, I can devote more of my limited attention and working memory capacity to my meaning-making efforts.)

I won't pretend that doing these things is easy for me – it isn't, at least not yet – but it's the only way that I can acquire the piano-playing expertise to which I aspire.

EPISTEMIC BELIEFS: WHAT WE THINK THINKING AND LEARNING *ARE*

Our **epistemic beliefs** are our beliefs about the general nature of "knowledge" and "learning." (You may also see such terms as *epistemological beliefs, epistemic cognition*, and *ways of knowing*.) Typically these beliefs are self-constructed; thus, they aren't necessarily accurate or productive. Some of the misconceptions I've previously identified in the book reflect counterproductive epistemic beliefs. Here are two more:

Misconception #20: That knowledge is largely a collection of discrete facts

Misconception #21: That we either know something or we don't

It should go without saying now that, for the most part, these two beliefs are wrong, wrong, wrong.

Epistemic beliefs include our self-constructed notions about the following issues:

- *To what degree is knowledge a certain, unchanging entity?* Is knowledge about a topic a permanent, unalterable "truth" or, instead, a dynamic entity that may continue to evolve over time?
- *How complex is knowledge?* Does knowledge consist of many discrete, isolated facts? Or can it be better characterized as a body of interrelated ideas?
- *How can new information best be verified as "truth"?* Should our criterion be a seemingly reliable source (e.g., a teacher, government official, religious leader, or Internet website)? Or, instead, should we depend on credible evidence and our own logical reasoning capabilities to critically evaluate the information?
- *How rapidly is knowledge typically acquired?* Is learning an almost instantaneous process, such that we either "get it" quickly or never get it at all? Or, instead, can we increasingly master a new topic or skill in step-by-step increments over an extended time period?
- *What underlying factors make us good or poor learners?* Are we born with a certain ability (or lack of ability) to learn things? Or, instead, is our learning success largely dependent on practice, persistence, and use of good strategies?[6]

Each of these issues reflects a *continuum* of possible beliefs, rather than an either-or dichotomy. For instance, with regard to how you determine what is and isn't "true," you might believe that you should rely both on outside sources you judge to be reliable (e.g., teachers) and on your own logical reasoning capabilities. If so, your belief would fall somewhere in the middle of the *how-can-information-best-be-verified* continuum.

Also, our epistemic beliefs can be somewhat specific to particular contexts and content domains.[7] For example, we know that certain things are indisputable facts. Grass is green (at least as perceived by the human eye), and our Earth revolves around the sun (rather than vice versa). Yet other parts of humankind's collective knowledge remain tentative and subject to further research; such is true for many aspects of the physical, biological, psychological, social, and medical sciences.

Some of our epistemic beliefs might lie well below the surface of our conscious awareness; in other words, they might take the form of *implicit* rather than explicit "knowledge."[8] Even so, they can have a profound impact on how we study and learn.[9] For example, if we believe that knowledge about a topic is merely a collection of isolated facts, we're apt to engage in rote learning – perhaps rehearsal – in an effort to drill those facts into our thick skulls. If we believe that knowledge is a certain, unchanging entity that we can acquire very quickly, we're likely to zero in on and steadfastly adhere to a particular perspective on a controversial issue; we won't be open to alternative and potentially more valid perspectives. And if we believe that we don't have any built-in, natural ability to learn math – hey, why bother even trying?

People's epistemic beliefs often evolve with age and experience.[10] For example, elementary school children are likely to believe that the "absolute truth" about virtually any topic is lurking out there somewhere. As they move into the middle school and secondary grades, some of them begin to understand that knowledge isn't necessarily an absolute, either-or, right-or-wrong entity – that it can occasionally have a *belief-rather-than-fact* quality and that two or more perspectives might be equally valid. And gradually some of them begin to understand that bona fide knowledge often involves knowing complex interrelationships among ideas as well as discrete facts.

Epistemic beliefs can continue to evolve in adulthood, especially for those of us who pursue college coursework or other advanced educational opportunities. At advanced levels, instructors and textbooks are more likely to portray knowledge and "truth" as tentative and uncertain rather than as undeniable fact. In addition, advanced instruction about a topic may foster an appreciation for critically analyzing and evaluating other people's claims and arguments – even the claims and arguments of experts.[11]

Developmentally speaking, you might think of epistemic beliefs about knowledge as possibly – but not always – morphing from a very naive conceptualization to an increasingly sophisticated one.[12] Three-year-olds typically have a *realist* view of knowledge, believing that it's essentially the same as what people say and do. For example, if you're only at this point in your epistemic development, you might believe me when I tell you that alligators wear sweaters to keep themselves warm in the winter. A year or so later, children transition to an *absolutist* view, in which they don't necessarily believe what other people tell them, but they're fairly certain that things are definitely either right or wrong, black or white. Some time after that – maybe in adolescence, maybe in adulthood, but maybe never – the absolutist view changes to a more *multiplist* one, in which knowledge can be various shades of gray with respect to its rightness/wrongness, and opposing opinions about a controversial topic may all be equally valid. A minority of adults eventually acquire an *evaluativist* view, in which perspectives that are consistent with logical principles and credible research findings are taken far more seriously than unsubstantiated ones. The more we can get beyond the basics of a certain discipline area – whether it be chemistry, psychology, history, literature, or some other domain – and explore the frontiers of the discipline's collective research and meaning-making efforts, the more likely we are to adopt an evaluativist view of that discipline's body of knowledge.

Only people with a *realist* view of knowledge might believe you if you tell them that alligators wear sweaters when they need to stay warm.

SELF-REGULATED LEARNING: MENTALLY TAKING CHARGE

Earlier I mentioned that effective learners engage in considerable self-direction. Most of our self-directed learning efforts fall within the realm of what psychologists call **self-regulated learning**. Self-regulated learning includes a number of cognitive processes, some of which I've already alluded to:

- *Setting goals for learning:* Identifying the desired end results of a learning activity – perhaps to get a general overview of a topic, gain a better understanding of cause-and-effect relationships, or simply acquire the kinds of information that might be assessed on an upcoming classroom exam.

- *Planning a viable approach:* Determining what mental and behavioral strategies are likely to be effective in completing the learning task – perhaps finding a quiet place to study, creating a concept map or two-dimensional table as a way of integrating and contrasting a body of interrelated ideas, or setting aside an hour each day to practice.

- *Motivating oneself to be productive:* Using self-motivational strategies to keep oneself on task – for instance, embellishing on a task to make it more interesting and enjoyable, or promising oneself to engage in a favorite activity after the task has been completed.

- *Self-controlling attention:* Trying to clear one's head of potentially distracting thoughts and diligently striving to keep one's attention focused where it needs to be.

- *Use of goal-relevant learning strategies:* Choosing and using the types of strategies (e.g., elaboration, mnemonics, critical-thinking processes) that can maximize the chances of success.

- *Self-monitoring throughout a learning activity:* Continually self-assessing one's current knowledge state to determine how much progress has been made.

- *Seeking help when it's needed:* Identifying times when someone else's expertise is called for and then taking active steps to get an expert's assistance.

- *Self-evaluation and self-reflection regarding one's final achievement level:* Self-assessing the final outcome, determining whether one has successfully accomplished one's goals, and using this information to plan approaches to future learning tasks.[13]

Among the most challenging aspects of self-regulation are its self-monitoring and self-evaluation aspects. Within this context, we have another common misconception:

Misconception #22: That we are reasonably good judges of what we know and don't know

This particular misconception is far, far from the truth. In studies of **comprehension monitoring** (you may also see the term *judgment of*

learning), researchers have found that many people of all ages don't carefully or accurately monitor their comprehension while they're studying
something new.[14] Thus, they may think they've learned something that
they've either misunderstood or not learned at all. In other words, they
have an **illusion of knowing** the material.[15] For example, as I reflect back
on my many years of college teaching, I can recall a few students who came
to my office door quite puzzled about why they did poorly on one of my
exams. "I studied *so hard*!!" they might tell me. I would invariably sit them
down and quiz them a bit about important ideas that classroom explanations and assigned readings had recently covered, as well as about possible
examples, implications, and applications of these ideas. "What implications does the concept of working memory [or long-term memory or self-
regulated learning or whatever] have for classroom instruction?" I might ask.
The response was usually something like this: "Well, working memory is
where you . . . you know . . . where you remember things . . . where . . . well,
I know what it is, but I can't explain it very well." I don't recall ever buying
into students' self-descriptions (and probably self-beliefs) that they were
just "poor test takers." Instead, I would recommend strategies for studying
more effectively – strategies that, given the content of my courses, they
should have been using for most of the semester.

People are more likely to be victims of this illusion of knowing when they
have overly simplistic epistemic beliefs about what it is to "learn" and "know"
something. And when they think they've mastered something they haven't
come even close to mastering, they're apt to stop studying it – something that
was probably the case for my self-diagnosed poor test takers.[16]

To be effective learners and rememberers, we must monitor our comprehension not only when we first study new material but also at some later
point in time. This brings us to yet another common misconception:

Misconception #23: That if we can recall something right after we
study it, then we will probably remember it later on as well

As you know, when we first encounter new information, it's in working
memory, which is at best only a very short-term repository of information.
Does it move on to long-term memory? Does it neurologically consolidate
so that it will stick around for a while? Only time and delayed comprehension monitoring will tell.[17] As I continue with my piano lessons these days,
I'm repeatedly reminded of the short-term nature of my working memory.
Things that my teacher tells me about music theory or effective finger
positions usually make immediate logical sense to me. But when I sit down

to practice the following day, I sometimes find myself thinking, "I know she talked about this issue, but what exactly did she tell me to do?" I have to return the following week, my head hung sheepishly low, and ask her to tell me again.

In general, the more metacognitively sophisticated we are, the more effective our learning – and the higher our achievement levels – will be. And as you've seen, the best metacognitive processes are very *strategic* ones, requiring an active, inquiring mind.

BEING STRATEGIC

I'm hoping that most of the strategies I've offered in previous chapters have already enhanced your metacognitive awareness. Here I offer a few additional strategies to enhance your learning prowess, along with some suggestions for enhancing the metacognitive capabilities of people with whom you might now or someday be working.

Enhancing Your Own Thinking and Learning in Everyday Life

- **Self-Strategy 7.1: Reflect on and critically evaluate your current epistemic beliefs**. For what topics is knowledge pretty much cut-and-dried, and for what topics is there still a good deal of uncertainty and room for debate? What is genuine *knowledge* about a topic like, anyway – to what degree is it comprised of discrete facts, and to what degree is it comprised of understandings of complex interrelationships? On whom and what do you rely in your efforts to determine the validity and truth of new information? What things about you make you a good or poor learner and rememberer? How much of your learning ability have you inherited, and how much have you acquired through experience and good strategies? Your answers to all of these questions can tell you a great deal about your future chances of mastering complex new topics and skills.
- **Self-Strategy 7.2: Regularly monitor your ongoing understandings of new material**. For example, quiz yourself after you've read a few pages of a textbook. Have other people quiz you as well. Compose a summary of what you've just heard or read. And definitely, definitely, definitely check yourself a few hours and days – ideally also a few weeks – after you've learned something, to see how much of it you can still remember and make sense of. Ideally, you should

self-assess the *specific* things you have and haven't mastered – for instance, "Okay, episodic memory is different from semantic memory in at least three key ways" (and you go on to tell yourself what their differences are) rather than "I think I finally understand this stuff."[18]

- **Self-Strategy 7.3: Also reflect on how well your current learning and study strategies are working for you.** How well have you been doing on exams and other assessments in any college courses you've been taking? How much can you recall of what you've been learning from athletic coaches, television documentaries, or music lessons? In general, have your learning efforts led to successful outcomes, or have they largely been a waste of your time? In other words, have your learning strategies been adequate for achieving your goals? If not, either revise or replace them.

- **Self-Strategy 7.4: Be wary of people who appear to have an absolutist view of the world.** Entirely too many people on the planet present themselves as experts on one topic or another. For example, I still shudder when I see a newly published book on "teaching to the right brain," "speed reading" techniques (which have largely been discredited[19]), or some other hogwash. And as I write this book during an especially contentious U.S. presidential campaign in 2016, I think with horror about candidates who are confidently asserting that they and they alone know best how to solve the country's and world's problems. I seriously doubt it, and their self-proclaimed expertise has convinced me that (a) they actually don't have a clue and (b) they'd be unlikely to seek the advice of people who *do* know something about the issues at hand.

  Yes, roses are red, and violets are blue. But even here we need to hedge a bit. Not all roses are red, and violets are really more purplish than blue; furthermore, some African violets are red, pink, or white. Aside from basic math facts – for instance, 2 and 2 always add up to 4 in a base-10 number system – very few things are absolutely true. At a minimum, try to take a *multiplist's* view of knowledge. Better still, aspire to being an *evaluativist* – someone who regularly inspects people's proclamations with logical reasoning and as much evidence as you can get.

Enhancing Other People's Thinking and Learning in Instructional Settings

- **Instructional Strategy 7.1: Teach and scaffold self-regulated learning skills.** Some children and adolescents spontaneously self-construct self-regulated learning skills during age-appropriate opportunities to study and learn independently.[20] But not all kids acquire these skills on their own – a problem that can persist into their adult lives. A lack of self-regulation skills is probably a key reason why so many adults drop out of online, study-it-yourself college courses.[21]

One effective way to foster self-regulated learning is to begin with **co-regulated learning**, in which two or more people share responsibility for planning and carrying out a learning task.[22] For instance, when assigning a new learning activity, you might give students particular goals to shoot for as they study, or you might describe specific criteria that they should use as they self-assess their progress. Alternatively, you might have students study something new in pairs or small groups in which each member is assigned a particular group-regulatory task. As students become more independently self-regulating over time, you can gradually remove the social scaffolding.

○ **Instructional Strategy 7.2: Help students develop realistic expectations for their memories and learning efforts.** Many students are overly optimistic about how much they can reasonably learn and remember within a limited time period. This is especially true for young children,[23] but I've witnessed the problem in college students as well. Perhaps the best way to foster more realism is to engage students in one or more learning activities in which they discover that they *can't* remember everything they've heard or read. Students must know that you won't be evaluating them on the basis of their unsatisfactory performance. Rather, the whole point of the exercise should be to help them get a sense of what they can and cannot expect their brains to do for them as they study new material.

○ **Instructional Strategy 7.3: Explicitly teach comprehension monitoring skills.** One especially effective approach is **self-questioning** – regularly asking oneself and then answering questions requiring either recall or elaborative processing.[24] Following are a few question stems that can get students started thinking in a self-interrogatory manner:
  ○ Explain why . . .
  ○ How might I use . . . to . . . ?
  ○ What might happen if . . . ?
  ○ How are . . . and . . . similar? How are they different?
  ○ What are some strengths and weaknesses of . . . ?
  ○ How might I relate this idea to something I've studied before?[25]

○ **Instructional Strategy 7.4: Gradually foster more sophisticated epistemic beliefs.** This strategy is more easily said than done, in part because students' beliefs may not be readily available for conscious inspection and evaluation.[26] One possible approach – which I'm obviously using in this book – is to explicitly describe *learning* as an active, constructive process that requires considerable mental work and to describe *knowledge* as something that involves many interconnections and continues to evolve with more experience and diligent studying. Another, probably better approach is to engage students in activities in which they (a) can successfully learn only if they persistently use appropriate cognitive processes and/or (b) must deal with controversial subject matter that includes many unresolved issues. For instance, you might have students conduct whole-class or small-group debates that address both the pros and cons of particular positions or perspectives on matters of history, government policy, or ethics. Or, instead, you might have students generate two or more hypotheses about an issue in physical, biological, or social science and then collect and analyze data to determine which of these hypotheses is consistent with the evidence. Such activities are most likely to promote epistemic development when students feel comfortable asking one another questions, tactfully critiquing one another's arguments, and critically analyzing and possibly revising their own beliefs.[27]

In your efforts to nurture more advanced epistemic beliefs in either yourself or others, however, you shouldn't expect dramatic changes overnight. Genuine epistemic development typically occurs only slowly, over a period of years. The challenge here is to promote *conceptual change*, a topic we turn to in Chapter 8.

NOTES

1. de Waal, 2016; Foote & Crystal, 2007; Kornell, 2009; Kornell, Son, & Terrace, 2007.
2. Flavell, 2000; Harris, 2006; Lillard, 1997; Wellman, 1990.
3. Afflerbach & Cho, 2010; Baker, 1989; Chan, Burtis, & Bereiter, 1997; Cromley, Snyder-Hogan, & Luciw-Dubas, 2010; Dole, Duffy, Roehler, & Pearson, 1991; Fox, 2009; Hacker, 1998.
4. Afflerbach & Cho, 2010; Alexander & the Disciplined Reading and Learning Research Laboratory, 2012; Azevedo & Witherspoon, 2009; Leu, O'Byrne, Zawilinski, McVerry, & Everett-Cacopardo, 2009.
5. Greene, Hutchinson, Costa, & Crompton, 2012; Kirschner & van Merriënboer, 2013; Niederhauser, 2008.

6. Bendixen & Rule, 2004; Chinn, Buckland, & Samarapungavan, 2011; Greene, Torney-Purta, & Azevedo, 2010; Hofer, 2004; Hofer & Pintrich, 2002; Schommer-Aikins, Bird, & Bakken, 2010; P. Wood & Kardash, 2002.
7. Buehl & Alexander, 2006; Muis, Bendixen, & Haerle, 2006; Schommer-Aikins, 2004.
8. Mason, 2010; Muis, 2007; Schraw & Moshman, 1995.
9. Bråten, Britt, Strømsø, & Rouet, 2011; Buehl & Alexander, 2005; DeBacker & Crowson, 2008; Hofer & Pintrich, 1997; Mason, 2010; Muis & Franco, 2009; Ricco, Pierce, & Medinilla, 2010; Schommer, 1994; Schommer-Aikins et al., 2010.
10. Hofer & Pintrich, 1997; Kuhn & Weinstock, 2002; Schommer, Calvert, Gariglietti, & Bajaj, 1997; Yang & Tsai, 2010.
11. Baxter Magolda, 2002; Hofer & Pintrich, 1997; Greene et al., 2010; Kuhn, 2001; Muis et al., 2006.
12. Kuhn & Franklin, 2006; Kuhn & Weinstock, 2002.
13. Duckworth & Seligman, 2005; Greene & Azevedo, 2009; Hacker, Dunlosky, & Graesser, 2009b; Kaplan & Berman, 2010; Karabenick & Sharma, 1994; Muis, 2007; Nolen, 1996; Ryan & Shim, 2012; Thiede, Anderson, & Therriault, 2003; Winne & Hadwin, 2008; Wolters, 2003; Zimmerman, 2008; Zimmerman & Moylan, 2009; Zusho & Barnett, 2011.
14. Dunlosky & Lipko, 2007; Nokes & Dole, 2004; Zhao & Linderholm, 2008.
15. Fernbach, Rogers, Fox, & Sloman, 2013; Stone, 2000; Thiede, Griffin, Wiley, & Redford, 2009; Zhao & Linderholm, 2008.
16. Dunning, Heath, & Suls, 2004; Kornell & Bjork, 2008b; Schneider, 2010.
17. Hacker et al., 2009b; Serra & Metcalfe, 2009; Weaver & Kelemen, 1997.
18. Dunlosky & Lipko, 2007; Zhao & Linderholm, 2008.
19. R. P. Carver, 1990; Rayner, Schotter, Masson, Potter, & Treiman, 2016.
20. Coplan & Arbeau, 2009; Corno & Mandinach, 2004; Paris & Paris, 2001; Zimmerman, 2004.
21. For example, see F. B. King, Harner, & Brown, 2000.
22. Bodrova & Leong, 1996; DiDonato, 2013; McCaslin & Hickey, 2001; Volet, Vaura, & Salonen, 2009; Vygotsky, 1934/1986.
23. Bjorklund & Green, 1992; Flavell, Friedrichs, & Hoyt, 1970.
24. Bugg & McDaniel, 2012; A. King, 1992; Otero, 2009; Rosenshine, Meister, & Chapman, 1996.
25. Questions based on those suggested by A. King, 1992, p. 309.
26. Mason, 2010; Muis, 2007; Schraw & Moshman, 1995.
27. Andre & Windschitl, 2003; Bendixen & Feucht, 2010; Kuhn, 2009; Muis et al., 2006; Rule & Bendixen, 2010; vanSledright & Limón, 2006.

8

Conceptual Change: Revising Our Understandings When Revisions Are Called For

It's time now to return to an important point I made previously in Chapter 3: *Our self-constructed understandings of the world aren't always accurate ones.* Sometimes we simply get our facts wrong. For example, when first encountering the Spanish word *vaca*, those non-Spanish-speaking people among us might erroneously think it means "vacation." It doesn't; a *vaca* is a cow. At other times, however, we've weaved one or more not-quite-right-or-completely-wrong ideas into a personal theory or worldview – something that subsequently influences how we interpret new information that comes our way. For example, if we've already come to the conclusion that this whole climate-change thing is a gigantic hoax collaboratively perpetuated by many of the world's scientists, we might continue to insist that any recent changes in climactic patterns are (a) simply manifestations of normal year-to-year or decade-to-decade variability and/or (b) the results of natural causes rather than human activities.[1]

Revising our beliefs about discrete facts can often be fairly easy. For instance, it shouldn't be too difficult to learn and remember that a *vaca* is a cow, not a vacation, although the *vaca*-vacation association might linger a bit and occasionally pop to the surface (recall the discussion of *interference* in Chapter 6). Revising a bunch of interconnected ideas or replacing them altogether – a process called **conceptual change** – can be far more challenging. Whether we're children or adults, we can be quite obstinate in holding onto certain misconceptions and counterproductive beliefs about the world, even after considerable instruction aimed at convincing us to think in more productive, scientifically supported ways.[2] Not only do we have to acquire new beliefs and ways of thinking, but we also have to dismantle – or at least to *inhibit* – some of our prior beliefs and inclinations.

Thus, if you're someone who would occasionally like to change other people's beliefs about a topic – and isn't that true for all of us? – you should keep in mind the following misconception about misconceptions:

Misconception #24: That we can easily change our current beliefs when we encounter new information that contradicts them

If mind changing were always a simple, effortless task, I wouldn't be devoting an entire chapter to the process – which, as you can see, I am.

ACQUIRING MISCONCEPTIONS: KNOWLEDGE CONSTRUCTION GONE AWRY

At this point in the book, I've presented 24 common misconceptions about human thinking and learning, and I'm still not done. Children and adults tend to have misconceptions about many other topics as well. For example, as a result of their ongoing efforts to make sense of the things they see and hear in their environment, children might believe that:

- The Earth is round only in the way that a pancake is round; the sun "comes up" on one side of the Earth in the morning and "goes down" on the other side at night.
- The North Pole is the Earth's top side, and the South Pole is its bottom; hence, someone who went to the South Pole would fall "down" into space.
- The lines that separate various countries or states/provinces on maps are also marked on the Earth's surface.
- Long ago, people and dinosaurs lived on the Earth at the same time and possibly interacted.[3]

Some misconceptions can persist well into adulthood, even after college-level instruction that specifically refutes them. Here are some examples:

- *That any moving object must have a force acting on it.* No, actually, thanks to inertia, once a force has set an object in motion, the object will continue to move in the same direction and at the same rate unless some other force (e.g., friction, gravity) impedes it or alters its course.
- *That whenever we look at something, some sort of energy travels from our eyes to the object.* Quite the opposite is true; for vision to be possible, rays from a light source must bounce off the object and then travel to the eye.

- *That it gets warmer in the summer than in the winter because the Earth is closer to the sun in the summer.* This notion doesn't account for the fact that people in the Southern Hemisphere have winter when folks in the Northern Hemisphere have summer. In reality, the seasons are the result of the angle at which the sun's rays hit the Earth's surface: The rays can arrive almost perpendicular to the ground in late spring and early summer but arrive at quite an angle – and so are more widely dispersed – during the winter.
- *That within the context of evolution, natural selection is the result of certain species needing to make changes in order to survive.* For instance, people might believe that "giraffes have long necks *so that* they can reach high food."[4] This logic entails a nonexistent causal relationship. Genetic mutations (e.g., genes that lead to a longer neck) happen randomly; those that work out well increase the chances of survival for those members of the species who inherit them. There is no *needing*-a-characteristic-*causes*-it-to-appear phenomenon involved in the process.[5]

We might also have a few misconceptions about ourselves, either as individuals or as typical members of the human race:

- *That, as individuals, we are so unique and exceptional that no one else could possibly understand us.* Although this misconception is especially prevalent during adolescence, it can continue into adulthood as well.[6]
- *That if we haven't succeeded at a particular activity in the past, we're unlikely to succeed at it in the future.* I've probably already convinced you that this isn't true, but I'll work even harder to do so in the discussion of *self-efficacy* in Chapter 9.
- *That intelligence and various learning abilities are just naturally built in – we either have them or we don't.* I've previously touched on this misconception in Chapters 3 and 7, and I'll address it further in Chapter 9.

WHY WE'RE OFTEN TOO STUBBORN TO CHANGE OUR MINDS

Why do we often fail to change our beliefs when conceptual change is clearly called for? Psychologists have offered a variety of explanations, each of which seems to contribute to our chronic pig-headedness.

Learning from Experience: Seeing Is Believing

The Earth is definitely flat, except for a few mountains or hills that stick up here and there. When we look at a globe, the South Pole is at the bottom, so obviously people who try to go there will fall off into space. Jackets and sweaters generate heat: We always feel warmer when we wear them. If we want to move something heavy, we must continue to push it until we get it when we want it; thus, any object needs a force acting on it in order to keep it in motion.

All four of the preceding statements are *false*, of course. But it's so easy to believe them – and to *keep* believing some of them – because they're consistent with our everyday realities.[7]

Our Need for Consistency: Elaboration Can Undermine Objective Self-Reflection

Much of the time, we humans are quite committed to drawing on our current understandings when we work to make sense of and elaborate on new information. Ideally, we want everything to hang together in our minds.[8] By now, this phenomenon should hardly be news to you.

A Retrieval Problem: We Don't Detect the Inconsistency

In Chapter 5, I mentioned that meaningful connection making can occur only if we're thinking about both the "old" and the "new" at the same time – that is, if both are simultaneously in working memory. But this doesn't always happen. Unless a situation provides retrieval cues that send us in the right directions in long-term memory, we might very well not retrieve our current beliefs. It's entirely possible for us to acquire new knowledge about a phenomenon while leaving our misconceptions untouched.[9] For instance, we might learn how the sun's rays hit our part of the Earth at different angles during different seasons and yet still hold tightly to our current belief that we're closer to the sun in the summer than in the winter. Sometimes, too, our current beliefs might take the form of *implicit* knowledge that isn't easily opened for conscious inspection.[10]

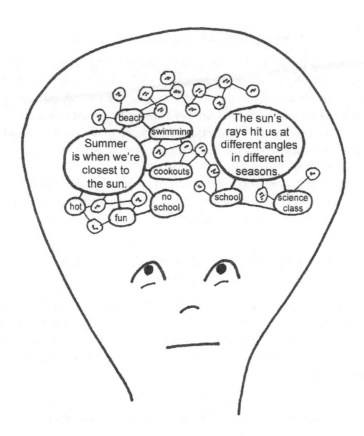

We don't necessarily discard our current misbeliefs when we acquire new, contradictory explanations.

Confirmation Bias: We Actively Seek Out Evidence That Supports Our Views, and We Steer Away from Evidence That Doesn't

Not only does our natural inclination to elaborate on new information predispose us to keep thinking what we've always been thinking, but we also work hard to *justify* our views and to discredit anything that might contradict them – a predisposition known as **confirmation bias**.[11] For example, if you're a regular user of Facebook or other social media, you've probably noticed that people are likely to post information that supports – rather than refutes – their current perspectives about a controversial issue. Rarely do they say, "Oops, sorry, I was wrong; here's the real scoop." And consider an incident that one researcher observed in a high school physics class. The class had been studying the idea that, other factors (such as air resistance) being equal, heavy and not-so-heavy objects fall at the same rate. To test this idea, the students built containers for eggs they would be dropping from a third-floor window, with the goal of keeping their eggs from breaking when they landed. A student named Barry adamantly refused to believe that light objects fall as quickly as heavy objects, so he added some nails to his container to give it extra weight. But on the day of the egg drop, his egg landed at about the same time as his classmates' eggs. His explanation: "The people weren't timing real good."[12]

We sometimes devote considerable mental effort to discrediting evidence that contradicts our current perspectives. I'll illustrate this point by reflecting on my own area of expertise: psychological science. As a university professor and (eventually) college textbook writer over the past 40 years, I've read countless articles and books on such topics as learning, cognition, motivation, and child development; I'm guessing that they've numbered in the tens of thousands. Thankfully, some of my colleagues in the field have modified their theoretical views on certain psychological phenomena as new research evidence has come to light. A few have even overhauled their entire psychological worldviews about what causes what – for instance, switching from behaviorist, stimulus-response perspectives to more cognitively oriented ones.[13] Yet other psychologists have not only held steadfastly to ideas that incoming evidence has increasingly called into question but in fact have actively sought out evidence or logic to support their shaky explanations.[14]

There might actually be a neurological basis to our tendency to stick with and possibly elaborate on what we already believe rather than revising our understandings in light of new evidence. Whenever we're learning new things, we're making adjustments to the neuron-based associations and pathways within our brains. Neurologically speaking, simply adding new ideas to what we already know and believe to be true is much, much easier than completely overhauling our personal theories or worldviews.[15]

To put it bluntly, we humans like to be right.

Motivated Reasoning: Our Motives and Emotions Can Take Precedence over Evidence and Logic

Not only do we like to be right, but in addition, we sometimes *really* don't like to be wrong, especially for motivational or emotional reasons – a phenomenon that some psychologists have called **motivated reasoning.**[16] For example, we may have certain goals we want to accomplish, such as keeping our reputations for being know-it-alls in a certain area of expertise; being wrong might seriously tarnish what others think of us. Or we might see any challenges to our ways of thinking as threatening our self-esteem and general sense of well-being. Sometimes new information clashes with our long-held views about topics near and dear to our hearts; views that we share with others in our cultural or religious group might fall into this category.

Simplistic Epistemic Beliefs: We Have It on Good Authority

Some of those naive beliefs about thinking and learning I described in Chapter 7 can play a significant role in determining whether and to what extent we undergo conceptual change when we should.[17] If knowledge is an unchanging entity that we either have or don't have, and if our best sources of "correct" information are people or documents that espouse irrefutable facts, why would we have any reason to change our opinions?

More and more, it seems, significant numbers of our species are adamantly rejecting well-documented scientific findings or historical facts – whether they be about climate change, the Holocaust, or the possible relationship between childhood immunizations and autism. (*Yes*, the Nazis killed more than six million people during the Holocaust of World War II, and *no*, scientists have found *no* convincing evidence that certain immunizations increase the likelihood of autism.[18]) Some psychologists have attributed such unyielding attitudes as reflecting either (a) misunderstandings of the nature of scientific inquiry – for instance, its focus on systematic data collection and analysis and its insistence on replication and subsequent validation – or else (b) complete rejection of science as an important source of information about what things are probably true and not true. All scientists are "biased," people might say, or they have "personal agendas," or they might be in cahoots in their efforts to propagate elaborate "hoaxes."[19] And people might assert that 95% or 99% certainty isn't good enough – that until something is 100% *proven* for all eternity, it can't possibly be taken seriously.

Social and Cultural Influences: Everybody Says So

Many of our beliefs and misbeliefs are in one way or another built into our social and cultural groups' ways of saying and doing things, to the point that we never question them.[20] For example, in our everyday language, we define a *transparent* object as "something we can see through," even though the "through-ing" is being done by light rays, *not* by our eyes. When we talk about traveling somewhere, we might say that we're going "up north" or "down south," even though the only up-ness or down-ness involved is what we see on a map or globe.

Who were the good guys and who were the bad guys in America's Civil War during the 1860s? Who were the good guys and who were the bad guys in the Russian Revolution of 1917? And at present, who are the good and bad guys in conflicts in various regions of the world – say, in Africa or the Middle East? The answers you give to such questions are typically based on what people around you have consistently told you is "true."

NUDGING OURSELVES AND OTHERS TOWARD CONCEPTUAL CHANGE: APPROACHES THAT SOMETIMES WORK

Occasionally other people successfully convince us to think differently about a topic or issue than we currently do. They might do so directly through face-to-face contact or indirectly through books, films, newscasts, and other media. But notice the word *nudging* in the heading for this section: Conceptual change can be a very slow process. Also notice the word *sometimes:* Despite other people's best efforts, it doesn't necessarily occur when it should.

It shouldn't surprise you to learn that meaningful learning is a key factor in bringing about conceptual change. Furthermore, conceptual change often requires review and practice and then more review and practice. Ideally, we cognitively process the new, contradictory information in considerable depth; that is, we spend a fair amount of time thinking about it and elaborating on it in *appropriate* ways – making logical sense of it, critically analyzing it, and mentally generating reasonable implications and applications. Formal and informal instruction that quickly and superficially glosses over many topics in an effort to "cover" them all can be a complete waste of everyone's time.[21]

Also effective – sometimes – is presenting evidence that both (a) is really hard to ignore and (b) creates a sense of mental discomfort. Developmental psychologists often call this mental discomfort **disequilibrium**; motivation theorists are more likely to use the term **cognitive dissonance**.[22] For example, one thing that most of us learn quite early in our lives is that rocks don't float; if we throw them into a lake or river, they quickly sink to the bottom. But some rocks *do* float; this is the case for pumice (cooled-down lava) because it tends to have many air pockets within it. In an effort to promote conceptual change regarding the rocks-always-sink misconception, one first-grade teacher showed her class a piece of granite and a piece of pumice and asked students to predict what would happen when she dropped the two rocks into a container of water. Naturally the students predicted that they would both sink. When the pumice floated instead of sinking, one girl grabbed her head and was visibly upset. "No! No! That's not right!" she exclaimed. "That doesn't go with my mind . . . it just doesn't go with my mind."[23]

Not all misconceptions can be dismantled by compelling physical demonstrations, however. Especially when subject matter involves abstract ideas, we're going to have to rely on one or more experts about how certain aspects of our world actually operate. Why would we take these experts seriously? As adults, we're more likely to be convinced if we can see competing explanations side by side, enabling us to compare their pros and cons, including the evidence and logic supporting and discrediting each one.[24]

If we're going to contribute in meaningful ways to our own and others' well-being, we need to keep ourselves up to date on what the physical, biological, social, and psychological sciences have to offer us and on what well-informed, thoughtful citizens have to say about issues that science can't easily resolve. Thus, we must continue to undergo conceptual change throughout our lives. Sorry to be a bit preachy here, but as an old saying goes, "There is nothing permanent except change."[25]

BEING STRATEGIC

Within the past 20 years, considerable research has been devoted to investigations of strategies that might effectively bring about conceptual change when it's called for. Most studies have focused on correcting other people's misconceptions rather than on encouraging self-revision. In the recommendations that follow, then, the three self-strategies are based on my own intuitions of what might conceivably work. The longer list of instructional strategies has a body of research literature to support it.

Enhancing Your Own Thinking and Learning in Everyday Life

- **Self-Strategy 8.1: Actively seek out evidence and logic that contradict your current beliefs**. If you can, try to fight the confirmation bias that almost certainly lurks within you. Regularly ask yourself questions such as these: "If so many people believe such-and-such, why do they think so?" "What evidence might I find or collect to discredit my current opinions about such-and-such?" "Can I accept and feel comfortable with the fact that I'm occasionally wrong about something?"

- **Self-Strategy 8.2: Remember that science is almost always a matter of probabilities rather than certainties, but systematically and repeatedly validated theories are as close to fact as they can possibly be.** A fair number of adults misinterpret the term *theory* to mean an abstract entity that is, by nature, only tentative and temporary.[26] It's true that some theories are quite tentative, and virtually anyone can publish, post, or boast an outlandish personal "theory" about one thing or another. In mainstream scientific communities, however, many theories are supported by a great deal of systematically collected data, with some researchers intentionally trying – yet often failing – to refute them. Theories that have stood the test of time tend to have mountains of evidence to back them up.

- **Self-Strategy 8.3: Difficult as it might sometimes be, try to keep an open mind about controversial issues.** On occasions when conceptual change is warranted, you're more likely to engage in it if you haven't mentally closed the door about the issue at hand – that is, if you haven't rigidly concluded that you already know the facts and don't need to consider the matter further. Thus, I'm suggesting that you adopt a general attitude of *open-mindedness* – a disposition I'll return to in Chapter 9.

  With respect to epistemic beliefs, I'm not advocating a *multiplist* position. More specifically, I'm not saying that you should treat opposing viewpoints as always having equal validity. Rather, I'm encouraging you to become an *evaluativist* – a person who regularly analyzes and critiques various perspectives regarding their credibility and probable veracity.

Enhancing Other People's Thinking and Learning in Instructional Settings

- **Instructional Strategy 8.1: Preassess students' current understandings.** You can more easily address students' misconceptions if you know what they are. Don't just ask students to spit back facts, figures, and formulas they might have previously memorized. Instead, ask them to explain and apply what they know or think they know.[27] Furthermore, ask probing questions that require students to get specific about what they mean. As an example, consider the seemingly simple question "What is rain?" A student once responded to this question by saying that "it's water that falls out of a cloud when the clouds evaporate." This wasn't right: Rain involves condensation rather than evaporation. But it turned out that the evaporation-condensation mix-up wasn't the only problem. After a series of follow-up questions, the student revealed quite an unusual understanding of rain: "Well, 'cause it comes down at little times like a salt shaker when you turn it upside down. It doesn't all come down at once 'cause there's little holes and it just comes out . . . holes in the clouds, letting the water out."[28] This student clearly had a long way to go in acquiring an accurate understanding of how rain happens.

○ **Instructional Strategy 8.2: Use physical models and verbal analogies to make abstract ideas more concrete and comprehensible**. Carefully chosen models and analogies can help students relate abstract ideas to things they can see or easily visualize.[29] For example, a teacher might use a flashlight (the sun) and a large ball (the Earth) to demonstrate how the sun's rays arrive at different angles during summer versus winter. And to help students understand that our species has lived on the Earth for a much shorter time than most people think, a teacher might say, "Imagine that the Earth's history is a twenty-four-hour day. We've lived here for only the very last minute of that day – just one minute before midnight."

○ **Instructional Strategy 8.3: Build on any kernels of truth that are embedded within students' misunderstandings**. Students' misconceived notions of the world aren't always completely wrong; some of them may be partly wrong but also partly right.[30] For instance, a child who thinks that the Earth is round like a pancake is certainly right about the "round" part. And the student who thought that rain is the result of evaporation was at least correct in the sense that evaporation is an essential component of the water cycle. Identifying and building on such kernels of truth can both encourage meaningful learning and also give students some confidence that they already know at least part of the story.

○ **Instructional Strategy 8.4: Conduct activities that are likely to create disequilibrium/cognitive dissonance**. The floating-pumice demonstration I described earlier illustrates this strategy.[31] Another potentially effective approach is to have students conduct experiments in which they test competing hypotheses about what causes what.[32] Still another is to conduct large- or small-group discussions regarding topics about which various group members are apt to have diverse opinions.[33] It's often hard for students to ignore or discredit the contradictory opinions and evidence presented by people who are, in most respects, very much like themselves.

○ **Instructional Strategy 8.5: Strive to correct students' misunderstandings about the nature of science.** Doing this involves not only explaining what genuine scientific inquiry involves but also actively engaging students in scientific inquiry.[34] Following are a few key principles of scientific reasoning that instructional activities should encompass:

   ○ Science involves the generation and testing of competing hypotheses regarding why various phenomena occur.

   ○ Legitimate explanations for phenomena require the support of systematically collected and objectively analyzed data.

   ○ Given the nature of statistical analysis techniques, it is virtually impossible to *prove* a hypothesis or theory; the best outcome is for a statistical analysis to confirm that there is an extremely high probability – maybe even 99.9% – that such-and-such is true.

   ○ Multiple replications of a study enhance the likelihood that the original study's findings weren't just a one-in-a-thousand fluke.

   It should be stressed, too, that these principles apply to scientific inquiry not only in the physical sciences, but also in the biological, social, and psychological sciences.

○ **Instructional Strategy 8.6: Ask students to make use of their newly acquired understandings.** The more that students apply what they've just learned, the more likely that their new understandings might overrule their previous misconceptions.[35] For example, if a person who's running in a marathon drops a water bottle, what does inertia tell us about where the water bottle is apt to land? Given what scientists believe to be true about the dinosaurs, why would sweaters *not* have helped most of them stay warm during cold spells? And given what we know about thermodynamics, why might a sweater actually help cold drinks *stay* cold on a hot summer day?

○ **Instructional Strategy 8.7: Continually monitor students' understandings to be sure that progress is being made.** One-shot explanations often don't stick; conceptual change can take a good deal of time and follow-up instruction. Furthermore, for reasons I've previously given you, some misconceptions can be quite tenacious and pop up much later, long after we think they've been abandoned.[36] Especially when misconceptions are apt to be counterproductive over the long run, ongoing monitoring of students' understandings is essential. Thus, it's important to have students explain and apply scientifically valid explanations not only immediately but also on subsequent occasions. Another good strategy is to ask students to choose between two or more possible explanations in classroom assignments and assessments.[37] Regularly requiring students to choose correct over not-so-right-or-completely-wrong explanations can help them inhibit those insidious misbeliefs.

o **Instructional Strategy 8.8: Try to convince students that it's in their own best interests to understand why other people think as they do**. At a minimum, students should come to realize that reasoned dialogue and debate about controversial topics are critical for the health of their society. Total consensus about many issues might not ever be possible, but a society's members can be more productive if they at least understand where other folks are coming from.[38] When dialoguing with one another, however, students must feel psychologically "safe" – that is, they must feel confident that their peers will treat them respectfully despite their opinions and that it's okay to admit that they're wrong and change their minds once in a while.[39]

Students must also feel confident that, with effort and persistence, they can eventually make sense of subject matter that might initially seem overwhelming and incomprehensible. In other words, they must have *controllable attributions* and high *self-efficacy for learning* – two concepts we'll delve into in Chapter 9.

NOTES

1. Gifford, 2011.
2. Chinn & Brewer, 1993; Lewandowsky et al., 2013; Vosniadou, 2008; Winer, Cottrell, Gregg, Fournier, & Bica, 2002.
3. Brewer, 2008; Brophy, Alleman, & Knighton, 2009; Gardner, Torff, & Hatch, 1996; Liben & Myers, 2007; Sneider & Pulos, 1983; Vosniadou, 1991; Vosniadou, Vamvakoussi, & Skopeliti, 2008.
4. Kelemen, 2012, pp. 67–68, italics added.
5. Chi, 2008; Chi, Kristensen, & Roscoe, 2012; diSessa, 1996; Kelemen, 2012; V. R. Lee, 2010; Linn & Eylon, 2011; Schneps & Sadler, 1989; Winer et al., 2002.
6. Elkind, 1981; Frankenberger, 2000.
7. D. B. Clark, 2006; diSessa, Elby, & Hammer, 2003; Linn & Eylon, 2011; Wiser & Smith, 2008.

8. Andiliou, Ramsay, Murphy, & Fast, 2012; Brewer, 2008; Kalyuga, 2010; Kendeou & van den Broek, 2005; Lewandowsky, Ecker, Seifert, Schwarz, & Cook, 2012.

9. Chi et al., 2012; Elby & Hammer, 2010; Kendeou & van den Broek, 2005; Sinatra et al., 2014.

10. Keil & Silberstein, 1996; Strike & Posner, 1992.

11. Bastardi, Uhlmann, & Ross, 2011; P. Fischer & Greitmeyer, 2010; E. R. Smith & Conrey, 2009; Stanovich, West, & Toplak, 2012; some theorists instead use such terms as *myside bias* and *selective exposure to confirmatory information.*

12. Hynd, 1998, p. 34.

13. As an example, see my discussion of verbal learning research in Ormrod, 2016a, chapter 6.

14. Sorry, I won't point fingers or name names here; you'll just have to take my word for it.

15. McClelland, 2013.

16. M. Feinberg & Willer, 2011; Gal & Rucker, 2010; Gregoire, 2003; Kunda, 1990; Porat, 2004; Sherman & Cohen, 2002; Sinatra et al., 2014; Southerland & Sinatra, 2003.

17. C. E. Nelson, 2012; Sinatra et al., 2014.

18. For two comprehensive literature reviews on possible links between childhood immunizations and autism, see Doja & Roberts, 2006; Madsen et al., 2002.

19. Chinn & Buckland, 2012; Lewandowsky et al., 2013; Sinatra et al., 2014; Thanukos & Scotchmoor, 2012.

20. Evans, 2008; Gopnik, Griffiths, & Lucas, 2015; Lewandowsky et al., 2012; Porat, 2004; Sinatra et al., 2014.

21. Beardsley, Bloom, & Wise, 2012; D. B. Clark, 2006; Lewandowsky et al., 2012; Linn, 2008; Pintrich, Marx, & Boyle, 1993.

22. For example, see Piaget, 1970 (for disequilibrium), and Festinger, 1957 (for cognitive dissonance).

23. Hennessey, 2003, p. 121.

24. Braasch, Goldman, & Wiley, 2013; Hynd, 2003; Lombardi, Nussbaum, & Sinatra, 2016; Mason, Gava, & Boldrin, 2008; Shanahan, 2004.

25. This saying has often been attributed to the ancient Greek philosopher Heraclitus. There is apparently some doubt about whether he said these exact words; however, he is well known for his belief that change is central to our world, and in *Kratylos*, Plato quotes him as saying, "Everything changes and nothing stands still."

26. Ormrod, 2016b; Thanukos & Scotchmoor, 2012.

27. D. E. Brown & Hammer, 2008; D. B. Clark, 2006; Roth, 1990.

28. Stepans, 1991, p. 94.

29. Clement, 2008; Furtak, Seidel, Iverson, & Briggs, 2012; Lehrer & Schauble, 2006; Sandoval, Sodian, Koerber, & Wong, 2014; Zohar & Aharon-Kraversky, 2005.
30. diSessa, 2006.
31. For several other good examples, see Chinn & Malhotra, 2002.
32. Echevarria, 2003; Hatano & Inagaki, 2003; Linn & Eylon, 2011.
33. Andriessen, 2006; Asterhan & Schwarz, 2007; Kuhn, 2015; Nussbaum & Edwards, 2011; Reznitskaya & Gregory, 2013.
34. Chinn & Buckland, 2012; Thanukos & Scotchmoor, 2012; Yang & Tsai, 2010.
35. Chinn & Malhotra, 2002; Linn & Eylon, 2011.
36. V. R Lee, 2010; Murphy, 2007; Vosniadou, 2008.
37. Little, Bjork, Bjork, & Angello, 2012; Sadler, Sonnert, Coyle, Cook-Smith, & Miller, 2013.
38. Eagly, Kulesa, Chen, & Chaiken, 2001; Lewandowsky et al., 2012; Sinatra, Southerland, McConaughy, & Demastes, 2003.
39. Hadjioannou, 2007; Nussbaum, 2008; Sinatra & Mason, 2008; Webb et al., 2008.

9

Bringing Other Factors into the Picture: How Emotions, Dispositions, and Attributions Affect Thinking and Learning

I'm sure you've realized by now that we *homo sapiens* – we supposedly "wise" creatures – don't always think in logical, impartial ways. It's now time to put another common misconception front and center:

Misconception #25: That, for the most part, we humans are rational creatures

As an example of how we can sometimes abandon all reason and rationality, consider this problem:

Several years ago you inherited an old car from your Uncle Harry. You've spent several thousand dollars getting the car in decent working order, and you've driven it around quite a bit. But now you've inherited a better car from your Aunt Harriet. You have two choices: You could (a) sell Uncle Harry's car for $1,500 in its present condition or (b) spend a couple thousand more in repairs and then sell it for $3,000. What should you do?[1]

Well, duh, take the $1,500. Simple math: If you choose the second option, your net gain is only $1,000. Yet some people can be lured by the higher sales price.[2]

Our focus in this chapter will be on three seemingly *non*cognitive factors that can affect our ability to think rationally, as well as our ability to think and learn more generally: emotion, personality characteristics, and motivation. As it turns out, each of these factors does, in fact, have cognitive elements. And once again I must remind you about the gazillion interconnections we have among the neurons and glial cells in our brains. The cells that are responsible for our supposedly rational cognitive processes are inextricably intertwined with those cells that are responsible for our emotional responses, our typical ways of behaving (i.e., our personalities), and our motives.[3]

HOT COGNITION: ADDING AN EMOTIONAL SIZZLE TO OUR THINKING AND LEARNING

As contemporary cognitive psychology was getting its feet off the ground in the mid-20th century, human thought processes were conceptualized as being predominantly emotion-free. But in contrast to such non-feeling, "cold" cognition, many psychologists now acknowledge that some of our thinking and learning involves **hot cognition** – cognitive processes that are infused with emotions.[4] For example, we're more likely to pay attention to, think about, and remember objects and events that evoke strong emotions – perhaps excitement, sadness, anger, horror, or disgust (see Chapters 4 and 6). Furthermore, emotions can either hinder us or help us in situations where conceptual change is called for (recall the discussions of *motivated reasoning, disequilibrium,* and *cognitive dissonance* in Chapter 8).

Cold cognition versus hot cognition

Our emotional responses to new information and events are such integral parts of the things we store in long-term memory that they can become important sources of information in and of themselves.[5] For example, when we recall a particular movie or television show we've watched, we're also likely to recall whether it made us happy, sad, or afraid. When we think about the various people we know, we might break into a smile or, instead, react with feelings of sadness, anger, or disgust. Also, we're apt to categorize objects and events based in part on how they make us feel, even though the category members might in other respects be quite different.[6] As an illustration, try this simple exercise:

1. Think of three things that make you happy.
2. Think of three things that make you sad.
3. Think of three things that make you angry.

I'm guessing that you could quickly think of three things in each category. For each item, the emotion was your starting point – your retrieval cue – that sent you along particular pathways in your long-term memory.

Emotions that we bring with us to any new learning or memory task can have a significant impact as well. For instance, we're more likely to keep our minds on a new task and to constructively elaborate on what we're learning if we're in a good mood rather than sad, bored, or otherwise in a foul frame of mind.[7] A good mood can also help us retrieve hard-to-find information we've previously stored in long-term memory[8]

One emotion that can pack quite a wallop is **anxiety** – that is, a feeling of apprehension and nervousness about what the outcomes of our efforts might be.[9] A little bit of anxiety can spur us into action to get things done – say, to study for an upcoming exam or prepare for a speech we need to give to a large crowd. And occasionally a great deal of anxiety can help us out – say, when we're running away from a person who wants to steal our backpack or purse. In general, however, a high level of anxiety does *not* work in our best interests, especially when we're facing a challenging situation that requires our minds as well as our bodies. Neurologically speaking, anxiety manifests itself in high levels of activation in the amygdala – an especially "emotional" part of the brain – along with suboptimal levels of activation in the more calm and rational prefrontal cortex.[10] Not only does high anxiety make us sweat and shake, but it also narrows our focus of attention, clutters up our working memory with worrisome thoughts, and restricts our search of long-term memory for potential problem solutions.[11] At the end of the chapter, I'll offer some strategies for keeping yourself and others cool, calm, and collected during situations that require considerable brainpower.

DISPOSITIONS: HOW PERSONALITY CHARACTERISTICS CAN INFLUENCE COGNITION

In psychology, **dispositions** are general, relatively stable inclinations to approach thinking, learning, and problem-solving tasks in particular ways; some psychologists call them *habits of mind*. One example of a disposition is *conscientiousness* – a tendency to address complex tasks in a careful, focused, and timely manner.[12] Another example is *consensus seeking* – an inclination to try to synthesize diverse perspectives into a single, cohesive whole rather than treat them as mutually exclusive alternatives.[13] Still a third is a tendency to engage in *critical thinking* on a regular basis.[14] Such dispositions are often correlated with – and may even play a causal role in – our long-term learning and achievement levels and our willingness to undergo conceptual change.[15]

In the following three subsections, I'll describe five noteworthy dispositions in more depth. After that, I'll alert you to a disposition-like concept that, despite its current popularity in education-related media, doesn't hold up under the scrutiny of sound research methods.

Need for Cognition and Intellectual Curiosity: A Thirst for New Cognitive Challenges

Two dispositions – the need for cognition and intellectual curiosity – overlap enough that it makes sense to talk about them together. A general **need for cognition** is a desire to be regularly engaged in mentally stimulating activities and cognitive challenges.[16] **Intellectual curiosity** (also known as *epistemic curiosity*) is an eagerness to gain knowledge about a wide range of topics – not necessarily for any personal or financial gain but, instead, simply as a means of gaining better understandings of certain aspects of the world.[17] People with these dispositions are more likely to mentally immerse themselves in, elaborate on, and remember what they're reading in a book or hearing in a lecture. They're also more likely to critically evaluate writers' and speakers' arguments for or against particular points of view and to acknowledge the ambiguities and uncertainties that exist within a mixed body of evidence.[18]

Are you curious about the basic principles of string theory? the strategies that Napoleon Bonaparte used to conquer much of Europe? the medicinal benefits of a horseshoe crab's blood? the reasons why some sequences of musical notes are quite melodic whereas other sequences are about as pleasant to the ear as fingernails scraping a chalkboard? And if you know you'll have to sit for a long time in, say, an airport, a doctor's office, or a restroom, do you bring reading materials, a puzzle book, or your cell phone to keep your mind occupied? If such things are true for you, you almost certainly have a need for cognition and some intellectual curiosity.

Open-Mindedness versus Need for Closure: Pondering Diverse
Perspectives or, Instead, Clinging to a Single "Right" Answer

Psychologists' meaning of the term **open-mindedness** is roughly equivalent to our everyday use of the word. In particular, open-minded individuals can flexibly consider alternative viewpoints and multiple sources of
evidence, and they suspend judgment about these viewpoints and sources
until they have enough information to draw reasonable, well-informed
conclusions.[19]

The virtual opposite of open-mindedness is a **need for closure** – a need
to find and adopt quick and simple answers regarding the "truth" about
complex, multifaceted issues. Individuals with a high need for closure
aren't comfortable with ambiguity and uncertainty; they want to know
what's "right" and what's "wrong" *now*, and once they've formed an
opinion about a topic, they're highly resistant to arguments and evidence
that might challenge it.[20]

As you might guess, open-minded people are far more amenable to
conceptual change than are people with a strong need for closure. In fact,
the latter group may feel personally threatened when other individuals
present contradictory information and opinions, and so they may dig their
heels even further into their current beliefs.[21]

Effortful Control: Showing Self-Restraint

Even as young children, we show differences in **effortful control** –
that is, in our ability to self-regulate our thoughts and behaviors and
to keep counterproductive impulses in check.[22] Effortful control is an
integral component of the *executive functions* I described in Chapter 4.
Those of us who are high in effortful control can (a) better keep our
minds on the things we should be focusing on, (b) plan a potentially
fruitful course of action when we need to accomplish something,
(c) think flexibly about important issues, and (d) control our emotions
while we're working. We're also more likely to (e) persist at challenging learning tasks and (f) resist appealing but nonproductive distractions. Thus, we high-control types tend to achieve at higher levels in
instructional settings.[23]

Effortful control appears to have its basis in certain areas of the brain,
including the relatively rational and controlling prefrontal cortex.[24]
Although preliminary research has been conducted on possible early
interventions,[25] how much we can actually improve the brain structures

that underlie our ability to control our thoughts and actions is still an open question. Teaching ourselves and others specific self-control *behaviors* is very much within our power, however, as you'll discover in Chapter 10.

Our Supposed "Learning Styles": Not All Research Is Good Research

I would be remiss if I didn't say something about learning styles, a topic that has recently commanded a great deal of attention in popular media and educational literature. Herein lies another widespread misconception:

> Misconception #26: That teaching to people's individual learning styles can have a significant impact on how effectively they learn

By and large, the research behind this learning-styles idea has used self-report questionnaires that ask people what their *preferences* are when they learn. Do they prefer to *see* new information (e.g., in a textbook) or to *hear* it (e.g., in a lecture)? Would they rather *write* things or *draw* things? Are they "morning people" or "night owls"? The psychometric qualities of such questionnaires – that is, the extent to which the questionnaires accurately and reliably measure certain personal characteristics – are very much in doubt. And tailoring instructional strategies to students' self-reported styles does little or nothing to enhance their academic achievement.[26]

I like to think that I'm a fairly open-minded scholar: I regularly revise my thinking about psychological and educational matters when there's compelling evidence to do so. But so far this whole learning-styles thing strikes me – as it has struck most of my professional colleagues – as being completely bogus. For the most part, good instruction for some people is good instruction for *all* people, and it's based on well-documented principles regarding human cognition and learning.

ATTRIBUTIONS: OUR BELIEFS ABOUT THE CAUSES OF OUR LEARNING SUCCESSES AND FAILURES

In our never-ending efforts to make sense of our world, we often strive to figure out what causes what, not only as the world exists independently of us but also as we interact with it. **Attributions** are our self-constructed beliefs about who and what are responsible for our personal successes and failures. For example, did we get a high or low grade on a recent exam because of how much we studied? because of how much inherited ability we have? because of how much our instructor likes or dislikes us? because of how healthy or sick we were that day? because we had a lucky day or a bad break? Our answers to such questions reflect our attributions about our academic and personal achievements and about our potential for improvement in various domains.

Attributions tend to vary in at least three key ways:[27]

- ***Locus ("place"):*** Sometimes our attributions have an *internal* locus: We attribute the causes of events to factors within ourselves. At other times, our attributions might have an *external* locus: We give credit to or blame other people or our environmental circumstances. Thinking that a recent exam grade was the result of how much we studied is an internal attribution. Thinking that we got a good or bad grade because our instructor either likes or dislikes us is an external attribution.
- ***Temporal stability:*** We attribute some outcomes to *stable* causes – to things that aren't likely to change much over time. We attribute other outcomes to *unstable* causes – to temporary factors that might differ from one day to the next. Thinking that we've done well or poorly on an exam because we're just naturally smart or stupid is a stable attribution. Thinking that our performance was due to sheer luck (or lack of it) is an unstable one.
- ***Personal controllability:*** In our own minds, some events might be *controllable*, whereas others might be *uncontrollable* and beyond our influence. Believing that an exam grade was the result of the specific study strategies we used is a controllable attribution, because we can always adjust our strategies if our current ones aren't working. Believing that the grade was the result of having a headache on exam day is an uncontrollable attribution.

Our attributions for our successes and failures can have major impacts on our learning and performance.[28] For example, we're more likely to expend effort, use effective learning strategies, and persist in the face of obstacles if we believe that effort, good strategies, and persistence will actually increase our chances of success. We're also likely to set ambitious goals for ourselves if we know that we either have or can learn what it takes to do well. Some psychologists use the term **self-efficacy for learning** when referring to the general optimism that some of us have – and most of us *should* have – about our future ability to acquire new information and skills.[29]

Human Intelligence: Is It Stable or Unstable, and Is It Controllable or Uncontrollable?

Exactly how optimistic should we be about our future learning potential? Just as psychologists differ in their opinions about how much intelligence is the result of heredity versus environment – traditionally known as a *nature-versus-nurture* question – so, too, do nonpsychologists have differing views about the matter. Some people have an **entity view** of intelligence: They believe that intelligence is a characteristic that's largely the result of heredity and thus is relatively stable and uncontrollable. Other folks have an **incremental view**: They think of intelligence as something that can and does improve with effort and practice.[30] Both of these views are examples of the *epistemic beliefs* previously described in Chapter 7.

This brings me back to a point I made in Chapter 3: Human intelligence appears to be the result of our inherited characteristics *and* of our environmental conditions *and* of the continuing interactions between the two. Furthermore, we can often act more intelligently when we have physical and cognitive tools and social support systems that can nurture and scaffold our thinking.[31] Thus, I must refute yet another common misconception:

> Misconception #27: That our intelligence is a stable characteristic that is out of our own and others' control

An entity view of intelligence can lead to a self-fulfilling prophecy in which belief becomes reality. More specifically, when people believe both that (a) intelligence is stable and uncontrollable and (b) they don't have very much of it, they're apt to set low goals for themselves and quickly give up in the face of easily surmountable obstacles. An incremental view tends to be more beneficial, although it can occasionally backfire if people underestimate how much effort future success might require.[32] Yes, we can definitely improve our abilities in a variety of domains, but we may need to work hard to make this happen.

Explanatory Styles: "I Can Do It!" versus "I *Can't* Do It Even If I Try!"

With time and experience, many of us become fairly consistent in the kinds of attributions we make for our successes and failures, and these general **explanatory styles** affect our expectations for our future achievement levels. Some of us regularly attribute our successes and failures to things we can control, such as our own effort and strategies – a style known as a **mastery orientation**. Unfortunately, others of us settle into a pattern of attributing events to circumstances over which we have little or no control – a style that in extreme cases is known as **learned helplessness**.[33]

Obviously, those of us with a mastery orientation come out ahead, even when our past achievement and ability levels have been no better than those of others. Mastery-oriented individuals set ambitious goals for themselves, persist at challenging tasks, and bounce back from occasional failures with a sense of optimism. In contrast, people with learned helplessness set their sights quite low and give up quickly when they encounter obstacles; they're also hampered by high anxiety, which can consume a good deal of their working-memory capacity. Once again, then, the result is a self-fulfilling prophecy: An expectation of failure leads to the reality of failure.[34]

Learned helplessness is sometimes the result of a personal history of *actual* helplessness. For example, victims of chronic domestic violence may eventually resign themselves to continuing abuse and pain. Students with diagnosed or undiagnosed learning abilities may acquire learned helplessness about their ability to read and write, especially if instruction hasn't been tailored to address their unique cognitive needs. And people who are convinced that they "can't do math" – typically because they've struggled with it in the past – tend to steer clear of math-related activities.[35]

Helplessness can also arise when we see other individuals having little or no control over their lives, as might happen when we see family or friends constantly victimized by seemingly endless violence at home or in the community.[36] And parents, teachers, and other influential adults can engender learned helplessness if they regularly find fault with our performance without also helping us *improve* our performance.[37]

Granted, there are times when we have absolutely no say about the things that happen to us. But we should take hold of what we *can* control and make desired things happen for us as much as possible.[38] Having an overall history of "Yes, I've done it!" can inoculate us against succumbing to learned helplessness when events occasionally tell us that "No, this time you can't."

BEING STRATEGIC

I imagine that you've already derived some self-strategies and instructional strategies from the preceding discussions of emotions, dispositions, and attributions. Following are my own suggestions.

Enhancing Your Own Thinking and Learning in Everyday Life

- **Self-Strategy 9.1: Try to keep unproductive emotions in check whenever you need to think about and learn something important**. What I'm talking about here is **emotion regulation**. For example, if you're fretting about something that's been bothering you, stop for a minute and decide on a course of action, write a note to yourself about your follow-up plans concerning that bothersome thing, and then get back to the business currently at hand. If you're bored to tears with the task you're trying to accomplish – and boredom can be a very unpleasant emotion at times – figure out a way to make the task more interesting and enjoyable, perhaps by turning it into a gamelike activity. If you're a bit upset about a recent event, try to put a positive spin on it – for instance, by treating it as a wake-up call that you need to do something differently next time or identifying a small silver lining in what might otherwise be a very dark cloud.[39] However, if you're so upset about something that you can't think straight, maybe it's time to set aside your task until you've worked through your emotions.

- **Self-Strategy 9.2: Rekindle your inner curiosity about the world in which you live**. As infants and young children, we humans seem to be naturally curious about our world.[40] What does my teddy bear taste like? Why is the sky blue? How do cell phones know where to find the people we're calling? But as we get older, some of us gradually lose our general sense of inquisitiveness.

  Reflect on how much your typical daily activities contribute to your general knowledge about the world. For instance, are you hooked on soap operas and other serial dramas to the point that you care deeply and passionately about completely made-up characters whose personal well-being doesn't matter even the tiniest bit in the Grand Scheme of Things? Or, instead, is one of your most important life goals to reach the highest possible level in a particular video game? I mean, really, is bingeing on television fiction or video games for much of the day a good use of your time?

By no means am I suggesting that you completely abandon activities that seemingly have no other purpose than to give you mindless entertainment. In fact, as you'll see in Chapter 10, engaging in such activities once in a while can actually be instrumental in helping you stay on task in more consequential endeavors. The trick is finding a productive balance between work and play.

- **Self-Strategy 9.3: Rather than assume that you can't do something, identify strategies and support mechanisms that might help you accomplish it**. So maybe you're not the best mathematician, basketball player, or artist in the world. Certainly you can improve yourself in these areas if you want to – and if you develop new and better strategies, seek out helpful tools and appropriate guidance, and exert reasonable effort. For example, turning to my own piano-learning experiences once again, I've concluded (just as I did when I took lessons as a child) that I'm probably not a "natural" at the keyboard. Nevertheless, by learning strategies for moving my fingers more efficiently, recognizing various scales and patterns in the printed music, and working on very different styles of music – all thanks to my lessons with a skillful teacher – and by also practicing as much as possible, I can now play "Moon River" and "Für Elise" a lot better than I could a year ago. My progress has been slow, but it's been progress nevertheless.

Enhancing Other People's Thinking and Learning in Instructional Settings

- ○ **Instructional Strategy 9.1: Keep students' anxiety about their learning and performance at productive levels**. At virtually all levels of education, from elementary school right on up through graduate school, some students come to class with debilitating levels of anxiety. And certain topics and classroom activities – such as math and tests – are notoriously anxiety arousing.[41] Although instructors obviously want to keep students motivated to do well, stressing out students about their performance is rarely helpful. I recall my first day of junior high school, when my seventh-grade science teacher stood at the front of the room and said something like "Only a third of you will do well in my class this year." Oy yoy yoy – this after leaving behind Mrs. Donaldson, my warm and caring sixth-grade teacher three months before. I subsequently found all kinds of reasons to be "sick" on the days I knew a science test would be given (although after several visits to the doctor, my mother eventually figured out that I was usually healthy as a horse). So, all right, maybe my science teacher didn't say the exact words I just quoted, but for the rest of the year those were the words I *remembered* her saying, and that's what mattered. I think I got a B in her class.

Regarding math, in my many years as a psychology professor, I occasionally taught statistics – a topic that immediately gets some students shaking in their boots. What seemed to work for my math-anxious students was to suggest that they find a math textbook that started with stuff they knew well (maybe simple algebra, or maybe just basic math facts) and tackle problems that they knew they could easily solve. Most of them would subsequently find that the basic statistics problems I introduced in the early days or weeks of my course – problems that involved, say, computing probabilities, means, or standard deviations – were actually easy-peasy. In the meantime, I gradually and gently moved to more complex topics, with lots of scaffolding for those who needed it. Anxiety down, mission accomplished.

As for tests and other important assessments, following are a few strategies that seem to work:

○ Give nongraded pretests to help students self-assess their current levels of understanding.

○ Allow students to use notes or other resources (e.g., dictionaries, calculators) if there's no inherent value in committing certain kinds of information to memory.

○ Keep assessments short enough that students can easily complete them within the allotted time period.

○ Judge students' performance on the basis of how well they've mastered the material, *not* on how well they perform relative to their classmates. In other words, don't grade "on the curve."

○ Occasionally give students second chances – for instance, by creating two forms of a single test, one for the initial assessment and the other for a possible retake.

○ Base end-of-term grades on many small assessments rather than on just two or three that might each have life-or-death implications for classroom success.[42]

And here's a biggie that should by now go without saying: Help students master both the subject matter and effective study strategies, thus maximizing the probability that students will do well and will *know* that they'll do well.

○ **Instructional Strategy 9.2: Encourage critical thinking as a general disposition**. In Chapter 5, I suggested a few probing questions that can foster critical thinking (e.g., "What evidence or logic is the author using?" and "What motives or biases might the author have?"). But in addition, I recommend creating an overall classroom climate in which critical thinking is both the expectation and the norm. One way you might do this is by regularly modeling critical thinking yourself – for instance by saying, "This research study hasn't convinced me that _[such-and-such]_ is true; the study didn't include a good control group." Another essential strategy is to give students many opportunities to practice critical thinking, perhaps in whole-group discussions, small-group debates, role-playing activities, or written critiques of persuasive arguments.[43] And let's not forget epistemic beliefs here: Students must ultimately believe that society's collective "knowledge" about any given topic should be open to continual review, reappraisal, and revision.

○ **Instructional Strategy 9.3: Take all the stuff about learning styles for what it's worth – not much**. If you encounter proclamations about the benefits of "teaching to students' learning styles" in popular media or professional journals, carefully scrutinize these sources for objective and credible evidence to back up the claims – and I don't mean "This is what students told us" evidence. In other words, engage in critical thinking as you read! And whatever you do, please don't use any of those alleged "learning-style inventories" you can so easily find on the Internet.

○ **Instructional Strategy 9.4: Communicate optimistic attributions**. The kinds of feedback you give students about their successes and failures can definitely have an impact.[44] Consider such statements as "This is certainly your lucky day" (attribution to uncontrollable and probably temporary luck) and "Hmm, maybe this isn't something you're good at" (attribution to an uncontrollable and stable ability level – an *entity* view of intelligence). Yikes! Statements such as the following are much better: "Your hard work has really paid off" (attribution to controllable effort), "Let me teach you some studying techniques that might help you here" (attribution to controllable strategies), and "The longer and harder you work at this, the better you'll get" (attribution to a controllable, *incremental* view of intelligence).

Another way you're likely to foster various kinds of attributions is in how you respond to students' failures. For example, do you give struggling students the kinds of assistance they need to master a topic or skill, or do you instead turn most of your attention to more "promising" individuals? I'm sure I don't need to tell you which approach is preferable. But you need to be careful here. Giving help when students don't really need it can communicate your belief that they don't have what it takes to accomplish something on their own.[45]

○ **Instructional Strategy 9.5: Help students discover that their effort, persistence, and good strategies actually make a difference**. Naturally, such discoveries can come from students' own experiences – ideally those that include appropriately tailored and scaffolded instruction. But students can also gain confidence about their learning abilities when they see how other people very similar to themselves have been able to achieve at high levels.[46] For example, a high school instrumental music teacher might ask beginning students to listen to pieces that last year's novices can now play, and a college professor might show students in a first-semester introductory research methods course the kinds of research projects that second-semester students have been able to conduct. And I've seen doctoral students become more optimistic about successfully completing their dissertations after looking at previous graduates' dissertations. Especially when you want to foster an incremental view of ability, some of the peer models you present might be those who have had to struggle a bit before eventually mastering a task, thereby driving home the idea that success sometimes requires hard work.[47]

But despite the best of intentions and despite knowing that we're potentially capable of great things, we don't always follow through and do what we've hoped we would do. Success doesn't involve only believing we can succeed; it always involves actively making success happen. And making it happen requires *self-regulated behavior*. Stay tuned, because I'll explain what I mean in Chapter 10.

NOTES

1. Problem modeled after a similar one in Halpern, 1998.
2. Halpern, 1998.
3. For example, see Benes, 2007; Forgas, 2008; Talmi, 2013.
4. Bower, 1994; Marcus, 2008; E. Peterson & Welsh, 2014; Pintrich, 2003.
5. Clore, Gasper, & Garvin, 2001; Forgas, 2008; Minsky, 2006.
6. Bower & Forgas, 2001.
7. Bohn-Gettler & Rapp, 2011; Pekrun et al., 2010; Schwarz & Skurnik, 2003.
8. Oatley & Nundy, 1996.
9. Beilock & Carr, 2001; Broadhurst, 1959; Cassady, 2010; Siegel, 2012; Yerkes & Dodson, 1908.

10. Sharot, Martorella, Delgado, & Phelps, 2007; Young, Wu, & Menon, 2012.
11. Ashcraft, 2002; Beilock & Carr, 2005; Fletcher & Cassady, 2010.
12. Hampson, 2008; Trautwein, Lüdtke, Schnyder, & Niggli, 2006.
13. Halpern, 1997.
14. Giancarlo & Facione, 2001; Halpern, 2008; Toplak & Stanovich, 2002.
15. Dai & Sternberg, 2004; Kuhn & Franklin, 2006; Perkins & Ritchhart, 2004; Southerland & Sinatra, 2003.
16. Cacioppo, Petty, Feinstein, & Jarvis, 1996; Kardash & Scholes, 1996; West, Toplak, & Stanovich, 2008.
17. Kang et al., 2009; von Stumm, Hell, & Chamorro-Premuzic, 2011.
18. Cacioppo et al., 1996; Kardash & Scholes, 1996; von Stumm, Hell, & Chamorro-Premuzic, 2011.
19. Sinatra, Kardash, Taasoobshirazi, & Lombardi, 2012; Southerland & Sinatra, 2003; West et al., 2008.
20. DeBacker & Crowson, 2009; Kruglanski & Webster, 1996; Roets & Van Hiel, 2011.
21. DeBacker & Crowson, 2009; Gal & Rucker, 2010; Kruglanski & Webster, 1996; Lombardi & Sinatra, 2012.
22. Else-Quest, Hyde, Goldsmith, & Van Hulle, 2006; Papageorgiou, Smith, Wu, Johnson, & Kirkham, 2014; Rothbart, 2011; Rothbart, Sheese, & Posner, 2007.
23. Rothbart, 2011; Rothbart & Hwang, 2005; Valiente, Lemery-Chalfant, & Swanson, 2010.
24. Rothbart et al., 2007; Tang & Tang, 2012.
25. For example, see Rothbart et al., 2007.
26. Kirschner & van Merriënboer, 2013; Kozhevnikov, Evans, & Kosslyn, 2014; Rogowsky, Calhoun, & Tallal, 2015.
27. Weiner, 1986, 2000, 2004.
28. Chen & Pajares, 2010; Dweck, 2000; Dweck & Molden, 2005; McClure et al., 2011; Pressley, Borkowski, & Schneider, 1987; Weiner, 1984; Yeager & Dweck, 2012.
29. The concept *self-efficacy for learning* has its origins in a theoretical perspective known as *social cognitive theory*; for example, see Bandura, 1997; Schunk & Pajares, 2004; Zimmerman & Kitsantas, 2005.
30. Dweck & Leggett, 1988; Dweck & Molden, 2005; Weiner, 1994.
31. Greeno, 2006; Hickey, 2011; van de Sande & Greeno, 2012.
32. Bandura, 1997; H. W. Stevenson, Chen, & Uttal, 1990; Zimmerman & Moylan, 2009.
33. Dweck, 2000; Mikulincer, 1994; C. Peterson, 2006; C. Peterson, Maier, & Seligman, 1993; Seligman, 1991. (Some of these sources use the terms *optimists* and *pessimists*.)
34. Dweck, 2000; Paris & Cunningham, 1996; C. Peterson et al., 1993; Ziegert, Kistner, Castro, & Robertson, 2001.

35. Bargai, Ben-Shakhar, & Shalev, 2007; C. S. Carver & Scheier, 2005; Hiroto & Seligman, 1975; Jameson, 2010; Núñez et al., 2005.
36. I. Brown & Inouye, 1978; C. Peterson et al., 1993.
37. Dweck, 2000; Hokoda & Fincham, 1995; Kamins & Dweck, 1999.
38. C. Peterson et al., 1993.
39. Fletcher & Cassady, 2010; Halperin, Porat, Tamir, & Gross, 2013; Pekrun, 2006; Wolters, 2003.
40. Callanan & Oakes, 1992; Lieberman, 1993; Piaget, 1952.
41. Cassady, 2010; Hoffman, 2010; Jameson, 2010; Zeidner & Matthews, 2005.
42. Ormrod, 2016a.
43. Halpern, 1998; Kuhn, 2015; Nussbaum & Edwards, 2011; Sandoval et al., 2014; Wineburg, Martin, & Monte-Sano, 2011.
44. Cimpian, Arce, Markman, & Dweck, 2007; Mueller & Dweck, 1998; Rattan, Good, & Dweck, 2012. In arguing for the importance of communicating controllable attributions, Dweck has recently been using the term *mindset* for the general explanatory style that parents, teachers, supervisors, and other influential individuals should foster (e.g., Dweck, 2006; Yeager & Dweck, 2012).
45. Graham, 1997; Graham & Barker, 1990; Weiner, 2005.
46. Dijkstra, Kuyper, van der Werf, Buunk, & van der Zee, 2008; Schunk & Pajares, 2005.
47. Kitsantas, Zimmerman, & Cleary, 2000; Schunk, Hanson, & Cox, 1987; Zimmerman & Kitsantas, 2002.

10

Self-Regulating Our Behavior: Turning Intentions into Actions

As schoolchildren, most of us had parents and teachers who nagged us to study and learn things that were presumably worth knowing. As adults, however, we need to be largely self-propelled in our learning activities. In other words, we need to have some internal *get-up-and-go* that moves us forward toward our desired goals.

Our get-up-and-go is certainly affected by some of the motivational variables described in Chapter 9 – variables such as the need for cognition, intellectual curiosity, productive attributions, and self-efficacy for learning. Yet even when we have the confidence that we can do something and a strong inclination to do it, we can't just suddenly tell ourselves "I need to get myself motivated" and then magically put ourselves in motion. Herein lies the last of my 28 common misconceptions:

Misconception #28: That getting something done is simply a matter of "turning on" an internal motivation "switch"

Nope, we don't have a simple on-off switch for our get-up-and-go. Not only must we be motivated to accomplish something, but we must also have concrete strategies for pointing ourselves in the right directions and keeping ourselves moving those ways – strategies that collectively comprise **self-regulated behavior**. In this chapter, I describe several key components of self-regulated behavior, all of which can make a difference in our learning and achievement.[1]

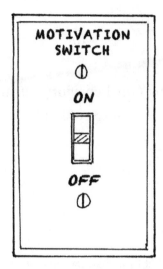

Unfortunately, our get-up-and-go isn't something we can just turn "on"
and "off" at will.

GOAL SETTING: GETTING SPECIFIC ABOUT WHAT
WE WANT TO ACCOMPLISH

In Chapter 7, I briefly mentioned goal setting as an element of self-regulated learning. There I was talking primarily about goals for a particular learning activity. We're more likely to learn and achieve at high levels if, in addition, we set long-term goals for our achievements – perhaps completing an online course, earning a college degree, or becoming an orthopedic surgeon.

The problem here is that some of our long-term goals are apt to be fairly abstract and a bit vague.[2] For example, what do we really mean when we say we want to "earn a college degree"? Are we talking about a bachelor's degree from a highly selective, prestigious university or, instead, an associate's degree from a local community college? Different kinds of goals require different kinds of actions in the short run. And what's the time frame in which we want to get that degree? Two years? Four years? Seven or eight years while we also have a full-time job? We need to pin everything down.

We also need to determine the specific standards by which we'll eventually judge our accomplishments as being successes or failures. For example, if we think we want to become a good basketball player, what does "good" mean? Are we shooting for a spot on a professional basketball team, or do we just want to be skillful enough to have enjoyable games at a neighborhood park? And if we want to earn a college degree, will we be happy with a 2.0 grade point average, or are we striving for a perfect 4.0? I don't recommend perfectionism, by the way. Not only can it make success almost impossible to achieve, but it can also drive our anxiety level sky high.

One good step in getting specific is to set a series of concrete, short-term goals that need to be accomplished along the way toward an abstract, longer-term one. For example, to achieve a long-term goal of earning a bachelor's degree within a 6-year time period, some of our shorter-term goals might be to complete at least three courses a semester, earn a grade of at least C in each course, commit to a major by the middle of our second year, and finish all required general education courses by the end of our third year.

Better still, we should identify some really concrete goals we want to accomplish within the upcoming days or weeks. Such **proximal goals** – say, finishing a textbook reading assignment by Friday or completing a 15-page research paper within the next two weeks – not only give us specific, accomplishable targets to shoot for but also enable us to regularly monitor our progress.[3] And the shorter term our goals are, the less likely we are to procrastinate in our efforts to meet them.[4]

Some psychologists have made a distinction between two types of goals we might set for ourselves in our learning activities. A **mastery goal** is one in which our main priority is to acquire new knowledge and skills for their own intrinsic value. In contrast, the chief aim of a **performance goal** is for us to look good (or at least *not* look *bad*) in the eyes of others, perhaps by getting a high score on an exam or becoming the star player on a competitive softball team. Often we'll have both kinds of goals at the same time – and achieving performance goals can tell us that we're making progress toward mastery – but in general mastery goals are the more beneficial of the two. When we focus on mastery goals, we're more likely to pay attention during instructional activities, engage in effective learning strategies, persevere in the face of temporary setbacks, and learn from our mistakes.[5]

ADVANCE PLANNING: IDENTIFYING A CONCRETE COURSE OF ACTION

Planning is another element of self-regulation that I briefly mentioned in Chapter 7. Once we've broken our long-term goals into a bunch of more concrete proximal goals, we also need to determine exactly how and by what date (or hour) we expect to accomplish each one. Once again, vagueness – "I'm hoping to get around to it some time next week" – doesn't work very well.

I'll give you an example in my own life. As I write these words this morning, I know that my deadline for submitting the completed book manuscript to my editor is July 1st – exactly six weeks from today. Yes, I've almost reached the end of the book, but right now I'm only writing the first draft. I still have to go back and read all 10 chapters, pouring over them with a fine-toothed mental comb to check for readability, possible inconsistencies, unnecessary repetitiveness, and, of course, grammatical and spelling errors. Then I need to double-check all the citations and compile a reference list. And I haven't even started on the figures and illustrative artwork. Barring unexpected circumstances (such as being hit by a truck), I'll get it all done because I have a concrete plan for the final six weeks, just as I've had a plan – complete with due dates for myself – for the entire book. I'll finish this chapter three days from now at the latest. As I look at my calendar, I see that I don't have too many commitments next week, so I should have four days to reread everything word by word, and I'll do that in the mornings and early afternoons – the times when I can best focus my attention on my work. Meanwhile, I'll spend one or two late afternoons *planning* how and when I'll create the figures and arts – it's supposed to rain on Sunday, so that might be a good day to do it. The week after next, I'll devote five full days to getting those figures and arts done. As for the citations and reference list – oh yeah, and the table of contents – I can save those for relatively brain-dead hours. And the final manuscript preparation – that'll probably take two full days. I should make my deadline with a few days to spare . . . once again, barring the hit-by-a-truck scenario.

One more thing about my plan: I will be in my office and at my desk for all of my subtasks. This is a strategy I've historically referred to as **self-imposed stimulus control**, although I've recently read a journal article in which the authors use the term *situational strategies for self-control*.[6] Regardless of what we want to call this approach, it involves picking a location where we can actually focus on the task before us. It should be a quiet one with few distractions. Needed resources should be close at hand – a strategy that might, in itself, require a little advance planning. And alerts for distracting smartphone apps – for me, these are alerts that my faraway partners have just taken their turns in our "Words with Friends" games – should be turned off, off, off.

Speaking of such things, I've just finished what I told myself I would do this morning. I'm giving myself a 45-minute lunch break now, and I can play "Words with Friends" while I eat. But I'm giving myself *only* 45 minutes, and then I'll be back at my desk to write at least two more sections.

SELF-INSTRUCTIONS: TELLING OURSELVES WHAT TO DO

I'm back at my desk now, 50 minutes after I left you for my lunch break. Yeah, okay, so I'm 5 minutes late. Let's both be more self-regulating now and get back on task.

A strategy known as either **self-instructions** or *self-talk* involves talking ourselves through whatever activity we're currently engaging in. For instance, have you ever talked to yourself when you've tried to master a new athletic skill – perhaps when you've been practicing a basketball layup shot or an overhand volleyball serve? Have you ever mumbled to yourself when you've tried to figure out how to use a new smartphone app? Have you asked yourself "Where are the bolts I need to connect Part B to Part A?" or "What the [expletive deleted] does *this* mean?" when you're trying to follow the directions for a recently purchased assemble-it-yourself item? If you're saying no to all of these questions, you're probably lying.

As children, we humans often talk our way through complex new tasks and activities. We don't completely abandon this strategy when we move into adolescence and on to adulthood, nor should we.[7] By talking our way through challenging tasks, either to remind ourselves of the steps we should be taking or else to make better sense of ambiguous information, we're essentially providing scaffolding for *ourselves* rather than having to rely on someone else to do it for us.

SELF-MONITORING: KEEPING TRACK OF OUR PROGRESS

When we engage in **self-monitoring**, we're regularly observing our own behaviors and checking to see both (a) how frequently we're engaging in those behaviors and (b) whether they show us that we're making progress toward our goals.[8] Once again we need to be specific and concrete. Using objective criteria can help. In some cases, we might simply want to count how often we do something, with the hopes that we'll exhibit productive behaviors more often and nonproductive ones less often. In other cases, we might rely on a small number of concrete evaluation criteria that either we or others have identified for our desired performance. And as we're trying to make sense of and remember information as we read textbooks and other works of nonfiction, we might engage in the *self-questioning* I described in Chapter 7.

We can have a bit of a "Catch-22" here – a situation in which we need to have one thing happen in order for another thing to happen, and yet that second, prerequisite thing can't happen without the first thing having already happened.[9] Hmm, maybe that doesn't make sense in the abstract, but let me explain how it can be a problem in self-monitoring. In particular, if we don't already know what we need to know, we can't be good judges of what it is that we currently know and don't know.[10] In other words, we might think that we've mastered something that we haven't mastered at all. As an example, I occasionally go to a piano lesson thinking that I'm playing one of my new pieces really well, but that's usually only because I'm hitting almost all of the notes correctly. But then my teacher will point out that I'm playing a section *forte* (loudly) when it should be *mezzo piano* (moderately softly) or that I'm playing a series of chords in a choppy manner when they should be flowing smoothly from one to the next. When it comes to self-monitoring, good self-regulators know when they need to seek an expert's feedback and advice.

I've just reminded myself that I haven't yet gotten in the hour of piano practice I told myself I would complete each day this week, and I didn't practice at all yesterday because I was out of town. Besides, I've just finished the sections I told myself I needed to write before I quit for the day. I'm feeling proud about achieving today's writing goal but feeling guilty about my lack of piano practice since my lesson two days ago. My feelings of pride and guilt will bring us (tomorrow for me but right now for you) to the next section on self-imposing consequences.

SELF-IMPOSING CONSEQUENCES: REINFORCING AND PUNISHING OURSELVES

Beginning as early as our preschool years, many of us feel good about the things we do well and can feel quite badly about the things we screw up. Such feelings can take the form of pride (for the good things) and guilt or shame (for the bad things).[11] Pride in our successes can boost our self-efficacy for learning and spur us on to even greater heights. Guilt and shame serve a somewhat different role, in that their unpleasantness can act as internal, self-administered punishment for poor performance. Yet they, too, can spur improvement *provided that* we attribute our not-great performance to unstable factors we can control, such as effort and strategies. All three emotions, then, are important elements of self-regulation.

Some researchers have found that self-imposing *external* consequences can enhance learning and achievement as well, especially when the consequences are potentially reinforcing ones.[12] For example, depending on the scale and complexity of a goal we've just accomplished, we might reach for a candy bar or bowl of potato chips (a habit I gave up after gaining 20 pounds), give ourselves an hour to watch a mindless television show, play video games for 30 minutes, treat ourselves to a day at a sports event or local shopping mall, or – perhaps if we've just graduated from college or completed a doctoral dissertation – go to the Bahamas for a few days of fun and relaxation.

We self-regulating individuals certainly don't need to have our noses to the grindstone every hour of the day, every day of the week, or every week or the year. Personally, I like to think of my own self-reinforcing activities as *contingent vegging* or *guilt-free self-indulgence*. The trick is to make self-reinforcement contingent on achieving our goals beforehand. Going to the Bahamas and *then* working toward a challenging goal just doesn't work.

BEING STRATEGIC

Self-regulation strategies become increasingly important as we move through the grade levels and then go on to further academic or professional education. And self-regulation strategies are critical if we want to keep learning throughout our lifespans. Accordingly, I offer a few final recommendations.

Enhancing Your Own Thinking and Learning in Everyday Life

- **Self-Strategy 10.1: Specify your goals for any new learning task.** For example, if you want to become a better player in a particular sport, what specific skills do you need to work on? If you want to be a better trumpet player or pianist, what kinds of music and in what particular contexts do you want to be able to play well? If you're taking a college course, what final grade do you want to get in the course? And consider the course requirements: Exactly what do you need to do to fulfill those requirements? Your goals should be specific and concrete enough that you'll know exactly when you've accomplished each one.

- **Self-Strategy 10.2: Make yourself a realistic schedule for any lengthy learning or performance task**. I strongly emphasize the word *realistic* here. After breaking down your ultimate goal into easily accomplishable proximal goals, list them all on a sheet of paper or computer spreadsheet. Assign reasonable due dates for each one, taking into account any other significant commitments and obligations you have in your life – for instance, your family, your job, your need for daily exercise, and that self-indulgent vegging you'll need to do in order to reinforce yourself for achieving your little subgoals along the way.

  In sticking to your schedule, a smidgen of anxiety about it can be useful. Don't stress yourself out (see Chapter 9), but worrying just a little bit about meeting your due dates can help you chip away at any insidious desire to procrastinate. If you're not a good self-nagger, give the task to your cell phone: Many smartphone apps are now available to do the nagging for you.

- **Self-Strategy 10.3: Regularly use concrete criteria to self-assess your progress**. For example, if you've created a schedule for yourself, make a huge checkmark beside each proximal goal you complete. If you're working on basketball layup shots, write down the percentage of shots you get in the basket each time you practice. If you're taking a college course, make use of the self-check quizzes that many digital textbooks (e-books) now include in every chapter. Unfortunately, such e-quizzes don't always focus on elaboration or other forms of meaningful learning – I've seen entirely too many that emphasize memorization of discrete facts – but they can at least give you a start in your comprehension-monitoring efforts.

- **Self-Strategy 10.4: Reinforce yourself for jobs well done**. Your self-reinforcements should be commensurate with your accomplishments – small with small, big with big. For example, if you finish the ambitious goal you've set for a single day's work, take an hour to do something you really want to do, even if it's just vegging in front of your television or computer screen. If you do as well on an assignment or exam as you had hoped to, give yourself a mental pat on the back and maybe go out for a drink with friends. If you've accomplished something really significant, take a day to go to the city, the ocean, or the mountains, or just spend the day binging on sports events or previous episodes of a favorite television series. And as long as you don't come across as arrogant and boastful, post an announcement on Facebook or some other social media site. Doing so will get you plenty of reinforcement from family and friends as well – praise for sure, and maybe a few smiley faces and other cheerful emojis.

Enhancing Other People's Thinking and Learning in Instructional Settings

○ **Instructional Strategy 10.1: Provide specific, proximal goals toward which students can direct their efforts**. In the elementary grades, goals can be as simple as "Here are the fifteen new spelling words you should try to learn this week" and "Let's see if you can write all of your multiplication facts in less time this Friday than you did last Friday." At more advanced levels, they might be presented as concrete objectives for a particular lesson or unit. Goals should focus not only on *what* should be learned but also on *how* it should be learned – for instance, through meaningful learning (explained in age-appropriate language) and regular practice.

○ **Instructional Strategy 10.2: Teach self-instructions that can help students guide themselves through complex skills**. For example, if you're teaching new dance steps to preschool children, you might encourage your students to say to themselves "Slide, jump, slide, jump, run, and stop" (for a "butterfly" sequence) and "Step, step, jump, one, two, three" (for a "cupcake" sequence).[13]

Task-specific mnemonics can come in handy here. For example, many high school math teachers suggest that students remember the sentence "Please excuse my dear Aunt Sally" as they perform the various procedures that complex mathematical expressions call for: First address the operations inside parentheses (cued by the *P* in *please*), then deal with the exponents (cued by the *E* in *excuse*), then do the multiplication and division (*my dear*), and finally do the addition and subtraction (*Aunt Sally*). Similarly, some physical education teachers suggest "BEEF" as a mnemonic for helping aspiring basketball players master a good free-throw technique: "Balance the ball," "elbows in," "elevate arms," and "follow through."

○ **Instructional Strategy 10.3: Especially when working with underachieving adolescents and adults, teach and scaffold long-term self-regulation strategies as well as short-term ones**. Students with a history of low achievement often need explicit guidance about how to plan their studying efforts, manage their time, and stay on top of assignments.[14] For example, you might teach students how to create to-do lists and note-to-self reminders for upcoming assignments. You might also teach them to make use of a paper calendar or smartphone calendar program, the latter of which can provide a hard-to-ignore sound alert a day or two before something needs to be finished. And showing students how to break a seemingly overwhelming project into small, manageable pieces – each with a self-imposed deadline – can help them take the project in stride and *not* procrastinate in getting it done.

○ **Instructional Strategy 10.4: Provide student-friendly self-assessment tools.** Remember that Catch-22 problem I described earlier? Students don't always know what to look for when they're trying to evaluate their own performance, and giving them concrete self-evaluation tools can help them self-monitor their progress. For example, you might provide a checklist of desired characteristics that students should be sure to address as they work on a complex, multifaceted task – perhaps writing a short story, preparing a persuasive argument for an upcoming debate, planning a scientific research project, or playing a musical instrument. You might create short self-check quizzes that enable students to test themselves on the contents of a recent lecture or reading assignment. And if you have the appropriate technological resources, you might encourage students to audiotape or videotape their performance and then carefully scrutinize it as an outside observer might.

○ **Instructional Strategy 10.5: Encourage students to reinforce themselves, sometimes externally but always internally**. When their self-reinforcement involves things external to themselves, students must know that a response-reinforcement contingency is essential. By definition, the desirable "consequences" – whether those consequences involve eating, drinking, playing video games, going shopping, or whatever – should come *after* students have accomplished their goals, not before.

But probably most effective are the internal pats on the back and feelings of pride that can come with success. Having a genuine sense of accomplishment after days, weeks, or years of hard work – that's the kind of self-reinforcement that can last a lifetime.

NOTES

1. Bandura, 2008; Duckworth & Seligman, 2005; Zimmerman & Schunk, 2001.
2. Bandura, 1997.
3. Belland, Kim, & Hannafin, 2013; R. B. Miller & Brickman, 2004; Schunk & Pajares, 2005.

4. Klassen & Usher, 2010; Rabin, Fogel, & Nutter-Upham, 2011; Wang, Sperling, & Haspel, 2015.
5. Midgley, 2002; Ormrod, 2016a.
6. Duckworth, Gendler, & Gross, 2016; Mahoney & Thoresen, 1974; Ormrod, 2016a.
7. Hatzigeorgiadis, Zourbanos, Galanis, & Theodorakis, 2011; Schunk, 1989; Veenman, 2011; Vygotsky, 1934/1986.
8. For example, see Schunk & Zimmerman, 1998; Zimmerman, 2004.
9. The term "Catch-22" originated with Joseph Heller's novel *Catch-22*, first published in 1961.
10. Atir, Rosenzweig, & Dunning, 2015; Dunning, Johnson, Ehrlinger, & Kruger, 2003.
11. Bandura, 1986, 2008; Kochanska, Gross, Lin, & Nichols, 2002; Lewis & Sullivan, 2005.
12. Greiner & Karoly, 1976; Hayes et al., 1985; Mace, Belfiore, & Hutchinson, 2001; H. C. Stevenson & Fantuzzo, 1986.
13. Vintere, Hemmes, Brown, & Poulson, 2004, p. 309.
14. Eilam, 2001; McCaslin & Hickey, 2001; Meltzer et al., 2007.

Appendix

Twenty-Eight Common Misconceptions about Thinking and Learning

CHAPTER 1

Misconception #1: That our minds mentally record every piece of information we encounter

Misconception #2: That our minds record information exactly as we receive it

Misconception #3: That occasional forgetfulness is a sign that something is wrong with our mental hardware

Misconception #4: That we intuitively know how we can best learn and remember something new

Misconception #5: That we intuitively know how we can most effectively teach other people new knowledge and skills

CHAPTER 2

Misconception #6: That we are born with virtually all the neurons we will ever have

Misconception #7: That the brain's left and right hemispheres have very different functions and can be independently trained and nurtured

Misconception #8: That each tiny bit of knowledge is located in a particular spot in the brain

Misconception #9: That most of us don't use more than 10% of our brain capacity

Misconception #10: That parents, teachers, and other adults need to do everything they can to minimize the loss of synapses in young children

Misconception #11: That the brain reaches full maturity within the first few years of life

CHAPTER 3

Misconception #12: That people who say things with a great deal of
certainty and conviction are likely to be giving us accurate
information

CHAPTER 4

Misconception #13: That information that can be remembered only
for a few hours, days, or weeks is in "short-term memory"
Misconception #14: That long-term memory has an upper limit on how
much information it can hold
Misconception #15: That all information stored in long-term memory
stays there until we die

CHAPTER 5

Misconception #16: That the best way to remember something is
to repeat it over and over in a short period of time
Misconception #17: That regular practice in memorizing verbal
materials is a good way to strengthen our minds for other, unrelated
purposes
Misconception #18: That studying any subject area that requires precise,
rigorous thinking is another good way to strengthen our minds

CHAPTER 6

Misconception #19: That if we can recall an event quite vividly and in
considerable detail, then the event almost certainly happened the way
we remember it happening

CHAPTER 7

Misconception #20: That knowledge is largely a collection of discrete
facts
Misconception #21: That we either know something or we don't
Misconception #22: That we are reasonably good judges of what we
know and don't know

Misconception #23: That if we can recall something right after we study it, then we will probably remember it later on as well

CHAPTER 8

Misconception #24: That we can easily change our current beliefs when we encounter new information that contradicts them

CHAPTER 9

Misconception #25: That, for the most part, we humans are rational creatures

Misconception #26: That teaching to people's individual learning styles can have a significant impact on how effectively they learn

Misconception #27: That our intelligence is a stable characteristic that is out of our own and others' control

CHAPTER 10

Misconception #28: That getting something done is simply a matter of "turning on" an internal motivation "switch"

REFERENCES

Adesope, O. O., Lavin, T., Thompson, T., & Ungerleider, C. (2010). A systematic review and meta-analysis of the cognitive correlates of bilingualism. *Review of Educational Research, 80*, 207–245.

Afflerbach, P., & Cho, B.-Y. (2010). Determining and describing reading strategies: Internet and traditional forms of reading. In H. S. Waters & W. Schneider (Eds.), *Metacognition, strategy use, and instruction* (pp. 201–225). New York, NY: Guilford.

Albert, D., Chein, J., & Steinberg, L. (2013). The teenage brain: Peer influences on adolescent decision making. *Current Directions in Psychological Science, 22*, 114–120.

Alexander, P. A., & Disciplined Reading and Learning Research Laboratory. (2012). Reading into the future: Competence for the 21st century. *Educational Psychologist, 47*, 259–280.

Alexander, P. A., & Jetton, T. L. (1996). The role of importance and interest in the processing of text. *Educational Psychology Review, 8*, 89–121.

Altmann, E. M., & Gray, W. D. (2002). Forgetting to remember: The functional relationship of decay and interference. *Psychological Science, 13*, 27–33.

Amsterlaw, J. (2006). Children's beliefs about everyday reasoning. *Child Development, 77*, 443–464.

Anderson, J. R. (1983). *The architecture of cognition.* Cambridge, MA: Harvard University Press.

Anderson, J. R. (2005). *Cognitive psychology and its implications* (6th ed.). New York, NY: Worth.

Anderson, J. R., Bothell, D., Byrne, M. D., Douglass, S., Lebiere, C., & Qin, Y. (2004). An integrated theory of the mind. *Psychological Review, 111*, 1036–1060.

Anderson, J. R., & Schooler, L. J. (1991). Reflections of the environment in memory. *Psychological Science, 2*, 396–408.

Anderson, M. C. (2009). Motivated forgetting. In A. Baddeley, M. W. Eysenck, & M. C. Anderson (Eds.), *Memory* (pp. 217–244). Hove, England: Psychology Press.

Anderson, M. C., & Levy, B. J. (2009). Suppressing unwanted memories. *Current Directions in Psychological Science, 18*, 189–194.

Andiliou, A., Ramsay, C. M., Murphy, P. K., & Fast, J. (2012). Weighing opposing positions: Examining the effects of intratextual persuasive messages on students' knowledge and beliefs. *Contemporary Educational Psychology, 37*, 113–127.

Andre, T., & Windschitl, M. (2003). Interest, epistemological belief, and intentional conceptual change. In G. M. Sinatra & P. R. Pintrich (Eds.), *Intentional conceptual change* (pp. 173–197). Mahwah, NJ: Erlbaum.

Andriessen, J. (2006). Arguing to learn. In R. K. Sawyer (Ed.), *The Cambridge handbook of the learning sciences* (pp. 443–459). Cambridge, England: Cambridge University Press.

Aplin, L. M., Farine, D. R., Morand-Ferron, J., Cockburn, A., Thornton, A., & Sheldon, B. C. (2015). Experimentally induced innovations lead to persistent culture via conformity in wild birds. *Nature, 518*, 538–541.

Arbib, M. (Ed.). (2005). *Action to language via the mirror neuron system.* New York, NY: Cambridge University Press.

Arrigo, J. M., & Pezdek, K. (1997). Lessons from the study of psychogenic amnesia. *Current Directions in Psychological Science, 6*, 148–152.

Ashcraft, M. H. (2002). Math anxiety: Personal, educational, and cognitive consequences. *Current Directions in Psychological Science, 11*, 181–184.

Aslin, R. N., & Newport, E. L. (2012). Statistical learning: From acquiring specific items to forming general rules. *Current Directions in Psychological Science, 21*, 170–176.

Asterhan, C. S. C., & Schwarz, B. B. (2007). The effects of monological and dialogical argumentation on concept learning in evolutionary theory. *Journal of Educational Psychology, 99*, 626–639.

Atir, S., Rosenzweig, E., & Dunning, D. (2015). When knowledge knows no bounds: Self-perceived expertise predicts claims of impossible knowledge. *Psychological Science, 26*, 1295–1303.

Atkins, S. M., Bunting, M. F., Bolger, D. J., & Dougherty, M. R. (2012). Training the adolescent brain: Neural plasticity and the acquisition of cognitive abilities. In V. F. Reyna, S. B. Chapman, M. R. Dougherty, & J. Confrey (Eds.), *The adolescent brain: Learning, reasoning, and decision making* (pp. 211–241). Washington, DC: American Psychological Association.

Atkinson, R. C., & Shiffrin, R. M. (1968). Human memory: A proposed system and its control processes. In K. W. Spence & J. T. Spence (Eds.), *The psychology of learning and motivation: Advances in research and theory* (Vol. 2). New York, NY: Academic Press.

Atkinson, R. K., Levin, J. R., Kiewra, K. A., Meyers, T., Kim, S., Atkinson, L. A., . . . Hwang, Y. (1999). Matrix and mnemonic text-processing adjuncts: Comparing and combining their components. *Journal of Educational Psychology, 91*, 342–357.

Atran, S., Medin, D. L., & Ross, N. O. (2005). The cultural mind: Environmental decision making and cultural modeling within and across populations. *Psychological Review, 112*, 744–776.

Ausubel, D. P. (1963). *The psychology of meaningful verbal learning.* New York, NY: Grune & Stratton.

Azevedo, R., & Witherspoon, A. M. (2009). Self-regulated learning with hypermedia. In D. J. Hacker, J. Dunlosky, & A. C. Graesser (Eds.), *Handbook of metacognition in education* (pp. 319–339). New York, NY: Routledge.

Bachevalier, J., Malkova, L., & Beauregard, M. (1996). Multiple memory systems: A neuropsychological and developmental perspective. In G. R. Lyon & N. A. Krasnegor (Eds.), *Attention, memory, and executive function* (pp. 185–198). Baltimore, MD: Paul H. Brookes.

Baddeley, A. D. (2001). Is working memory still working? *American Psychologist, 56*, 851–864.

Baddeley, A. D. (2007). *Working memory, thought and action.* Oxford, England: Oxford University Press.

Baddeley, A. D., Eysenck, M. W., & Anderson, M. C. (2009). *Memory.* Hove, England: Psychology Press.

Baer, J., & Garrett, T. (2010). Teaching for creativity in an era of content standards and accountability. In R. A. Beghetto & J. C. Kaufman (Eds.), *Nurturing creativity in the classroom* (pp. 6–23). New York, NY: Cambridge University Press.

Bahrick, H. P. (1984). Semantic memory content in permastore: Fifty years of memory for Spanish learned in school. *Journal of Experimental Psychology: General, 113*, 1–29.

Baillargeon, R., & DeVos, J. (1991). Object permanence in young infants: Further evidence. *Child Development, 62*, 1227–1246.

Baird, B., Smallwood, J., Mrazek, M. D., Kam, J. W. Y., Franklin, M. S., & Schooler, J. W. (2012). Inspired by distraction: Mind wandering facilitates creative incubation. *Psychological Science, 23*, 1117–1122.

Baker, L. (1989). Metacognition, comprehension monitoring, and the adult reader. *Educational Psychology Review, 1*, 3–38.

Balch, W., Bowman, K., & Mohler, L. (1992). Music-dependent memory in immediate and delayed word recall. *Memory and Cognition, 20*, 21–28.

Baldwin, C. L. (2007). Cognitive implications of facilitating echoic persistence. *Memory and Cognition, 35*, 774–780.

Bandura, A. (1986). *Social foundations of thought and action: A social cognitive theory.* Englewood Cliffs, NJ: Prentice Hall.

Bandura, A. (1997). *Self-efficacy: The exercise of control.* New York, NY: Freeman.

Bandura, A. (2008). Toward an agentic theory of the self. In H. W. Marsh, R. G. Craven, & D. M. McInerney (Eds.), *Self-processes, learning, and enabling human potential* (pp. 15–49). Charlotte, NC: Information Age.

Banich, M. T. (2009). Executive function: The search for an integrated account. *Current Directions in Psychological Science, 18*, 89–94.

Barab, S. A., & Dodge, T. (2008). Strategies for designing embodied curriculum. In J. M. Spector, M. D. Merrill, J. van Merriënboer, & M. P. Driscoll (Eds.), *Handbook of research on educational communications and technology* (3rd ed., pp. 97–110). New York, NY: Erlbaum.

Bargai, N., Ben-Shakhar, G., & Shalev, A. Y. (2007). Posttraumatic stress disorder and depression in battered women: The mediating role of learned helplessness. *Journal of Family Violence, 22*, 267–275.

Bargh, J. A., & Morsella, E. (2008). The unconscious mind. *Perspectives on Psychological Science, 3*, 73–79.

Barkley, R. A. (1996). Critical issues in research on attention. In G. R. Lyon & N. A. Krasnegor (Eds.), *Attention, memory, and executive function* (pp. 307–326). Baltimore, MD: Paul H. Brookes.

Baroody, A. J., Eiland, M. D., Purpura, D. J., & Reid, E. E. (2013). Can computer-assisted discovery learning foster first graders' fluency with the most basic addition combinations? *American Educational Research Journal, 50*, 533–573.

Barron, E., Riby, L. M., Greer, J., & Smallwood, J. (2011). Absorbed in thought: The effect of mind wandering on the processing of relevant and irrelevant events. *Psychological Science, 22*, 596–601.

Barrouillet, P., & Camos, V. (2012). As time goes by: Temporal constraints in working memory. *Current Directions in Psychological Science, 2*, 413–419.

Bastardi, A., Uhlmann, E. L., & Ross, L. (2011). Wishful thinking: Belief, desire, and the motivated evaluation of scientific evidence. *Psychological Science, 22*, 731–732.

Bauer, P. J., DeBoer, T., & Lukowski, A. F. (2007). In the language of multiple memory systems: Defining and describing developments in long-term declarative memory. In L. M. Oakes & P. J. Bauer (Eds.), *Short- and long-term memory in infancy and early childhood: Taking the first steps toward remembering* (pp. 240–270). New York, NY: Oxford University Press.

Bäuml, K.-H. T., & Samenieh, A. (2010). The two faces of memory retrieval. *Psychological Science, 21*, 793–795.

Baxter Magolda, M. B. (2002). Epistemological reflection: The evolution of epistemological assumptions from age 18 to 30. In B. K. Hofer & P. R. Pintrich (Eds.), *Personal epistemology: The psychology of beliefs about knowledge and knowing* (pp. 89–102). Mahwah, NJ: Erlbaum.

Beardsley, P. M., Bloom, M. V., & Wise, S. B. (2012). Challenges and opportunities for teaching and designing effective K–12 evolution curricula. In K. S. Rosengren, S. K. Brem, E. M. Evans, & G. M. Sinatra (Eds.), *Evolution challenges: Integrating research and practice in teaching and learning about evolution* (pp. 287–310). Oxford, England: Oxford University Press.

Beeman, M. J., & Chiarello, C. (1998). Complementary right- and left-hemisphere language comprehension. *Current Directions in Psychological Science, 7*, 2–8.

Behrmann, M. (2000). The mind's eye mapped onto the brain's matter. *Current Directions in Psychological Science, 9*, 50–54.

Beilock, S. L., & Carr, T. H. (2001). On the fragility of skilled performance: What governs choking under pressure? *Journal of Experimental Psychology: General, 130*, 701–725.

Beilock, S. L., & Carr, T. H. (2004). From novice to expert performance: Memory, attention, and the control of complex sensorimotor skills. In A. M. Williams & N. J. Hodges (Eds.), *Skill acquisition in sport: Research, theory, and practice* (pp. 309–327). London, England: Routledge.

Beilock, S. L., & Carr. T. H. (2005). When high-powered people fail: Working memory and "choking under pressure" in math. *Psychological Science, 16*, 101–105.

Belland, B. R., Kim, C., & Hannafin, M. J. (2013). A framework for designing scaffolds that improve motivation and cognition. *Educational Psychologist, 48*, 243–270.

Bendixen, L. D., & Feucht, F. C. (Eds.). (2010). *Personal epistemology in the classroom: Theory, research, and implications for practice.* Cambridge, England: Cambridge University Press.

Bendixen, L. D., & Rule, D. C. (2004). An integrative approach to personal epistemology: A guiding model. *Educational Psychologist, 39,* 69–80.

Benes, F. M. (2007). Corticolimbic circuitry and psychopathology: Development of the corticolimbic system. In D. Coch, G. Dawson, & K. W. Fischer (Eds.), *Human behavior, learning, and the developing brain: Atypical development* (pp. 331–361). New York, NY: Guilford.

Benton, S. L., Kiewra, K. A., Whitfill, J. M., & Dennison, R. (1993). Encoding and external-storage effects on writing processes. *Journal of Educational Psychology, 85,* 267–280.

Bergman, E. T., & Roediger, H. L., III. (1999). Can Bartlett's repeated reproduction experiments be replicated? *Memory & Cognition, 27,* 937–947.

Berlyne, D. E. (1960). *Conflict, arousal, and curiosity.* New York, NY: McGraw-Hill.

Bernstein, D. M., & Loftus, E. F. (2009). The consequences of false memories for food preferences and choices. *Perspectives on Psychological Science, 4,* 135–139.

Berntsen, D. (2010). The unbidden past: Involuntary autobiographical memories as a basic mode of remembering. *Current Directions in Psychological Science, 19,* 138–142.

Best, J. R., & Miller, P. H. (2010). A developmental perspective on executive function. *Child Development, 81,* 1641–1660.

Bialystok, E. (2001). *Bilingualism in development: Language, literacy, and cognition.* Cambridge, England: Cambridge University Press.

Bjorklund, D. F., & Green, B. L. (1992). The adaptive nature of cognitive immaturity. *American Psychologist, 47,* 46–54.

Bodrova, E., & Leong, D. J. (1996). *Tools of the mind: The Vygotskian approach to early childhood education.* Upper Saddle River, NJ: Merrill/Prentice Hall.

Boesch, C. (2012). From material to symbolic cultures: Culture in primates. In J. Valsiner (Ed.), *The Oxford handbook of culture and psychology* (pp. 677–694). New York, NY: Oxford University Press.

Bohn-Gettler, C. M., & Rapp, D. N. (2011). Depending on my mood: Mood-driven influences on text comprehension. *Journal of Educational Psychology, 103,* 562–577.

Booth, J. R. (2007). Brain bases of learning and development of language and reading. In D. Coch, K. W. Fischer, & G. Dawson (Eds.), *Human behavior, learning, and the developing brain: Typical development* (pp. 279–300). New York, NY: Guilford.

Bower, G. H. (1994). Some relations between emotions and memory. In P. Ekman & R. J. Davidson (Eds.), *The nature of emotion: Fundamental questions* (pp. 303–305). New York, NY: Oxford University Press.

Bower, G. H., Black, J. B., & Turner, T. J. (1979). Scripts in memory for text. *Cognitive Psychology, 11,* 177–220.

Bower, G. H., & Forgas, J. P. (2001). Mood and social memory. In J. P. Forgas (Ed.), *Handbook of affect and social cognition* (pp. 95–120). Mahwah, NJ: Erlbaum.

Bower, G. H., Karlin, M. B., & Dueck, A. (1975). Comprehension and memory for pictures. *Memory and Cognition, 3,* 216–220.

Bowers, J. S., Mattys, S. L., & Gage, S. H. (2009). Preserved implicit knowledge of a forgotten childhood language. *Psychological Science, 20,* 1064–1069.

Braasch, J. L. G., Goldman, S. R., & Wiley, J. (2013). The influences of text and reader characteristics on learning from refutations in science texts. *Journal of Educational Psychology, 105*, 561–578.

Brainerd, C. J., & Reyna, V. F. (1992). Explaining "memory free" reasoning. *Psychological Science, 3*, 332–339.

Brainerd, C. J., & Reyna, V. F. (1998). When things that were never experienced are easier to "remember" than things that were. *Psychological Science, 9*, 484–489.

Brainerd, C. J., & Reyna, V. F. (2002). Fuzzy-trace theory and false memory. *Current Directions in Psychological Science, 11*, 164–169.

Brainerd, C. J., & Reyna, V. F. (2005). *The science of false memory*. Oxford, England: Oxford University Press.

Bramham, C. R., & Messaoudi, E. (2005). BDNF function in adult synaptic plasticity: The synaptic consolidation hypothesis. *Progress in Neurobiology, 76*, 99–125.

Bransford, J. D., Franks, J. J., Vye, N. J., & Sherwood, R. D. (1989). New approaches to instruction: Because wisdom can't be told. In S. Vosniadou & A. Ortony (Eds.), *Similarity and analogical reasoning* (pp. 470–497). Cambridge, England: Cambridge University Press.

Bråten, I., Britt, M. A., Strømsø, H. I., & Rouet, J.-F. (2011). The role of epistemic beliefs in the comprehension of multiple expository texts: Toward an integrated model. *Educational Psychologist, 46*, 48–70.

Breitmeyer, B. B., & Ganz, L. (1976). Implications of sustained and transient channels for theories of visual pattern masking, saccadic suppression, and information processing. *Psychological Review, 83*, 1–36.

Brewer, W. F. (2008). Naive theories of observational astronomy: Review, analysis, and theoretical implications. In S. Vosniadou (Ed.), *International handbook of research on conceptual change* (pp. 155–204). New York, NY: Routledge.

Broadhurst, P. L. (1959). The interaction of task difficulty and motivation: The Yerkes-Dodson law revived. *Acta Psychologica, 16*, 321–338.

Brody, N. (1992). *Intelligence* (2nd ed.). San Diego, CA: Academic Press.

Bromme, R., Kienhues, D., & Porsch, T. (2010). Who knows what and who can we believe? Epistemological beliefs are beliefs about knowledge (mostly) to be attained from others. In L. D. Bendixen & F. C. Feucht (Eds.), *Personal epistemology in the classroom: Theory, research, and implications for practice* (pp. 163–193). Cambridge, England: Cambridge University Press.

Bronfenbrenner, U. (1999). Is early intervention effective? Some studies of early education in familial and extra-familial settings. In A. Montagu (Ed.), *Race and IQ* (expanded ed., pp. 343–378). New York, NY: Oxford University Press.

Brooks-Gunn, J. (2003). Do you believe in magic? What we can expect from early childhood intervention programs. *Social Policy Report, 17*(1), 3–14.

Brophy, J. E., Alleman, J., & Knighton, B. (2009). *Inside the social studies classroom*. New York, NY: Routledge.

Brown, D. E., & Hammer, D. (2008). Conceptual change in physics. In S. Vosniadou (Ed.), *International handbook of research on conceptual change* (pp. 127–154). New York, NY: Routledge.

Brown, I., & Inouye, D. K. (1978). Learned helplessness through modeling: The role of perceived similarity in competence. *Journal of Personality and Social Psychology, 36*, 900–908.

Bruer, J. T. (1999). *The myth of the first three years: A new understanding of early brain development and lifelong learning.* New York, NY: Free Press.

Bryck, R. L., & Fisher, P. A. (2012). Training the brain: Practical applications of neural plasticity from the intersection of cognitive neuroscience, developmental psychology, and prevention science. *American Psychologist, 67,* 87–100.

Buckner, R. L., & Petersen, S. E. (1996). What does neuroimaging tell us about the role of prefrontal cortex in memory retrieval? *Seminars in the Neurosciences, 8,* 47–55.

Buehl, M. M., & Alexander, P. A. (2005). Motivation and performance differences in students' domain-specific epistemological belief profiles. *American Educational Research Journal, 42,* 697–726.

Buehl, M. M., & Alexander, P. A. (2006). Examining the dual nature of epistemological beliefs. *International Journal of Educational Research, 45,* 28–42.

Bugg, J. M., & McDaniel, M. A. (2012). Selective benefits of question self-generation and answering for remembering expository text. *Journal of Educational Psychology, 104,* 922–931.

Byrnes, J. P. (2001). *Minds, brains, and learning: Understanding the psychological and educational relevance of neuroscientific research.* New York, NY: Guilford.

Cacioppo, J. T., Petty, R. E., Feinstein, J. A., & Jarvis, W. B. G. (1996). Dispositional differences in cognitive motivation: The life and times of individuals varying in need for cognition. *Psychological Bulletin, 119,* 197–253.

Calfee, R. (1981). Cognitive psychology and educational practice. In D. C. Berliner (Ed.), *Review of Research in Education* (Vol. 9, pp. 3–73). Washington, DC: American Educational Research Association.

Callanan, M. A., & Oakes, L. M. (1992). Preschoolers' questions and parents' explanations: Causal thinking in everyday activity. *Cognitive Development, 7,* 213–233.

Campo, P., Maest, F., Ortiz, T., Capilla, A., Fernandez, S., & Fernandez, A. (2005). Is medial temporal lobe activation specific to encoding long-term memories? *Neuroimage, 25,* 34–42.

Carey, S. (1985). *Conceptual change in childhood.* Cambridge, MA: MIT Press.

Carmichael, L., Hogan, H. P., & Walters, A. A. (1932). An experimental study of the effect of language on the reproduction of visually perceived form. *Journal of Experimental Psychology, 15,* 73–86.

Carver, C. S., & Scheier, M. F. (2005). Engagement, disengagement, coping, and catastrophe. In A. Elliot & C. Dweck (Eds.), *Handbook of competence and motivation* (pp. 527–547). New York, NY: Guilford.

Carver, R. P. (1990). *Reading rate: A review of research and theory.* San Diego, CA: Academic Press.

Case, R., & Okamoto, Y., in collaboration with Griffin, S., McKeough, A., Bleiker, C., Henderson, B., & Stephenson, K. M. (1996). The role of central conceptual structures in the development of children's thought. *Monographs of the Society for Research in Child Development, 61*(1–2, Serial No. 246).

Cassady, J. C. (2010). Test anxiety: Contemporary theories and implications for learning. In J. C. Cassady (Ed.), *Anxiety in schools: The causes, consequences, and solutions for academic anxieties* (pp. 7–26). New York, NY: Peter Lang.

Castelli, D. M., Hillman, C. H., Buck, S. M., & Erwin, H. E. (2007). Physical fitness and academic achievement in third- and fifth-grade students. *Journal of Sport & Exercise Psychology, 29,* 239–252.

Cattell, R. B. (1987). *Intelligence: Its structure, growth, and action.* Amsterdam, The Netherlands: North-Holland.

Ceci, S. J. (2003). Cast in six ponds and you'll reel in something: Looking back on 25 years of research. *American Psychologist, 58,* 855–864.

Chan, C., Burtis, J., & Bereiter, C. (1997). Knowledge building as a mediator of conflict in conceptual change. *Cognition and Instruction, 15,* 1–40.

Chein, J. M., & Schneider, W. (2012). The brain's learning and control architecture. *Current Directions in Psychological Science, 21,* 78–84.

Chen, J. A., & Pajares, F. (2010). Implicit theories of ability of grade 6 science students: Relation to epistemological beliefs and academic motivation and achievement in science. *Contemporary Educational Psychology, 35,* 75–87.

Cheng, P. W. (1985). Restructuring versus automaticity: Alternative accounts of skill acquisition. *Psychological Review, 92,* 414–423.

Chi, M. T. H. (2008). Three types of conceptual change: Belief revision, mental model transformation, and categorical shift. In S. Vosniadou (Ed.), *International handbook of research on conceptual change* (pp. 61–82). New York, NY: Routledge.

Chi, M. T. H., Kristensen, A. K., & Roscoe, R. D. (2012). Misunderstanding emergent causal mechanism in natural selection. In K. S. Rosengren, S. K. Brem, E. M. Evans, & G. M. Sinatra (Eds.), *Evolution challenges: Integrating research and practice in teaching and learning about evolution* (pp. 145–173). Oxford, England: Oxford University Press.

Chinn, C. A., & Brewer, W. F. (1993). The role of anomalous data in knowledge acquisition: A theoretical framework and implications for science instruction. *Review of Educational Research, 63,* 1–49.

Chinn, C. A., & Buckland, L. A. (2012). Model-based instruction: Fostering change in evolutionary conceptions and in epistemic practices. In K. S. Rosengren, S. K. Brem, E. M. Evans, & G. M. Sinatra (Eds.), *Evolution challenges: Integrating research and practice in teaching and learning about evolution* (pp. 211–232). Oxford, England: Oxford University Press.

Chinn, C. A., Buckland, L. A., & Samarapungavan, A. (2011). Expanding the dimensions of epistemic cognition: Arguments from philosophy and psychology. *Educational Psychologist, 46,* 141–167.

Chinn, C. A., & Malhotra, B. A. (2002). Children's responses to anomalous scientific data: How is conceptual change impeded? *Journal of Educational Psychology, 94,* 327–343.

Chomsky, N. (2006). *Language and mind* (3rd ed.). Cambridge, England: Cambridge University Press.

Chrobak, Q. M., & Zaragoza, M. S. (2012). When forced fabrications become truth: Causal explanations and false memory development. *Journal of Experimental Psychology: General, 142,* 827–844.

Cimpian, A., Arce, H.-M. C., Markman, E. M., & Dweck, C. S. (2007). Subtle linguistic cues affect children's motivation. *Psychological Science, 18,* 314–316.

Clark, D. B. (2006). Longitudinal conceptual change in students' understanding of thermal equilibrium: An examination of the process of conceptual restructuring. *Cognition and Instruction, 24*, 467–563.

Clark, J. M., & Paivio, A. (1991). Dual coding theory and education. *Educational Psychology Review, 3*, 149–210.

Clement, J. (2008). The role of explanatory models in teaching for conceptual change. In S. Vosniadou (Ed.), *International handbook of research on conceptual change* (pp. 417–452). New York, NY: Routledge.

Clore, G. L., Gasper, K., & Garvin, E. (2001). Affect as information. In J. P. Forgas (Ed.), *Handbook of affect and social cognition* (pp. 121–144). Mahwah, NJ: Erlbaum.

Cohen, G. (2000). Hierarchical models in cognition: Do they have psychological reality? *European Journal of Cognitive Psychology, 12*(1), 1–36.

Cohen, L. B., & Cashon, C. H. (2006). Infant cognition. In W. Damon & R. M. Lerner (Series Eds.), D. Kuhn & R. Siegler (Vol. Eds.), *Handbook of child psychology: Vol. 2. Cognition, perception, and language* (6th ed., pp. 214–251). New York, NY: Wiley.

Cohn, S., Hult, R. E., & Engle, R. W. (1990, April). *Working memory, notetaking, and learning from a lecture.* Paper presented at the annual meeting of the American Educational Research Association, Boston, MA.

Colbert, S. M., & Peters, E. R. (2002). Need for closure and jumping-to-conclusions in delusion-prone individuals. *Journal of Nervous and Mental Disease, 190*(1), 27–31.

Cole, M., & Cagigas, X. E. (2010). Cognition. In M. H. Bornstein (Ed.), *Handbook of cultural developmental science* (pp. 127–142). New York, NY: Psychology Press.

Cole, M., & Hatano, G. (2007). Cultural-historical activity theory: Integrating phylogeny, cultural history, and ontogenesis in cultural psychology. In S. Kitayama & D. Cohen (Eds.), *Handbook of cultural psychology* (pp. 109–135). New York, NY: Guilford.

Collins, A. M. (2006). Cognitive apprenticeship. In R. K. Sawyer (Ed.), *The Cambridge handbook of the learning sciences* (pp. 47–60). Cambridge, England: Cambridge University Press.

Collins, A. M., & Loftus, E. F. (1975). A spreading-activation theory of semantic processing. *Psychological Review, 82*, 407–428.

Coplan, R. J., & Arbeau, K. A. (2009). Peer interactions and play in early childhood. In K. H. Rubin, W. M. Bukowski, & B. Laursen (Eds.), *Handbook of peer interactions, relationships, and groups* (pp. 143–161). New York, NY: Guilford.

Corno, L., & Mandinach, E. B. (2004). What we have learned about student engagement in the past twenty years. In D. M. McNerney & S. Van Etten (Eds.), *Big theories revisited* (pp. 299–328). Greenwich, CT: Information Age.

Cothern, N. B., Konopak, B. C., & Willis, E. L. (1990). Using readers' imagery of literary characters to study text meaning construction. *Reading Research and Instruction, 30*, 15–29.

Cowan, N. (2007). What infants can tell us about working memory development. In L. M. Oakes & P. J. Bauer (Eds.), *Short- and long-term memory in infancy and early childhood: Taking the first steps toward remembering* (pp. 126–150). New York, NY: Oxford University Press.

Cowan, N. (2010). The magical mystery four: How is working memory capacity limited, and why? *Current Directions in Psychological Science, 19,* 51–57.

Cowan, N., Nugent, L. D., Elliott, E. M., & Saults, J. S. (2000). Persistence of memory for ignored lists of digits: Areas of developmental constancy and change. *Journal of Experimental Child Psychology, 76,* 151–172.

Cowan, N., Wood, N. L., Nugent, L. D., & Treisman, M. (1997). There are two word-length effects in verbal short-term memory: Opposed effects of duration and complexity. *Psychological Science, 8,* 290–295.

Craik, F. I. M. (2006). Distinctiveness and memory: Comments and a point of view. In R. R. Hunt & J. B. Worthen (Eds.), *Distinctiveness and memory* (pp. 425–442). Oxford, England: Oxford University Press.

Craik, F. I. M., & Watkins, M. J. (1973). The role of rehearsal in short-term memory. *Journal of Verbal Learning and Verbal Behavior, 12,* 598–607.

Cromley, J. G., Snyder-Hogan, L. E., & Luciw-Dubas, U. A. (2010). Cognitive activities in complex science text and diagrams. *Contemporary Educational Psychology, 35,* 59–74.

Crowley, K., & Jacobs, M. (2002). Building islands of expertise in everyday family activity. In G. Leinhardt, K. Crowley, & K. Knutson (Eds.), *Learning conversations in museums* (pp. 333–356). Mahwah, NJ: Erlbaum.

Dai, D. Y., & Sternberg, R. J. (2004). Beyond cognitivism: Toward an integrated understanding of intellectual functioning and development. In D. Y. Dai & R. J. Sternberg (Eds.), *Motivation, emotion, and cognition: Integrative perspectives on intellectual functioning and development* (pp. 3–38). Mahwah, NJ: Erlbaum.

Daneman, M. (1987). Reading and working memory. In J. R. Beech & A. M. Colley (Eds.), *Cognitive approaches to reading* (pp. 57–86). Chichester, England: Wiley.

Dansereau, D. F. (1995). Derived structural schemas and the transfer of knowledge. In A. McKeough, J. Lupart, & A. Marini (Eds.), *Teaching for transfer: Fostering generalization in learning* (pp. 93–122). Mahwah, NJ: Erlbaum.

Darwin, C. R. (1859). *On the origin of species by means of natural selection.* London, England: John Murray.

Datta, L. G. (1962). Learning in the earthworm, *Lumbricus terrestris. American Journal of Psychology, 75,* 531–553.

Davachi, L., & Dobbins, I. G. (2008). Declarative memory. *Current Directions in Psychological Science, 17,* 112–118.

de Jong, T. (2011). Instruction based on computer simulations. In R. E. Mayer & P. A. Alexander (Eds.), *Handbook of research on learning and instruction* (pp. 446–466). New York, NY: Routledge.

De La Paz, S., & Felton, M. K. (2010). Reading and writing from multiple source documents in history: Effects of strategy instruction with low to average high school writers. *Contemporary Educational Psychology, 35,* 174–192.

De La Paz, S., & McCutchen, D. (2011). Learning to write. In R. E. Mayer & P. A. Alexander (Eds.), *Handbook of research on learning and instruction* (pp. 32–54). New York, NY: Routledge.

de Waal, F. (2016). *Are we smart enough to know how smart animals are?* New York, NY: W. W. Norton.

DeBacker, T. K., & Crowson, H. M. (2008). Measuring need for closure in classroom learners. *Contemporary Educational Psychology, 33*, 711–732.

DeBacker, T. K., & Crowson, H. M. (2009). The influence of need for closure on learning and teaching. *Educational Psychology Review, 21*, 303–323.

DeCasper, A. J., & Spence, M. J. (1986). Prenatal maternal speech influences newborns' perception of speech sounds. *Infant Behavior and Development, 9*, 133–150.

Dehaene, S. (2007). A few steps toward a science of mental life. *Mind, Brain, and Education, 1*(1), 28–47.

Delaney, P. F., Sahakyan, L., Kelley, C. M., & Zimmerman, C. A. (2010). Remembering to forget: The amnesic effect of daydreaming. *Psychological Science, 21*, 1036–1042.

Dewar, K. M., & Xu, F. (2010). Induction, overhypothesis, and the origin of abstract knowledge: Evidence from 9-month-old infants. *Psychological Science, 21*, 1871–1877.

Dewhurst, S. A., & Conway, M. A. (1994). Pictures, images, and recollective experience. *Journal of Experimental Psychology: Learning, Memory, and Cognition, 20*, 1088–1098.

Di Vesta, F. J., & Gray, S. G. (1972). Listening and notetaking. *Journal of Educational Psychology, 63*, 8–14.

Diamond, M., & Hopson, J. (1998). *Magic trees of the mind.* New York, NY: Dutton.

DiDonato, N. C. (2013). Effective self- and co-regulation in collaborative learning groups: An analysis of how students regulate problem solving of authentic interdisciplinary tasks. *Instructional Science, 41*, 25–47.

Dijksterhuis, A., & Nordgren, L. F. (2006). A theory of unconscious thought. *Perspectives on Psychological Science, 1*, 95–109.

Dijksterhuis, A., & Strick, M. (2016). A case for thinking without consciousness. *Perspectives on Psychological Science, 11*, 117–132.

Dijkstra, P., Kuyper, H., van der Werf, G., Buunk, A. P., & van der Zee, Y. G. (2008). Social comparison in the classroom: A review. *Review of Educational Research, 78*, 828–879.

Dinges, D. F., & Rogers, N. L. (2008). The future of human intelligence: Enhancing cognitive capability in a 24/7 world. In P. C. Kyllonen, R. D. Roberts, & L. Stankov (Eds.), *Extending intelligence: Enhancement and new constructs* (pp. 407–430). New York, NY: Erlbaum/Taylor & Francis.

Dirix, C. E. H., Nijhuis, J. G., Jongsma, H. W., & Hornstra, G. (2009). Aspects of fetal learning and memory. *Child Development, 80*, 1251–1258.

diSessa, A. A. (1996). What do "just plain folk" know about physics? In D. R. Olson & N. Torrance (Eds.), *The handbook of education and human development: New models of learning, teaching, and schooling* (pp. 709–730). Cambridge, MA: Blackwell.

diSessa, A. A. (2006). A history of conceptual change research. In R. K. Sawyer (Ed.), *The Cambridge handbook of the learning sciences* (pp. 265–281). Cambridge, England: Cambridge University Press.

diSessa, A. A., Elby, A., & Hammer, D. (2003). J's epistemological stance and strategies. In G. M. Sinatra & P. R. Pintrich (Eds.), *Intentional conceptual change* (pp. 237–290). Mahwah, NJ: Erlbaum.

Dodge, K. A., Malone, P. S., Lansford, J. E., Miller, S., Pettit, G. S., & Bates, J. E. (2009). A dynamic cascade model of the development of substance-use onset. *Monographs of the Society for Research in Child Development, 74*(3, Serial No. 294), 1–119.

Doja, A., & Roberts, W. (2006). Immunizations and autism: A review of the literature. *Canadian Journal of Neurological Sciences, 33,* 341–346.

Dole, J. A., Duffy, G. G., Roehler, L. R., & Pearson, P. D. (1991). Moving from the old to the new: Research on reading comprehension instruction. *Review of Educational Research, 61,* 239–264.

Dooling, D. J., & Christiaansen, R. E. (1977). Episodic and semantic aspects of memory for prose. *Journal of Experimental Psychology: Human Learning and Memory, 3,* 428–436.

Draganski, B., Gaser, C., Busch, V., Schuierer, G., Bogdahn, U., & May, A. (2004). Changes in grey matter induced by training. *Nature, 427,* 311–312.

Duckworth, A. L., Gendler, T. S., & Gross, J. J. (2016). Situational strategies for self-control. *Perspectives on Psychological Science, 11,* 35–55.

Duckworth, A. L., & Seligman, M. E. P. (2005). Self-discipline outdoes IQ in predicting academic performance of adolescents. *Psychological Science, 16,* 939–944.

Dunlosky, J., & Lipko, A. R. (2007). Metacomprehension: A brief history and how to improve its accuracy. *Current Directions in Psychological Science, 16,* 228–232.

Dunlosky, J., Rawson, K. A., Marsh, E. J., Nathan, M. J., & Willingham, D. T. (2013). Improving students' learning with effective learning techniques: Promising directions from cognitive and educational psychology. *Psychological Science in the Public Interest, 14,* 4–58.

Dunning, D., Heath, C., & Suls, J. M. (2004). Flawed self-assessment: Implications for health, education, and the workplace. *Psychological Science in the Public Interest, 5,* 69–106.

Dunning, D., Johnson, K., Ehrlinger, J., & Kruger, J. (2003). Why people fail to recognize their own incompetence. *Current Directions in Psychological Science, 12,* 83–87.

Dweck, C. S. (2000). *Self-theories: Their role in motivation, personality, and development.* Philadelphia, PA: Psychology Press.

Dweck, C. S. (2006). *Mindset: The new psychology of success.* New York, NY: Ballantine Books.

Dweck, C. S., & Leggett, E. L. (1988). A social-cognitive approach to motivation and personality. *Psychological Review, 95,* 256–273.

Dweck, C. S., & Molden, D. C. (2005). Self-theories: Their impact on competence motivation and acquisition. In A. J. Elliot & C. S. Dweck (Eds.), *Handbook of competence and motivation* (pp. 122–140). New York, NY: Guilford.

Eagly, A. H., Kulesa, P., Chen, S., & Chaiken, S. (2001). Do attitudes affect memory? Tests of the congeniality hypothesis. *Current Directions in Psychological Science, 10,* 5–9.

Echevarria, M. (2003). Anomalies as a catalyst for middle school students' knowledge construction and scientific reasoning during science inquiry. *Journal of Educational Psychology, 95,* 357–374.

Edelson, D. C., & Reiser, B. J. (2006). Making authentic practices accessible to learners. In R. K. Sawyer (Ed.), *The Cambridge handbook of the learning sciences* (pp. 335–354). Cambridge, England: Cambridge University Press.

Eilam, B. (2001). Primary strategies for promoting homework performance. *American Educational Research Journal, 38*, 691–725.

Einstein, G. O., & McDaniel, M. A. (2005). Prospective memory: Multiple retrieval processes. *Current Directions in Psychological Science, 14*, 286–290.

Elby, A., & Hammer, D. (2010). Epistemological resources and framing: A cognitive framework for helping teachers interpret and respond to their students' epistemologies. In L. D. Bendixen & F. C. Feucht (Eds.), *Personal epistemology in the classroom: Theory, research, and implications for practice* (pp. 409–434). Cambridge, England: Cambridge University Press.

Elkind, D. (1981). *Children and adolescents: Interpretive essays on Jean Piaget* (3rd ed.). New York, NY: Oxford University Press.

Else-Quest, N. M., Hyde, J. S., Goldsmith, H. H., & Van Hulle, C. A. (2006). Gender differences in temperament: A meta-analysis. *Psychological Bulletin, 132*, 33–72.

Erickson, K. I., Voss, M. W., Prakash, R. S., Basak, C., Szabo, A., Chaddock, L., . . . Kramer, A. F. (2011). Exercise training increases size of hippocampus and improves memory. *Proceedings of the National Academy of Sciences, USA, 108*, 3017–3022.

Ericsson, K. A. (1996). *The road to excellence: The acquisition of expert performance in the arts and science, sports, and games*. Mahwah, NJ: Erlbaum.

Evans, E. M. (2008). Conceptual change and evolutionary biology: A developmental analysis. In S. Vosniadou (Ed.), *International handbook of research on conceptual change* (pp. 263–294). New York, NY: Routledge.

Feinberg, I., & Campbell, I. G. (2013). Longitudinal sleep EEG trajectories indicate complex patterns of adolescent brain maturation. *American Journal of Physiology: Regulatory, Integrative, and Comparative Physiology, 304*(4), R296–R303. doi: 10.1152/ajpregu.00422.2012

Feinberg, M., & Willer, R. (2011). Apocalypse soon? Dire messages reduce belief in global warming by contradicting just-world beliefs. *Psychological Science, 22*, 34–38.

Feinstein, J. S., Duff, M. C., & Tranel, D. (2010). Sustained experience of emotion after loss of memory in patients with amnesia. *PNAS, 107*, 7674–7679.

Fernández-Espejo, D., Bekinschtein, T., Monti, M. M., Pickard, J. D., Junque, C., Coleman, M. R., & Owen, A. M. (2011). Diffusion weighted imaging distinguishes the vegetative state from the minimally conscious state. *Neuroimage, 54*, 103–112.

Fernbach, P. M., Rogers, T., Fox, C. R., & Sloman, S. A. (2013). Political extremism is supported by an illusion of understanding. *Psychological Science, 24*, 939–946.

Festinger, L. (1957). *A theory of cognitive dissonance*. Stanford, CA: Stanford University Press.

Feuerstein, R., Feuerstein, R. S., & Falik, L. H. (2010). *Beyond smarter: Mediated learning and the brain's capacity for change*. New York, NY: Teachers College Press.

Figner, B., & Weber, E. U. (2011). Who takes risks when and why? Determinants of risk taking. *Current Directions in Psychological Science, 20*, 211–216.

Fischer, G. (2009). Learning in communities: A distributed intelligence perspective. In J. M. Carroll (Ed.), *Learning in communities: Interdisciplinary perspectives on human centered information technology* (pp. 11–16). London, England: Springer-Verlag.

Fischer, P., & Greitemeyer, T. (2010). A new look at selective-exposure effects: An integrative model. *Current Directions in Psychological Science, 19*, 384–389.

Fivush, R., Haden, C., & Reese, E. (2006). Elaborating on elaborations: Role of maternal reminiscing style in cognitive and socioemotional development. *Child Development, 77*, 1568–1588.

Flavell, J. H. (2000). Development of children's knowledge about the mental world. *International Journal of Behavioral Development, 24*(1), 15–23.

Flavell, J. H., Friedrichs, A. G., & Hoyt, J. D. (1970). Developmental changes in memorization processes. *Cognitive Psychology, 1*, 324–340.

Flavell, J. H., Miller, P. H., & Miller, S. A. (2002). *Cognitive development* (4th ed.). Upper Saddle River, NJ: Prentice Hall.

Fletcher, K. L., & Cassady, J. C. (2010). Overcoming academic anxieties: Promoting effective coping and self-regulation strategies. In J. C. Cassady (Ed.), *Anxiety in schools: The causes, consequences, and solutions for academic anxieties* (pp. 177–200). New York, NY: Peter Lang.

Foer, J. (2011). *Moonwalking with Einstein: The art and science of remembering everything*. New York, NY: Penguin.

Foley, M. A., Harris, J., & Herman, S. (1994). Developmental comparisons of the ability to discriminate between memories for symbolic play enactments. *Developmental Psychology, 30*, 206–217.

Foote, A. L., & Crystal, J. D. (2007). Metacognition in the rat. *Current Biology, 17*, 551–555.

Forgas, J. P. (2008). Affect and cognition. *Perspectives on Psychological Science, 3*, 94–101.

Fox, E. (2009). The role of reader characteristics in processing and learning from informational text. *Review of Educational Research, 79*, 197–261.

Frankenberger, K. D. (2000). Adolescent egocentrism: A comparison among adolescents and adults. *Journal of Adolescence, 23*, 343–354.

Frensch, P. A., & Rünger, D. (2003). Implicit learning. *Current Directions in Psychological Science, 12*, 13–18.

Freud, S. (1922). *Beyond the pleasure principle*. London, England: International Psychoanalytic Press.

Freud, S. (1957). Repression. In J. Strachey (Ed.), *The standard edition of the complete psychological works of Sigmund Freud* (Vol. 14, pp. 146–158). London, England: Hogarth Press. (Original work published 1915.)

Fuchs, L. S., Geary, D. C., Compton, D. L., Fuchs, D., Schatschneider, C., Hamlett, C. L., ... Changas, P. (2013). Effects of first-grade number knowledge tutoring with contrasting forms of practice. *Journal of Educational Psychology, 105*, 58–77.

Furnham, A. (2003). Belief in a just world: Research progress over the past decade. *Personality and Individual Differences, 34,* 795–817.

Furtak, E. M., Seidel, T., Iverson, H., & Briggs, D. C. (2012). Experimental and quasi-experimental studies of inquiry-based science teaching: A meta-analysis. *Review of Educational Research, 82,* 300–329.

Gal, D., & Rucker, D. D. (2010). When in doubt, shout! Paradoxical influences of doubt on proselytizing. *Psychological Science, 21,* 1701–1707.

Gallese, V., Gernsbacher, M. A., Heyes, C., Hickok, G., & Iacoboni, M. (2011). Mirror neuron forum. *Perspectives on Psychological Science, 6,* 369–407.

Gallimore, R., & Tharp, R. (1990). Teaching mind in society: Teaching, schooling, and literate discourse. In L. C. Moll (Ed.), *Vygotsky and education: Instructional implications and applications of sociohistorical psychology* (pp. 175–205). Cambridge, England: Cambridge University Press.

Galván, A. (2012). Risky behavior in adolescents: The role of the developing brain. In V. F. Reyna, S. B. Chapman, M. R. Dougherty, & J. Confrey (Eds.), *The adolescent brain: Learning, reasoning, and decision making* (pp. 267–289). Washington, DC: American Psychological Association.

Galván, A., Hare, T. A., Parra, C. E., Penn, J., Voss, H., Glover, G., & Casey, B. J. (2006). Earlier development of the accumbens relative to orbitofrontal cortex might underlie risk-taking behavior in adolescents. *Journal of Neuroscience, 26,* 6885–6892.

Gardner, H. (1999). *Intelligence reframed: Multiple intelligences for the 21st century.* New York, NY: Basic Books.

Gardner, H., Torff, B., & Hatch, T. (1996). The age of innocence reconsidered: Preserving the best of the progressive traditions in psychology and education. In D. R. Olson & N. Torrance (Eds.), *The handbook of education and human development: New models of learning, teaching, and schooling* (pp. 28–55). Cambridge, MA: Blackwell.

Garry, M., & Gerrie, M. P. (2005). When photographs create false memories. *Current Directions in Psychological Science, 14,* 321–325.

Gelman, S. A. (2003). *The essential child: Origins of essentialism in everyday thought.* New York, NY: Oxford University Press.

Geraerts, E., Lindsay, D. S., Merckelbach, H., Jelicic, M., Raymaekers, L., Arnold, M. M., & Schooler, J. W. (2009). Cognitive mechanisms underlying recovered-memory experiences of childhood sexual abuse. *Psychological Science, 20,* 92–98.

Ghetti, S., & Alexander, K. W. (2004). "If it happened, I would remember it": Strategic use of event memorability in the rejection of false autobiographical events. *Child Development, 75,* 542–561.

Giancarlo, C. A., & Facione, P. A. (2001). A look across four years at the disposition toward critical thinking among undergraduate students. *Journal of General Education, 50,* 29–55.

Giedd, J. N., Stockman, M., Weddle, C., Liverpool, M., Wallace, G. L., Lee, N. R., . . . Lenroot, R. K. (2012). Anatomic magnetic resonance imaging of the developing child and adolescent brain. In V. F. Reyna, S. B. Chapman, M. R. Dougherty, & J. Confrey (Eds.), *The adolescent brain: Learning, reasoning, and decision making* (pp. 15–35). Washington, DC: American Psychological Association.

Gifford, R. (2011). The dragons of inaction: Psychological barriers that limit climate change mitigation and adaptation. *American Psychologist, 66,* 290–302.

Goel, V., Tierney, M., Sheesley, L., Bartolo, A., Vartanian, O., & Grafman, J. (2007). Hemispheric specialization in human prefrontal cortex for resolving certain and uncertain inferences. *Cerebral Cortex, 17,* 2245–2250.

Gogtay, N., Giedd, J. N., Lusk, L., Hayashi, K. M., Greenstein, D., Vaituzis, A. C., . . . Thompson, P. M. (2004). Dynamic mapping of human cortical development during childhood through early adulthood. *Proceedings of the National Academy of Sciences, USA, 101,* 8174–8179.

Gold, J. M., Murray, R. F., Sekuler, A. B., Bennett, P. J., & Sekuler, R. (2005). Visual memory decay is deterministic. *Psychological Science, 16,* 769–774.

Goldin-Meadow, S., & Beilock, S. L. (2010). Action's influence on thought: The case of gesture. *Perspectives on Psychological Science, 5,* 664–674.

Goldin-Meadow, S., Cook, S. W., & Mitchell, Z. A. (2009). Gesturing gives children new ideas about math. *Psychological Science, 20,* 267–272.

Goldman-Rakic, P. S. (1986). Setting the stage: Neural development before birth. In S. L. Friedman, K. A. Klivington, & R. W. Peterson (Eds.), *The brain, cognition, and education.* Orlando, FL: Academic Press.

Gonsalves, B. D., & Cohen, N. J. (2010). Brain imaging, cognitive processes, and brain networks. *Perspectives on Psychological Science, 5,* 744–752.

Gonsalves, B. D., Reber, P. J., Gitelman, D. R., Parrish, T. B., Mesulam, M.-M., & Paller, K. A. (2004). Neural evidence that vivid imagining can lead to false remembering. *Psychological Science, 15,* 655–660.

Goodman, C. S., & Tessier-Lavigne, M. (1997). Molecular mechanisms of axon guidance and target recognition. In W. M. Cowan, T. M. Jessell, & S. L. Zipursky (Eds.), *Molecular and cellular approaches to neural development* (pp. 108–137). New York, NY: Oxford University Press.

Goodman, G. S., Ghetti, S., Quas, J. A., Edelstein, R. S., Alexander, K. W., Redlich, A. D., . . . Jones, D. P. H. (2003). A prospective study of memory for child sexual abuse: New findings relevant to the repressed-memory controversy. *Psychological Science, 14,* 113–118.

Goodman, G. S., & Quas, J. A. (2008). Repeated interviews and children's memory: It's more than just how many. *Current Directions in Psychological Science, 17,* 386–390.

Gopnik, A., Griffiths, T. L., & Lucas, C. G. (2015). When younger learners can be better (or at least more open-minded) than older ones. *Current Directions in Psychological Science, 24,* 87–92.

Gorus, E., De Raedt, R., Lambert, M., Lemper, J.-C., & Mets, T. (2008). Reaction times and performance variability in normal aging, mild cognitive impairment, and Alzheimer's disease. *Journal of Geriatric Psychiatry and Neurology, 21,* 204–218.

Grabe, M. (1986). Attentional processes in education. In G. D. Phye & T. Andre (Eds.), *Cognitive classroom learning: Understanding, thinking, and problem solving* (pp. 49–82). Orlando, FL: Academic Press.

Graham, S. (1997). Using attribution theory to understand social and academic motivation in African American youth. *Educational Psychologist, 32,* 21–34.

Graham, S., & Barker, G. (1990). The downside of help: Anattributional-developmental analysis of helping behavior as a low ability cue. *Journal of Educational Psychology, 82*, 7–14.

Greene, J. A., & Azevedo, R. (2009). A macro-level analysis of SRL processes and their relations to the acquisition of a sophisticated mental model of a complex system. *Contemporary Educational Psychology, 34*, 18–29.

Greene, J. A., Hutchinson, L. A., Costa, L.-J., & Crompton, H. (2012). Investigating how college students' task definitions and plans relate to self-regulated learning processing and understanding of a complex science topic. *Contemporary Educational Psychology, 37*, 307–320.

Greene, J. A., Torney-Purta, J., & Azevedo, R. (2010). Empirical evidence regarding relations among a model of epistemic and ontological cognition, academic performance, and educational level. *Journal of Educational Psychology, 102*, 234–255.

Greeno, J. G. (2006). Learning in activity. In R. K. Sawyer (Ed.), *The Cambridge handbook of the learning sciences* (pp. 79–96). Cambridge, England: Cambridge University Press.

Greeno, J. G., Collins, A. M., & Resnick, L. B. (1996). Cognition and learning. In D. C. Berliner & R. C. Calfee (Eds.), *Handbook of educational psychology* (pp. 15–46). New York, NY: Macmillan.

Gregoire, M. (2003). Is it a challenge or a threat? A dual-process model of teachers' cognition and appraisal processes during conceptual change. *Educational Psychology Review, 15*, 147–179.

Greiner, J. M., & Karoly, P. (1976). Effects of self-control training on study activity and academic performance: An analysis of self-monitoring, self-reward, and systematic planning components. *Journal of Counseling Psychology, 23*, 495–502.

Hacker, D. J. (1998). Self-regulated comprehension during normal reading. In D. J. Hacker, J. Dunlosky, & A. C. Graesser (Eds.), *Metacognition in educational theory and practice* (pp. 165–191). Mahwah, NJ: Erlbaum.

Hacker, D. J., Dunlosky, J., & Graesser, A. C. (2009a). A growing sense of "agency." In D. J. Hacker, J. Dunlosky, & A. C. Graesser (Eds.), *Handbook of metacognition in education* (pp. 1–4). New York, NY: Routledge.

Hacker, D. J., Dunlosky, J., & Graesser, A. C. (Eds.). (2009b). *Handbook of metacognition in education*. New York, NY: Routledge.

Hadjioannou, X. (2007). Bringing the background to the foreground: What do classroom environments that support authentic discussions look like? *American Educational Research Journal, 44*, 370–399.

Haier, R. J. (2001). PET studies of learning and individual differences. In J. L. McClelland & R. S. Siegler (Eds.), *Mechanisms of cognitive development: Behavioral and neural perspectives* (pp. 123–145). Mahwah, NJ: Erlbaum.

Hall, J. F. (1971). *Verbal learning and retention*. Philadelphia, PA: J. B. Lippincott.

Hall, N. C., Hladkyj, S., Perry, R. P., & Ruthig, J. C. (2004). The role of attributional retraining and elaborative learning in college students' academic development. *Journal of Social Psychology, 144*, 591–612.

Halperin, E., Porat, R., Tamir, M., & Gross, J. J. (2013). Can emotion regulation change political attitudes in intractable conflicts? From the laboratory to the field. *Psychological Science, 24*, 106–111.

Halpern, D. F. (1997). *Critical thinking across the curriculum: A brief edition of thought and knowledge.* Mahwah, NJ: Erlbaum.

Halpern, D. F. (1998). Teaching critical thinking for transfer across domains: Dispositions, skills, structure, training, and metacognitive monitoring. *American Psychologist, 53,* 449–455.

Halpern, D. F. (2008). Is intelligence critical thinking? Why we need a new definition of intelligence. In P. C. Kyllonen, R. D. Roberts, & L. Stankov (Eds.), *Extending intelligence: Enhancement and new constructs* (pp. 349–370). New York, NY: Erlbaum/Taylor & Francis.

Hampson, S. E. (2008). Mechanisms by which childhood personality traits influence adult well-being. *Current Directions in Psychological Science, 17,* 264–268.

Han, X., Chen, M., Wang, F., Windrem, M., Wang, S., Shanz, S., . . . Nedergaard, M. (2013). Forebrain engraftment by human glial progenitor cells enhances synaptic plasticity and learning in adult mice. *Cell Stem Cell, 12,* 342–353.

Harris, P. L. (2006). Social cognition. In W. Damon & R. M. Lerner (Series Eds.), D. Kuhn & R. Siegler (Vol. Eds.), *Handbook of child psychology: Vol. 2. Cognition, perception, and language* (6th ed., pp. 811–858). New York, NY: Wiley.

Hartmann, W. K., Miller, R., & Lee, P. (1984). *Out of the cradle: Exploring the frontiers beyond Earth.* New York, NY: Workman.

Hasher, L., & Zacks, R. T. (1984). Automatic processing of fundamental information. *American Psychologist, 39,* 1372–1388.

Hassin, R. R. (2013). Yes it can: On the functional abilities of the human unconscious. *Perspective on Psychological Science, 8,* 195–207.

Hatano, G., & Inagaki, K. (2003). When is conceptual change intended? A cognitive-sociocultural view. In G. M. Sinatra & P. R. Pintrich (Eds.), *Intentional conceptual change* (pp. 407–427). Mahwah, NJ: Erlbaum.

Hatzigeorgiadis, A., Zourbanos, N., Galanis, E., & Theodorakis, Y. (2011). Self-talk and sports performance: A meta-analysis. *Perspectives on Psychological Science, 6,* 348–356.

Hayes, S. C., Rosenfarb, I., Wulfert, E., Munt, E. D., Korn, Z., & Zettle, R. D. (1985). Self-reinforcement effects: An artifact of social standard setting? *Journal of Applied Behavior Analysis, 18,* 201–214.

Healey, M. K., Campbell, K. L., Hasher, L., & Ossher, L. (2010). Direct evidence for the role of inhibition in resolving interference in memory. *Psychological Science, 21,* 1464–1470.

Hebb, D. O. (1949). *The organization of behavior: A neuropsychological theory.* New York, NY: Wiley.

Heller, J. (1961). *Catch-22.* New York, NY: Simon & Schuster.

Hennessey, M. G. (2003). Metacognitive aspects of students' reflective discourse: Implications for intentional conceptual change teaching and learning. In G. M. Sinatra & P. R. Pintrich (Eds.), *Intentional conceptual change* (pp. 103–132). Mahwah, NJ: Erlbaum.

Heron, W. (1957). The pathology of boredom. *Scientific American, 196*(1), 52–56.

Hertzog, C., Kramer, A. F., Wilson, R. S., & Lindenberger, U. (2009). Enrichment effects on adult cognitive development: Can the functional capacity of older adults be preserved and enhanced? *Psychological Science in the Public Interest, 9,* 1–65.

Heuer, F., & Reisberg, D. (1990). Vivid memories of emotional events: The accuracy of remembered minutiae. *Memory and Cognition, 18,* 496–506.

Heyes, C. M., & Galef, B. G., Jr. (Eds.). (1996). *Social learning in animals: The roots of culture.* San Diego, CA: Academic Press.

Hickey, D. J. (2011). Participation by design: Improving individual motivation by looking beyond it. In D. M. McInerney, R. A. Walker, & G. A. D. Liem (Eds.), *Sociocultural theories of learning and motivation: Looking back, looking forward* (pp. 137–161). Charlotte, NC: Information Age.

Hidi, S., & Renninger, K. A. (2006). The four-phase model of interest development. *Educational Psychologist, 41,* 111–127.

Hintzman, D. L. (2011). Research strategy in the study of memory: Fads, fallacies, and the search for "coordinates of truth." *Perspectives on Psychological Science, 6,* 253–271.

Hiroto, D. S., & Seligman, M. E. P. (1975). Generality of learned helplessness in man. *Journal of Personality and Social Psychology, 31,* 311–327.

Hirst, W., & Phelps, E. A. (2016). Flashbulb memories. *Current Directions in Psychological Science, 25,* 36–41.

Hofer, B. K. (2004). Epistemological understanding as a metacognitive process: Thinking aloud during online searching. *Educational Psychologist, 39,* 43–55.

Hofer, B. K., & Pintrich, P. R. (1997). The development of epistemological theories: Beliefs about knowledge and knowing and their relation to learning. *Review of Educational Research, 67,* 88–140.

Hofer, B. K., & Pintrich, P. R. (Eds.). (2002). *Personal epistemology: The psychology of beliefs about knowledge and knowing.* Mahwah, NJ: Erlbaum.

Hoffman, B. (2010). "I think I can, but I'm afraid to try": The role of self-efficacy beliefs and mathematics anxiety in mathematics problem-solving efficiency. *Learning and Individual Differences, 20,* 276–283.

Hokoda, A., & Fincham, F. D. (1995). Origins of children's helplessness and mastery achievement patterns in the family. *Journal of Educational Psychology, 87,* 375–385.

Holland, R. W., Hendriks, M., & Aarts, H. (2005). Smells like clean spirit: Nonconscious effects of scent on cognition and behavior. *Psychological Science, 16,* 689–693.

Howe, M. L. (2011). The adaptive nature of memory and its illusions. *Current Directions in Psychological Science, 20,* 312–315.

Hsee, C. K., Yang, A. X., & Wang, L. (2010). Idleness aversion and the need for justifiable busyness. *Psychological Science, 21,* 926–930.

Hunt, R. R., & Worthen, J. B. (Eds.). (2006). *Distinctiveness and memory.* Oxford, England: Oxford University Press.

Huttenlocher, P. R. (1979). Synaptic density in human frontal cortex – developmental changes and effects of aging. *Brain Research, 163,* 195–205.

Huttenlocher, P. R. (1990). Morphometric study of human cerebral cortex development. *Neuropsychologia, 28,* 517–527.

Huttenlocher, P. R. (1993). Morphometric study of human cerebral cortex development. In M. H. Johnson (Ed.), *Brain development and cognition: A reader.* Cambridge, MA: Blackwell.

Huttenlocher, P. R., & Dabholkar, A. S. (1997). Regional differences in synaptogenesis in human cerebral cortex. *Journal of Comparative Neurology, 387,* 167–178.

Hyde, K. L., Lerch, J., Norton, A., Forgeard, M., Winner, E., Evans, A. C., & Schlaug, G. (2009). Musical training shapes structural brain development. *Journal of Neuroscience, 29,* 3019–3025.

Hynd, C. (1998). Conceptual change in a high school physics class. In B. Guzzetti & C. Hynd (Eds.), *Perspectives on conceptual change: Multiple ways to understand knowing and learning in a complex world* (pp. 27–36). Mahwah, NJ: Erlbaum.

Hynd, C. (2003). Conceptual change in response to persuasive messages. In G. M. Sinatra & P. R. Pintrich (Eds.), *Intentional conceptual change* (pp. 291–315). Mahwah, NJ: Erlbaum.

Immordino-Yang, M. H., Christodoulou, J. A., & Singh, V. (2012). Rest is not idleness: Implications of the brain's default mode for human development and education. *Perspectives on Psychological Science, 7,* 352–364.

Immordino-Yang, M. H., & Fischer, K. W. (2007). Dynamic development of hemispheric biases in three cases: Cognitive/hemispheric cycles, music, and hemispherectomy. In D. Coch, K. W. Fischer, & G. Dawson (Eds.), *Human behavior, learning, and the developing brain: Typical development* (pp. 74–111). New York, NY: Guilford.

Inagaki, K., & Hatano, G. (2006). Young children's conception of the biological world. *Current Directions in Psychological Science, 15,* 177–181.

Jackson, D. L., Ormrod, J. E., & Salih, D. J. (1999, April). *Promoting students' achievement by teaching them to generate higher-order self-questions.* Paper presented at the annual meeting of the American Educational Research Association, Montreal, Quebec, Canada.

James, W. (1890). *Principles of psychology.* New York, NY: Holt.

Jameson, M. M. (2010). Math anxiety: Theoretical perspectives on potential influences and outcomes. In J. C. Cassady (Ed.), *Anxiety in schools: The causes, consequences, and solutions for academic anxieties* (pp. 45–58). New York, NY: Peter Lang.

John-Steiner, V., & Mahn, H. (1996). Sociocultural approaches to learning and development: A Vygotskian framework. *Educational Psychologist, 31,* 191–206.

Jones, M. S., Levin, M. E., Levin, J. R., & Beitzel, B. D. (2000). Can vocabulary-learning strategies and pair-learning formats be profitably combined? *Journal of Educational Psychology, 92,* 256–262.

Jung, R. E., & Haier, R. J. (2007). The parieto-frontal integration theory (P-FIT) of intelligence: Converging neuroimaging evidence. *Behavioral and Brain Sciences, 30,* 135–154.

Kahne, J. E., & Sporte, S. E. (2008). Developing citizens: The impact of civic learning opportunities on students' commitment to civic participation. *American Educational Research Journal, 45,* 738–766.

Kail, R. (1990). *The development of memory in children* (3rd ed.). New York, NY: W. H. Freeman.

Kaku, M. (2014). *The future of the mind: The scientific quest to understand, enhance, and empower the mind.* New York, NY: Doubleday.

Kalyuga, S. (2010). Schema acquisition and sources of cognitive load. In J. L. Plass, R. Moreno, & R. Brünken (Eds.), *Cognitive load theory* (pp. 48–64). Cambridge, England: Cambridge University Press.

Kamins, M. L., & Dweck, C. S. (1999). Person versus process praise and criticism: Implications for contingent self-worth and coping. *Developmental Psychology, 35*, 835–847.

Kane, M. J., Brown, L. H., McVay, J. C., Silvia, P. J., Myin-Germeys, I., & Kwapil, T. R. (2007). For whom the mind wanders, and when: An experience-sampling study of working memory and executive control in daily life. *Psychological Science, 18*, 614–621.

Kang, M. J., Hsu, M., Krajbich, I. M., Loewenstein, G., McClure, S. M., Wang, J. T.-Y., & Camerer, C. F. (2009). The wick in the candle of learning: Epistemic curiosity activates reward circuitry and enhances memory. *Psychological Science, 20*, 963–973.

Kaplan, S., & Berman, M. G. (2010). Directed attention as a common resource for executive functioning and self-regulation. *Perspectives on Psychological Science, 5*, 43–57.

Karabenick, S. A., & Sharma, R. (1994). Seeking academic assistance as a strategic learning resource. In P. R. Pintrich, D. R. Brown, & C. E. Weinstein (Eds.), *Student motivation, cognition, and learning: Essays in honor of Wilbert J. McKeachie* (pp. 189–212). Hillsdale, NJ: Erlbaum.

Kardash, C. A. M., & Scholes, R. J. (1996). Effects of pre-existing beliefs, epistemological beliefs, and need for cognition on interpretation of controversial issues. *Journal of Educational Psychology, 88*, 260–271.

Karl, S. R., & Varma, S. (2010, April–May). *The conflict between decimal numbers and whole numbers.* Paper presented at the annual meeting of the American Educational Research Association, Denver, CO.

Karpicke, J. D. (2012). Retrieval-based learning: Active retrieval promotes meaningful learning. *Current Directions in Psychological Science, 21*, 157–163.

Keil, F. C., & Newman, G. E. (2008). Two tales of conceptual change: What changes and what remains the same. In S. Vosniadou (Ed.), *International handbook on conceptual change* (pp. 83–101). New York, NY: Routledge.

Keil, F. C., & Silberstein, C. S. (1996). Schooling and the acquisition of theoretical knowledge. In D. R. Olson & N. Torrance (Eds.), *The handbook of education and human development: New models of learning, teaching, and schooling* (pp. 621–645). Cambridge, MA: Blackwell.

Kelemen, D. (2012). Teleological minds: How natural intuitions about agency and purpose influence learning about evolution. In K. S. Rosengren, S. K. Brem, E. M. Evans, & G. M. Sinatra (Eds.), *Evolution challenges: Integrating research and practice in teaching and learning about evolution* (pp. 66–92). Oxford, England: Oxford University Press.

Kendeou, P., & van den Broek, P. (2005). The effects of readers' misconceptions on comprehension of scientific text. *Journal of Educational Psychology, 97*, 235–245.

Kensinger, E. A. (2007). Negative emotion enhances memory accuracy: Behavioral and neuroimaging evidence. *Current Directions in Psychological Science, 16*, 213–218.

Keogh, B. K. (2003). *Temperament in the classroom.* Baltimore, MD: Brookes.

Kiewra, K. A. (1989). A review of note-taking: The encoding-storage paradigm and beyond. *Educational Psychology Review, 1,* 147–172.

Killeen, P. R. (2001). The four causes of behavior. *Current Directions in Psychological Science, 10,* 136–140.

Kim, J., Lim, J.-S., & Bhargava, M. (1998). The role of affect in attitude formation: A classical conditioning approach. *Journal of the Academy of Marketing Science, 26,* 143–152.

King, A. (1992). Comparison of self-questioning, summarizing, and notetaking-review as strategies for learning from lectures. *American Educational Research Journal, 29,* 303–323.

King, A. (1999). Discourse patterns for mediating peer learning. In A. M. O'Donnell & A. King (Eds.), *Cognitive perspectives on peer learning* (pp. 87–115). Mahwah, NJ: Erlbaum.

King, F. B., Harner, M., & Brown, S. W. (2000). Self-regulatory behavior influences in distance learning. *International Journal of Instructional Media, 27,* 147–155.

Kintsch, W. (1977). Reading comprehension as a function of text structure. In A. S. Reber & D. L. Scarborough (Eds.), *Toward a psychology of reading* (pp. 227–256). New York, NY: Wiley.

Kirby, M., Maggi, S., & D'Angiulli, A. (2011). School start times and the sleep–wake cycle of adolescents: A review of critical evaluation of available evidence. *Educational Researcher, 40,* 56–61.

Kirschner, P. A., & van Merriënboer, J. J. G. (2013). Do learners really know best? Urban legends in education. *Educational Psychologist, 48,* 169–183.

Kitsantas, A., Zimmerman, B. J., & Cleary, T. (2000). The role of observation and emulation in the development of athletic self-regulation. *Journal of Educational Psychology, 92,* 811–817.

Kiyonaga, A., & Egner, T. (2014). The working memory Stroop effect: When internal representations clash with external stimuli. *Psychological Science, 25,* 1619–1629.

Klassen, R. M., & Usher, E. L. (2010). Self-efficacy in educational settings: Recent research and emerging directions. In S. Karabenick & T. C. Urdan (Eds.), *Advances in motivation and achievement: Vol. 16A. The decade ahead: Theoretical perspectives on motivation and achievement* (pp. 1–33). Bingley, England: Emerald Group Publishing.

Klauda, S. L., & Guthrie, J. T. (2008). Relationships of three components of reading fluency to reading comprehension. *Journal of Educational Psychology, 100,* 310–321.

Knoll, L. J., Magis-Weinberg, L., Speekenbrink, M., & Blakemore, S. (2015). Social influence on risk perception during adolescence. *Psychological Science, 26,* 583–592.

Kochanska, G., Gross, J. N., Lin, M.-H., & Nichols, K. E. (2002). Guilt in young children: Development, determinants, and relations with a broader system of standards. *Child Development, 73,* 461–482.

Koffka, K. (1935). *Principles of Gestalt psychology.* New York, NY: Harcourt, Brace.

Köhler, W. (1929). *Gestalt psychology.* New York, NY: Liveright.

Kolb, B., Gibb, R., & Robinson, T. E. (2003). Brain plasticity and behavior. *Current Directions in Psychological Science, 12,* 1–5.

Koltko-Rivera, M. E. (2004). The psychology of worldviews. *Review of General Psychology, 8,* 3–58.

Koob, A. (2009). *The root of thought.* Upper Saddle River, NJ: Pearson.

Kornell, N. (2009). Metacognition in human and animals. *Current Directions in Psychological Science, 18,* 11–15.

Kornell, N., & Bjork, R. A. (2008a). Learning concepts and categories: Is spacing the "enemy of induction"? *Psychological Science, 19,* 585–592.

Kornell, N., & Bjork, R. A. (2008b). Optimizing self-regulated study: The benefits – and costs – of dropping flashcards. *Memory, 16,* 125–136.

Kornell, N., Castell, A. D., Eich, T. S., & Bjork, R. A. (2010). Spacing as the friend of both memory and induction in young and old adults. *Psychology and Aging, 25,* 498–503.

Kornell, N., Son, L. K., & Terrace, H. S. (2007). Transfer of metacognitive skills and hint seeking in monkeys. *Psychological Science, 18,* 64–71.

Kosslyn, S. M. (1985). Mental imagery ability. In R. J. Sternberg (Ed.), *Human abilities: An information-processing approach* (pp. 151–172). New York, NY: W. H. Freeman.

Kosslyn, S. M. (1994). *Image and brain: The resolution of the imagery debate.* Cambridge, MA: MIT Press.

Kounios, J., & Beeman, M. (2009). The *Aha!* moment: The cognitive neuroscience of insight. *Current Directions in Psychological Science, 18,* 210–216.

Kozhevnikov, M., Evans, C., & Kosslyn, S. M. (2014). Cognitive style as environmentally sensitive individual differences in cognition: A modern synthesis and applications in education, business, and management. *Psychological Science in the Public Interest, 15,* 3–33.

Krapp, A., Hidi, S., & Renninger, K. A. (1992). Interest, learning, and development. In K. A. Renninger, S. Hidi, & A. Krapp (Eds.), *The role of interest in learning and development* (pp. 3–25). Hillsdale, NJ: Erlbaum.

Kruglanski, A. W., & Webster, D. M. (1996). Motivated closing of the mind: Seizing and freezing. *Psychological Review, 103,* 263–283.

Kuhbandner, C., Spitzer, B., & Pekrun, R. (2011). Read-out of emotional information from iconic memory: The longevity of threatening stimuli. *Psychological Science, 22,* 695–700.

Kuhn, D. (2001). How do people know? *Psychological Science, 12,* 1–8.

Kuhn, D. (2009). The importance of learning about knowing: Creating a foundation for development of intellectual values. *Child Development Perspectives, 3,* 112–117.

Kuhn, D. (2015). Thinking together and alone. *Educational Researcher, 44,* 46–53.

Kuhn, D., & Crowell, A. (2011). Dialogic argumentation as a vehicle for developing young adolescents' thinking. *Psychological Science, 22,* 545–552.

Kuhn, D., & Franklin, S. (2006). The second decade: What develops (and how)? In W. Damon & R. M. Lerner (Series Eds.), D. Kuhn & R. Siegler (Vol. Eds.), *Handbook of child psychology: Vol. 2. Cognition, perception, and language* (6th ed., pp. 953–993). New York, NY: Wiley.

Kuhn, D., & Park, S.-H. (2005). Epistemological understanding and the development of intellectual values. *International Journal of Educational Research, 43,* 111–124.

Kuhn, D., & Pease, M. (2010). The dual components of developing strategy use: Production and inhibition. In H. S. Waters & W. Schneider (Eds.), *Metacognition, strategy use, and instruction* (pp. 135–159). New York, NY: Guilford.

Kuhn, D., & Weinstock, M. (2002). What is epistemological thinking and why does it matter? In B. K. Hofer & P. R. Pintrich (Eds.), *Personal epistemology: The psychology of beliefs about knowledge and knowing* (pp. 121–144). Mahwah, NJ: Erlbaum.

Kunda, Z. (1990). The case for motivated reasoning. *Psychological Bulletin, 108,* 480–498.

Kurlansky, M. (1997). *Cod: A biography of the fish that changed the world.* New York, NY: Walker Publishing.

Langer, E. J. (2000). Mindful learning. *Current Directions in Psychological Science, 9,* 220–223.

Lee, J., & Shute, V. J. (2010). Personal and social-contextual factors in K–12 academic performance: An integrative perspective on student learning. *Educational Psychologist, 45,* 185–202.

Lee, O. (1999). Science knowledge, world views, and information sources in social and cultural contexts: Making sense after a natural disaster. *American Educational Research Journal, 36,* 187–219.

Lee, V. R. (2010, April–May). *Misconstruals or more? The interactions of orbit diagrams and explanations of the seasons.* Paper presented at the annual meeting of the American Educational Research Association, Denver, CO.

Leelawong, K., & Biswas, G. (2008). Designing learning by teachable agents: The Betty's Brain system. *International Journal of Artificial Intelligence, 18*(3), 181–208.

LeFevre, J., Bisanz, J., & Mrkonjic, J. (1988). Cognitive arithmetic: Evidence for obligatory activation of arithmetic facts. *Memory and Cognition, 16,* 45–53.

Lehrer, R., & Schauble, L. (2006). Cultivating model-based reasoning in science education. In R. K. Sawyer (Ed.), *The Cambridge handbook of the learning sciences* (pp. 371–387). Cambridge, England: Cambridge University Press.

Lenroot, R. K., & Giedd, J. N. (2007). The structural development of the human brain as measured longitudinally with magnetic resonance imaging. In D. Coch, K. W. Fischer, & G. Dawson (Eds.), *Human behavior, learning, and the developing brain: Typical development* (pp. 50–73). New York, NY: Guilford.

Leopold, C., & Mayer, R. E. (2015). An imagination effect in learning from scientific text. *Journal of Educational Psychology, 107,* 47–63.

Lervåg, A., & Hulme, C. (2009). Rapid automatized naming (RAN) taps a mechanism that places constraints on the development of early reading fluency. *Psychological Science, 20,* 1040–1048.

Leu, D. J., O'Byrne, W. I., Zawilinski, L., McVerry, J. G., & Everett-Cacopardo, H. (2009). Expanding the new literacies conversation. *Educational Researcher, 38,* 264–269.

Leuner, B., Mendolia-Loffredo, S., Kozorovitskiy, Y., Samburg, D., Gould, E., & Shors, T. J. (2004). Learning enhances the survival of new neurons beyond the time when the hippocampus is required for memory. *Journal of Neuroscience, 24,* 7477–7481.

Lewandowsky, S., Ecker, U. K. H., Seifert, C. M., Schwarz, N., & Cook, J. (2012). Misinformation and its correction: Continued influence and successful debiasing. *Psychological Science in the Public Interest, 13,* 106–131.

Lewandowsky, S., Oberauer, K., & Gignac, G. E. (2013). NASA faked the moon landing – therefore, (climate) science is a hoax: An anatomy of the motivated rejection of science. *Psychological Science, 24,* 622–633.

Lewis, M., & Sullivan, M. W. (2005). The development of self-conscious emotions. In A. J. Elliot & C. S. Dweck (Eds.), *Handbook of competence and motivation* (pp. 185–201). New York, NY: Guilford Press.

Liben, L. S., & Myers, L. J. (2007). Developmental changes in children's understanding of maps: What, when, and how? In J. M. Plumert & J. P. Spencer (Eds.), *The emerging spatial mind* (pp. 193–218). New York, NY: Oxford University Press.

Lichtman, J. W. (2001). Developmental neurobiology overview: Synapses, circuits, and plasticity. In D. B. Bailey, Jr., J. T. Bruer, F. J. Symons, & J. W. Lichtman (Eds.), *Critical thinking about critical periods* (pp. 27–42). Baltimore, MD: Brookes.

Lieberman, A. (1993). *The emotional life of the toddler.* New York, NY: Free Press.

Lillard, A. S. (1997). Other folks' theories of mind and behavior. *Psychological Science, 8,* 268–274.

Lindsay, P. H., & Norman, D. A. (1977). *Human information processing.* New York, NY: Academic Press.

Linn, M. C. (2008). Teaching for conceptual change: Distinguish or extinguish ideas. In S. Vosniadou (Ed.), *International handbook on conceptual change* (pp. 694–722). New York, NY: Routledge.

Linn, M. C., & Eylon, B.-S. (2011). *Science learning and instruction: Taking advantage of technology to promote knowledge integration.* New York, NY: Routledge.

Little, J. L., Bjork, E. L., Bjork, R. A., & Angello, G. (2012). Multiple-choice tests exonerated, at least of some charges: Fostering test-induced learning and avoiding test-induced forgetting. *Psychological Science, 23,* 1337–1344.

Loftus, E. F. (1991). Made in memory: Distortions in recollection after misleading information. In G. H. Bower (Ed.), *The psychology of learning and motivation: Advances in research and theory* (Vol. 27, pp. 187–215). San Diego, CA: Academic Press.

Loftus, E. F. (1992). When a lie becomes memory's truth: Memory distortion after exposure to misinformation. *Current Directions in Psychological Science, 1,* 121–123.

Loftus, E. F. (1993). The reality of repressed memories. *American Psychologist, 48,* 518–537.

Loftus, E. F. (2003). Make-believe memories. *American Psychologist, 58,* 867–873.

Loftus, E. F. (2004). Memories of things unseen. *Current Directions in Psychological Science, 13,* 145–147.

Loftus, E. F., & Loftus, G. R. (1980). On the permanence of stored information in the human brain. *American Psychologist, 35,* 409–442.

Logie, R. H. (2011). The functional organization and capacity limits of working memory. *Current Directions in Psychological Science, 20,* 240–245.

Lombardi, D., Nussbaum, E. M., & Sinatra, G. M. (2016). Plausibility judgments in conceptual change and epistemic cognition. *Educational Psychologist, 51,* 35–56.

Lombardi, D., & Sinatra, G. M. (2012). College students' perceptions about the plausibility of human-induced climate change. *Research in Science Education, 42,* 201–217.

Lu, H., Zou, Q., Gu, H., Raichle, M. E., Stein, E. A., & Yang, Y. (2012). Rat brains also have a default mode network. *PNAS, 109,* 3979–3984.

Lu, Z.-L., & Sperling, G. (2003). Measuring sensory memory: Magnetoencephalography habituation and psychophysics. In Z.-L. Lu & L. Kaufman (Eds.), *Magnetic source imaging of the human brain* (pp. 319–342). Mahwah, NJ: Erlbaum.

Lu, Z.-L., Williamson, S. J., & Kaufman, L. (1992). Physiological measurements predict the lifetime for human auditory memory of a tone. *Science, 258,* 1668–1670.

Luciana, M., Conklin, H. M., Hooper, C. J., & Yarger, R. S. (2005). The development of nonverbal working memory and executive control processes in adolescents. *Child Development, 76,* 697–712.

Luna, B., Paulsen, D. J., Padmanabhan, A., & Geier, C. (2013). The teenage brain: Cognitive control and motivation. *Current Directions in Psychological Science, 22,* 94–100.

Luna, B., & Sweeney, J. A. (2004). The emergence of collaborative brain function: fMRI studies of the development of response inhibition. *Annals of the New York Academy of Sciences, 1021,* 296–309.

Lundberg, U., & Forsman, L. (1971). Adrenal-medullary and adrenal-cortical responses to understimulation and overstimulation: Comparison between Type A and Type B persons. *Biological Psychology, 9*(2), 79–89.

Luria, A. R. (1987). *The mind of a mnemonist: A little book about a vast memory* (L. Solotaroff, Trans.). Cambridge, MA: Harvard University Press.

Mace, F. C., Belfiore, P. J., & Hutchinson, J. M. (2001). Operant theory and research on self-regulation. In B. Zimmerman & D. Schunk (Eds.), *Learning and academic achievement: Theoretical perspectives* (pp. 39–65). Mahwah, NJ: Erlbaum.

MacLeod, C. M. (1988). Forgotten but not gone: Savings for pictures and words in long-term memory. *Journal of Experimental Psychology: Learning, Memory, and Cognition, 14,* 195–212.

MacLeod, M. D., & Saunders, J. (2008). Retrieval inhibition and memory distortion: Negative consequences of an adaptive process. *Current Directions in Psychological Science, 17,* 26–30.

Madsen, K. M., Hviid, A., Vestergaard, M., Schendel, D., Wohlfahrt, J., Thorsen, P., . . . Melbye, M. (2002). A population-based study of measles, mumps, and rubella vaccination and autism. *New England Journal of Medicine, 347,* 1477–1482.

Maguire, E. A., Gadian, D. G., Johnsrude, I. S., Good, C. D., Ashburnre, J., Frackowiak, R., & Frith, C. D. (2000). Navigation-related structural change in the hippocampi of taxi drivers. *Proceedings of the National Academy of Sciences, USA, 97,* 4398–4403.

Mahoney, M. J., & Thoresen, C. E. (1974). *Self-control: Power to the person.* Monterey, CA: Brooks-Cole.

Mandler, J. M. (2007). On the origins of the conceptual system. *American Psychologist, 62,* 741–751.

Marcus, G. (2008). *Kluge: The haphazard construction of the human mind.* Boston, MA: Houghton Mifflin.

Mareschal, D., Johnson, M. H., Sirois, S., Spratling, M. W., Thomas, M. S. C., & Westermann, G. (2007). *Neuroconstructivism: Vol. 1. How the brain constructs cognition.* Oxford, England: Oxford University Press.

Marmolejo, E. K., Wilder, D. A., & Bradley, L. (2004). A preliminary analysis of the effects of response cards on student performance and participation in an upper division university course. *Journal of Applied Behavior Analysis, 37,* 405–410.

Marsh, E. J. (2007). Retelling is not the same as recalling: Implications for memory. *Current Directions in Psychological Science, 16,* 16–20.

Mason, L. (2010). Beliefs about knowledge and revision of knowledge: On the importance of epistemic beliefs for intentional conceptual change in elementary and middle school students. In L. D. Bendixen & F. C. Feucht (Eds.), *Personal epistemology in the classroom: Theory, research, and implications for practice* (pp. 258–291). Cambridge, England: Cambridge University Press.

Mason, L., Gava, M., & Boldrin, A. (2008). On warm conceptual change: The interplay of text, epistemological beliefs, and topic interest. *Journal of Educational Psychology, 100,* 291–309.

Masten, A. S., Herbers, J. E., Desjardins, C. D., Cutuli, J. J., McCormick, C. M., Sapienza, J. K., . . . Zelazo, P. D. (2012). Executive function skills and school success in young children experiencing homelessness. *Educational Researcher, 41,* 375–384.

Mather, M., & Sutherland, M. R. (2011). Arousal-biased competition in perception and memory. *Perspectives on Psychological Science, 6,* 114–133.

Mayer, R. E. (2010). Fostering scientific reasoning with multimedia instruction. In H. S. Waters & W. Schneider (Eds.), *Metacognition, strategy use, and instruction* (pp. 160–175). New York, NY: Guilford Press.

Mayer, R. E. (2011). Instruction based on visualizations. In R. E. Mayer & P. A. Alexander (Eds.), *Handbook of research on learning and instruction* (pp. 427–445). New York, NY: Routledge.

Mayer, R. E., & Wittrock, M. C. (1996). Problem-solving transfer. In D. C. Berliner & R. C. Calfee (Eds.), *Handbook of educational psychology* (pp. 47–62). New York, NY: Macmillan.

Mayer, R. E., & Wittrock, M. C. (2006). Problem solving. In P. A. Alexander & P. H. Winne (Eds.), *Handbook of educational psychology* (2nd ed., pp. 287–303). Mahwah, NJ: Erlbaum.

Mazzoni, G., & Memon, A. (2003). Imagination can create false autobiographical memories. *Psychological Science, 14,* 186–188.

McCall, R. B., & Plemons, B. W. (2001). The concept of critical periods and their implications for early childhood services. In D. B. Bailey, Jr., J. T. Bruer, F. J. Symons, & J. W. Lichtman (Eds.), *Critical thinking about critical periods* (pp. 267–287). Baltimore, MD: Brookes.

McCaslin, M., & Hickey, D. T. (2001). Self-regulated learning and academic achievement: A Vygotskian view. In B. Zimmerman & D. Schunk (Eds.), *Self-*

regulated learning and academic achievement: Theory, research, and practice (2nd ed., pp. 227–252). Mahwah, NJ: Erlbaum.

McClelland, J. L. (2013). Incorporating rapid neocortical learning of new schema-consistent information into complementary learning systems theory. *Journal of Experimental Psychology: General, 142,* 1190–1210.

McClure, J., Meyer, L. H., Garisch, J., Fischer, R., Weir, K. F., & Walkey, F. H. (2011). Students' attributions for their best and worst marks: Do they relate to achievement? *Contemporary Educational Psychology, 36,* 71–81.

McDaniel, M. A., & Masson, M. E. J. (1985). Altering memory representations through retrieval. *Journal of Experimental Psychology: Learning, Memory, and Cognition, 11,* 371–385.

McDevitt, T. M., & Ormrod, J. E. (2016). *Child development and education* (6th ed.). Columbus, OH: Pearson.

McGivern, R. F., Andersen, J., Byrd, D., Mutter, K. L., & Reilly, J. (2002). Cognitive efficiency on a match to sample task decreases at the onset of puberty in children. *Brain and Cognition, 50*(1), 73–89.

McGuigan, F., & Salmon, K. (2004). The time to talk: The influence of the timing of adult-child talk on children's event memory. *Child Development, 75,* 669–686.

McNally, R. J. (2003). Recovering memories of trauma: A view from the laboratory. *Current Directions in Psychological Science, 12,* 32–35.

Meltzer, L. (Ed.). (2007). *Executive function in education: From theory to practice.* New York, NY: Guilford.

Meltzer, L., Pollica, L. S., & Barzillai, M. (2007). Executive function in the classroom: Embedding strategy instruction into daily teaching practices. In L. Meltzer (Ed.), *Executive function in education: From theory to practice* (pp. 165–193). New York, NY: Guilford.

Metzger, M. J., Flanagin, A. J., & Zwarun, L. (2003). College student Web use, perceptions of information credibility, and verification behavior. *Computers and Education, 41,* 271–290.

Midgley, C. (Ed.). (2002). *Goals, goal structures, and patterns of adaptive learning.* Mahwah, NJ: Erlbaum.

Mikulincer, M. (1994). *Human learned helplessness: A coping perspective.* New York, NY: Plenum Press.

Miller, G. A. (1956). The magical number seven, plus or minus two: Some limits on our capacity for processing information. *Psychological Review, 63,* 81–97.

Miller, G. A. (2010). Mistreating psychology in the decades of the brain. *Perspectives on Psychological Science, 5,* 716–743.

Miller, R. B., & Brickman, S. J. (2004). A model of future-oriented motivation and self-regulation. *Educational Psychology Review, 16,* 9–33.

Minogue, J., & Jones, M. G. (2006). Haptics in education: Exploring an untapped sensory modality. *Review of Educational Research, 76,* 317–348.

Minsky, M. (2006). *The emotion machine: Commonsense thinking, artificial intelligence, and the future of the human mind.* New York, NY: Simon & Schuster.

Mitchell, D. B. (2006). Nonconscious priming after 17 years: Invulnerable implicit memory? *Psychological Science, 17,* 925–929.

Moon, J. (2008). *Critical thinking: An exploration of theory and practice.* London, England: Routledge.

Mosborg, S. (2002). Speaking of history: How adolescents use their knowledge of history in reading the daily news. *Cognition and Instruction, 20*, 323–358.

Mueller, C. M., & Dweck, C. S. (1998). Intelligence praise can undermine motivation and performance. *Journal of Personality and Social Psychology, 75*, 33–52.

Muis, K. R. (2007). The role of epistemic beliefs in self-regulated learning. *Educational Psychologist, 42*, 173–190.

Muis, K. R., Bendixen, L. D., & Haerle, F. C. (2006). Domain-generality and domain-specificity in personal epistemology research: Philosophical and empirical reflections in the development of a theoretical framework. *Educational Psychology Review, 18*, 3–54.

Muis, K. R., & Franco, G. M. (2009). Epistemic beliefs: Setting the standards for self-regulated learning. *Contemporary Educational Psychology, 34*, 306–318.

Murata, A., Fadiga, L., Fogassi, L., Gallese, V., Raos, V., & Rizzolatti, G. (1997). Object representation in the ventral premotor cortex (area F5) of the monkey. *Journal of Neurophysiology, 78*, 2226–2230.

Murphy, P. K. (2007). The eye of the beholder: The interplay of social and cognitive components in change. *Educational Psychologist, 42*, 41–53.

Murphy, P. K., & Mason, L. (2006). Changing knowledge and beliefs. In P. A. Alexander & P. H. Winne (Eds.), *Handbook of educational psychology* (2nd ed., pp. 305–324). Mahwah, NJ: Erlbaum.

Murphy, P. K., Wilkinson, I. A. G., & Soter, A. O. (2011). Instruction based on discussion. In R. E. Mayer & P. A. Alexander (Eds.), *Handbook of research on learning and instruction* (pp. 382–407). New York, NY: Routledge.

Nadel, L., & Jacobs, W. J. (1998). Traumatic memory is special. *Current Directions in Psychological Science, 7*, 154–157.

Nee, D. E., Berman, M. G., Moore, K. S., & Jonides, J. (2008). Neuroscientific evidence about the distinction between short- and long-term memory. *Current Directions in Psychological Science, 17*, 102–106.

Neisser, U., & Harsch, N. (1992). Phantom flashbulbs: False recollections of hearing the news about *Challenger*. In E. Winograd & U. Neisser (Eds.), *Affect and accuracy in recall: Studies of "flashbulb" memories* (pp. 9–31). Cambridge, England: Cambridge University Press.

Nell, V. (2002). Why young men drive dangerously: Implications for injury prevention. *Current Directions in Psychological Science, 11*, 75–79.

Nelson, C. A., III, Thomas, K. M., & de Haan, M. (2006). Neural bases of cognitive development. In W. Damon & R. M. Lerner (Series Eds.), D. Kuhn & R. Siegler (Vol. Eds.), *Handbook of child psychology. Vol. 2: Cognition, perception, and language* (6th ed., pp. 3–57). New York, NY: Wiley.

Nelson, C. E. (2012). Why don't undergraduates really "get" evolution: What can faculty do? In K. S. Rosengren, S. K. Brem, E. M. Evans, & G. M. Sinatra (Eds.), *Evolution challenges: Integrating research and practice in teaching and learning about evolution* (pp. 311–347). Oxford, England: Oxford University Press.

Nelson, K. (1996). *Language in cognitive development: The emergence of the mediated mind*. Cambridge, England: Cambridge University Press.

Nelson, T. O. (1978). Detecting small amounts of information in memory: Savings for nonrecognized items. *Journal of Experimental Psychology: Human Learning and Memory, 4*, 453–468.

Nesbit, J. C., & Adesope, O. O. (2006). Learning with concept and knowledge maps: A meta-analysis. *Review of Educational Research, 76,* 413–448.

Neville, H. J., Stevens, C., Pakulak, E., Bell, T. A., Fanning, J., Klein, S., & Isbell, E. (2013). Family-based training program improves brain function, cognition, and behavior in lower socioeconomic status preschoolers. *PNAS, U.S.A., 110,* 12138–12143.

Newcombe, N. S., Drummey, A. B., Fox, N. A., Lie, E., & Ottinger-Albergs, W. (2000). Remembering early childhood: How much, how, and why (or why not). *Current Directions in Psychological Science, 9,* 55–58.

Ni, Y., & Zhou, Y.-D. (2005). Teaching and learning fraction and rational numbers: The origins and implications of whole number bias. *Educational Psychologist, 40,* 27–52.

Niederhauser, D. S. (2008). Educational hypertext. In J. M. Spector, M. D. Merrill, J. van Merriënboer, & M. P. Driscoll (Eds.), *Handbook of research on educational communications and technology* (3rd ed., pp. 199–210). New York, NY: Erlbaum.

Nisbett, R. E. (2009). *Intelligence and how to get it.* New York, NY: Norton.

Nisbett, R. E., Aronson, J., Blair, C., Dickens, W., Flynn, J., Halpern, D. F., & Turkheimer, E. (2012). Intelligence: New findings and theoretical developments. *American Psychologist, 67,* 130–159.

Nokes, J. D., & Dole, J. A. (2004). Helping adolescent readers through explicit strategy instruction. In T. L. Jetton & J. A. Dole (Eds.), *Adolescent literacy research and practice* (pp. 162–182). New York, NY: Guilford.

Nolen, S. B. (1996). Why study? How reasons for learning influence strategy selection. *Educational Psychology Review, 8,* 335–355.

Nørby, S. (2015). Why forget? On the adaptive value of memory loss. *Perspectives on Psychological Science, 10,* 551–578.

Novak, J. D. (1998). *Learning, creating, and using knowledge: Concept maps as facilitative tools in schools and corporations.* Mahwah, NJ: Erlbaum.

Núñez, J. C., González-Pienda, J. A., González-Pumariega, S., Roces, C., Alvarez, L., González, P., . . . Rodríguez, S. (2005). Subgroups of attributional profiles in students with learning disabilities and their relation to self-concept and academic goals. *Learning Disabilities Research and Practice, 20,* 86–97.

Nussbaum, E. M. (2008). Collaborative discourse, argumentation, and learning: Preface and literature review. *Contemporary Educational Psychology, 33,* 345–359.

Nussbaum, E. M., & Edwards, O. V. (2011). Critical questions and argument stratagems: A framework for enhancing and analyzing students' reasoning practices. *Journal of the Learning Sciences, 20,* 443–488.

Nuthall, G. (2000). The anatomy of memory in the classroom: Understanding how students acquire memory processes from classroom activities in science and social studies units. *American Educational Research Journal, 37,* 247–304.

Oakes, L. M., & Bauer, P. J. (Eds.). (2007). *Short- and long-term memory in infancy and early childhood: Taking the first steps toward remembering.* New York, NY: Oxford University Press.

Oatley, K., & Nundy, S. (1996). Rethinking the role of emotions in education. In D. R. Olson & N. Torrance (Eds.), *The handbook of education and human development: New models of learning, teaching, and schooling* (pp. 257–274). Cambridge, MA: Blackwell.

Oberauer, K., & Hein, L. (2012). Attention to information in working memory. *Current Directions in Psychological Science, 21*, 164–169.

Oberheim, N. A., Takano, T., Han, X., He, W., Lin, J. H. C., Wang, F., ... Nedergaard, M. (2009). Uniquely hominid features of adult human astrocytes. *Journal of Neuroscience, 29*, 3276–3287.

Ólafsdóttir, H. F., Carpenter, F., & Barry, C. (2016). Coordinated grid and place cell replay during rest. *Nature Neuroscience*. Advance online publication. doi: 10.1038/nn.4291

Olson, M. A., & Fazio, R. H. (2001). Implicit attitude formation through classical conditioning. *Psychological Science, 12*, 413–417.

Ormrod, J. E. (2015). *Essentials of educational psychology* (4th ed.). Columbus, OH: Pearson.

Ormrod, J. E. (2016a). *Human learning* (7th ed.). Columbus, OH: Pearson.

Ormrod, J. E. (2016b). Teaching *across* rather than *within* theories of learning: A "big ideas" approach to organizing educational psychology courses. In M. C. Smith & N. DeFrates-Densch (Eds.), *Challenges and innovations in educational psychology teaching and learning* (Chapter 1, pp. 3–14). Charlotte, NC: Information Age.

Ornstein, R. (1997). *The right mind: Making sense of the hemispheres*. San Diego, CA: Harcourt Brace.

Osgood, C. E. (1949). The similarity paradox in human learning: A resolution. *Psychological Review, 56*, 132–143.

Otero, J. (2009). Question generation and anomaly detection in texts. In D. J. Hacker, J. Dunlosky, & A. C. Graesser (Eds.), *Handbook of metacognition in education* (pp. 47–59). New York, NY: Routledge.

Öztekin, I., Davachi, L., & McElree, B. (2010). Are representations in working memory distinct from representations in long-term memory? Neural evidence in support of a single store. *Psychological Science, 21*, 1123–1133.

Paller, K. A., Voss, J. L., & Westerberg, C. E. (2009). Investigating the awareness of remembering. *Perspectives on Psychological Science, 4*, 185–199.

Palmiero, M., Belardinelli, M. O., Nardo, D., Sestieri, C., Di Matteo, R., D'Ausillo, A., & Romani, G. L. (2009). Mental imagery generation in different modalities activates sensory-motor areas. *Cognitive Processing, 10*(Supplement 2), S268–S271.

Pansky, A., & Koriat, A. (2004). The basic-level convergence effect in memory distortions. *Psychological Science, 15*, 52–59.

Papageorgiou, K. A., Smith, T. J., Wu, R., Johnson, M. H., Kirkham, N. Z., & Ronald, A. (2014). Individual differences in infant fixation duration related to attention and behavioral control in childhood. *Psychological Science, 25*, 1371–1379.

Paris, S. G., & Cunningham, A. E. (1996). Children becoming students. In D. C. Berliner & R. C. Calfee (Eds.), *Handbook of educational psychology* (pp. 117–147). New York, NY: Macmillan.

Paris, S. G., & Paris, A. H. (2001). Classroom applications of research on self-regulated learning. *Educational Psychologist, 36*, 89–101.

Parker, E. S., Cahill, L., & McGaugh, J. L. (2006). A case of unusual autobiographical remembering. *Neurocase, 12*, 35–49.

Parker, J. (1995). Age differences in source monitoring of performed and imagined actions on immediate and delayed tests. *Journal of Experimental Child Psychology, 60,* 84–101.

Pashler, H. (1992). Attentional limitations in doing two tasks at the same time. *Current Directions in Psychological Science, 1,* 44–48.

Pashler, H., Rohrer, D., Cepeda, N. J., & Carpenter, S. K. (2007). Enhancing learning and retarding forgetting: Choices and consequences. *Psychonomic Bulletin & Review, 14,* 187–193.

Patihis, L., Ho, L. Y., Tingen, I. W., Lilienfeld, S. O., & Loftus, E. F. (2014). Are the "memory wars" over? A scientist-practitioner gap in beliefs about repressed memory. *Psychological Science, 25,* 519–530.

Payne, J. D., & Kensinger, E. A. (2010). Sleep's role in the consolidation of emotional episodic memories. *Current Directions in Psychological Science, 19,* 290–295.

Pea, R. D. (1993). Practices of distributed intelligence and designs for education. In G. Salomon (Ed.), *Distributed cognitions: Psychological and educational considerations* (pp. 47–87). Cambridge, England: Cambridge University Press.

Pekrun, R. (2006). The control-value theory of achievement emotions: Assumptions, corollaries, and implications for educational research and practice. *Educational Psychology Review, 18,* 315–341.

Pekrun, R., Goetz, T., Daniels, L. M., Stupnisky, R. H., & Perry, R. P. (2010). Boredom in achievement settings: Exploring control–value antecedents and performance outcomes of a neglected emotion. *Journal of Educational Psychology, 102,* 531–549.

Pellegrini, A. D., & Bjorklund, D. F. (1997). The role of recess in children's cognitive performance. *Educational Psychologist, 32,* 35–40.

Pelucchi, B., Hay, J. F., & Saffran, J. R. (2009). Statistical learning in a natural language by 8-month-old infants. *Child Development, 80,* 674–685.

Pereira, F., Detre, G., & Botvinick, M. (2011). Generating text from functional brain images. *Frontiers in Human Neuroscience, 5*(72). doi: 10.3389/fnhum.2011.00072

Perfect, T. J. (2002). When does eyewitness confidence predict performance? In T. J. Perfect & B. L. Schwartz (Eds.), *Applied metacognition* (pp. 95–120). Cambridge, England: Cambridge University Press.

Perkins, D. N., & Ritchhart, R. (2004). When is good thinking? In D. Y. Dai & R. J. Sternberg (Eds.), *Motivation, emotion, and cognition: Integrative perspectives on intellectual functioning and development* (pp. 351–384). Mahwah, NJ: Erlbaum.

Perkins, D. N., & Salomon, G. (1989). Are cognitive skills context-bound? *Educational Researcher, 18*(1), 16–25.

Peterson, C. (2006). *A primer in positive psychology.* New York, NY: Oxford University Press.

Peterson, C., Maier, S. F., & Seligman, M. E. P. (1993). *Learned helplessness: A theory for the age of personal control.* New York, NY: Oxford University Press.

Peterson, E., & Welsh, M. C. (2014). The development of hot and cold executive functions: Are we getting warmer? In S. Goldstein & J. Naglieri (Eds.), *Handbook of executive function* (pp. 45–67). New York, NY: Springer.

Peterson, L. R., & Peterson, M. J. (1959). Short-term retention of individual items. *Journal of Experimental Psychology, 58*, 193–198.

Peverly, S. T., Brobst, K. E., Graham, M., & Shaw, R. (2003). College adults are not good at self-regulation: A study on the relationship of self-regulation, note taking, and test taking. *Journal of Educational Psychology, 95*, 335–346.

Pezdek, K., Finger, K., & Hodge, D. (1997). Planting false childhood memories: The role of event plausibility. *Psychological Science, 8*, 437–441.

Piaget, J. (1952). *The origins of intelligence in children* (M. Cook, Trans.). New York, NY: W. W. Norton.

Piaget, J. (1970). Piaget's theory. In P. H. Mussen (Ed.), *Carmichael's manual of psychology* (pp. 703–732). New York, NY: Wiley.

Pianta, R. C., Barnett, W. S., Burchinal, M., & Thornburg, K. R. (2009). The effects of preschool education: What we know, how public policy is or is not aligned with the evidence base, and what we need to know. *Psychological Science in the Public Interest, 10*, 49–88.

Pillow, B. H. (2002). Children's and adults' evaluation of the certainty of deductive inferences, inductive inferences, and guesses. *Child Development, 73*, 779–792.

Pintrich, P. R. (2003). A motivational science perspective on the role of student motivation in learning and teaching contexts. *Journal of Educational Psychology, 95*, 667–686.

Pintrich, P. R., Marx, R. W., & Boyle, R. A. (1993). Beyond cold conceptual change: The role of motivational beliefs and classroom contextual factors in the process of conceptual change. *Review of Educational Research, 63*, 167–199.

Plass, J. L., Moreno, R., & Brünken, R. (Eds.). (2010). *Cognitive load theory.* Cambridge, England: Cambridge University Press.

Porat, D. A. (2004). *It's not written here, but this is what happened:* Students' cultural comprehension of textbook narratives on the Israeli-Arab conflict. *American Educational Research Journal, 41*, 963–996.

Porter, S., & Peace, K. A. (2007). The scars of memory: A prospective, longitudinal investigation of the consistency of traumatic and positive emotional memories in adulthood. *Psychological Science, 18*, 435–441.

Posner, M. I., & Rothbart, M. K. (2007). *Educating the human brain.* Washington, DC: American Psychological Association.

Poston, B., Van Gemmert, A. W. A., Barduson, B., & Stelmach, G. E. (2009). Movement structure in young and elderly adults during goal-directed movements of the left and right arm. *Brain and Cognition, 69*, 30–38.

Pressley, M., Borkowski, J. G., & Schneider, W. (1987). Cognitive strategies: Good strategy users coordinate metacognition and knowledge. In R. Vasta & G. Whitehurst (Eds.), *Annals of child development* (Vol. 5, pp. 80–129). New York, NY: JAI Press.

Pressley, M., Levin, J. R., & Delaney, H. D. (1982). The mnemonic keyword method. *Review of Educational Research, 52*, 61–91.

Pressley, M., Yokoi, L., Van Meter, P., Van Etten, S., & Freebern, G. (1997). Some of the reasons why preparing for exams is so hard: What can be done to make it easier? *Educational Psychology Review, 9*, 1–38.

Price, J., with Davis, B. (2008). *The woman who can't forget: The extraordinary story of living with the most remarkable memory known to science*. New York, NY: Free Press.

Prince, S. E., Tsukiura, T., & Cabeza, R. (2007). Distinguishing the neural correlates of episodic memory encoding and semantic memory retrieval. *Psychological Science, 18*, 144–151.

Pritchard, R. (1990). The effects of cultural schemata on reading processing strategies. *Reading Research Quarterly, 25*, 273–295.

Proctor, R. W., & Dutta, A. (1995). *Skill acquisition and human performance*. Thousand Oaks, CA: Sage.

Quinn, P. C. (2007). On the infant's prelinguistic conception of spatial relations: Three developmental trends and their implications for spatial language learning. In J. M. Plumert & J. P. Spencer (Eds.), *The emerging spatial mind* (pp. 117–141). New York, NY: Oxford University Press.

Raaijmakers, J. G. W., & Jakab, E. (2013). Is forgetting caused by inhibition? *Current Directions in Psychological Science, 22*, 205–209.

Rabin, L. A., Fogel, J., & Nutter-Upham, K. E. (2011). Academic procrastination in college students: The role of self-reported executive function. *Journal of Clinical and Experimental Neuropsychology, 33*, 344–357.

Ramey, C. T., & Ramey, S. L. (1998). Early intervention and early experience. *American Psychologist, 53*, 109–120.

Ramsay, C. M., & Sperling, R. A. (2010). Designating reader perspective to increase comprehension and interest. *Contemporary Educational Psychology, 35*, 215–227.

Rasch, B., & Born, J. (2008). Reactivation and consolidation of memory during sleep. *Current Directions in Psychological Science, 17*, 188–192.

Ratey, J. J. (2001). *A user's guide to the brain: Perception, attention, and the four theaters of the brain*. New York, NY: Vintage Books.

Rattan, A., Good, C., & Dweck, C. S. (2012). "It's ok – Not everyone can be good at math": Instructors with an entity theory comfort (and demotivate) students. *Journal of Personality and Social Psychology, 48*, 731–737.

Ray, W. J., Odenwald, M., Neuner, F., Schauer, M., Ruf, M., Wienbruch, C., … Elbert, T. (2006). Decoupling neural networks from reality: Dissociative experiences in torture victims are reflected in abnormal brain waves in left frontal cortex. *Psychological Science, 17*, 825–829.

Rayner, K., Schotter, E. R., Masson, M. E. J., Potter, M. C., & Treiman, R. (2016). So much to read, so little time: How do we read, and can speed reading help? *Psychological Science in the Public Interest, 17*(1), 4–34.

Rebok, G. W., Ball, K., Guey, L. T., Jones, R. N., Kim, H.-Y., King, J. W., … Willis, S. L. (2014). Ten-year effects of the ACTIVE cognitive training trial on cognition and everyday functioning in older adults, *Journal of the American Geriatrics Society, 62*(1), 16–24.

Reisberg, D. (Ed.). (1992). *Auditory imagery*. Hillsdale, NJ: Erlbaum.

Reyna, V. F., Chapman, S. B., Dougherty, M. R., & Confrey, J. (Eds.). (2012). *The adolescent brain: Learning, reasoning, and decision making*. Washington, DC: American Psychological Association.

Reynolds, R. E., & Shirey, L. L. (1988). The role of attention in studying and learning. In C. E. Weinstein, E. T. Goetz, & P. A. Alexander (Eds.), *Learning and study strategies: Issues in assessment, instruction, and evaluation*. San Diego, CA: Academic Press.

Reynolds, R. E., Taylor, M. A., Steffensen, M. S., Shirey, L. L., & Anderson, R. C. (1982). Cultural schemata and reading comprehension. *Reading Research Quarterly, 17*, 353–366.

Reznick, S. (2007). Working memory in infants and toddlers. In L. M. Oakes & P. J. Bauer (Eds.), *Short- and long-term memory in infancy and early childhood: Taking the first steps toward remembering* (pp. 3–26). New York, NY: Oxford University Press.

Reznitskaya, A., & Gregory, M. (2013). Student thought and classroom language: Examining the mechanisms of change in dialogic teaching. *Educational Psychologist, 48*, 114–133.

Ricco, R., Pierce, S. S., & Medinilla, C. (2010). Epistemic beliefs and achievement motivation in early adolescence. *Journal of Early Adolescence, 30*, 305–340.

Risley, T. R., & Hart, B. (2006). Promoting early language development. In N. F. Watt, C. Ayoub, R. H. Bradley, J. E. Puma, & W. A. LeBoeuf (Eds.), *The crisis in young mental health: Critical issues and effective programs: Vol. 4. Early intervention programs and policies* (pp. 83–88). Westport, CT: Praeger.

Ristic, J., & Enns, J. T. (2015). The changing face of attentional development. *Current Directions in Psychological Science, 24*, 24–31.

Rizzolatti, G., & Sinigaglia, C. (2008). *Mirrors in the brain: How our minds share actions and emotions* (F. Anderson, Trans.). Oxford, England: Oxford University Press.

Robinson, D. H., & Kiewra, K. A. (1995). Visual argument: Graphic organizers are superior to outlines in improving learning from text. *Journal of Educational Psychology, 87*, 455–467.

Roediger, H. L., Dudai, Y., & Fitzpatrick, S. M. (2007). *Science of memory: Concepts*. New York, NY: Oxford University Press.

Roets, A., & Van Hiel, A. (2011). Allport's prejudiced personality today: Need for closure as the motivated cognitive basis of prejudice. *Current Directions in Psychological Science, 20*, 349–354.

Rogoff, B. (1990). *Apprenticeship in thinking: Cognitive development in social context*. New York, NY: Oxford University Press.

Rogowsky, B. A., Calhoun, B. M., & Tallal, P. (2015). Matching learning style to instructional method: Effects on comprehension. *Journal of Educational Psychology, 107*, 64–78.

Rohrer, D., Dedrick, R. F., & Stershic, S. (2015). Interleaved practice improves mathematics learning. *Journal of Educational Psychology, 107*, 900–908.

Rohrer, D., & Pashler, H. (2010). Recent research on human learning challenges conventional instructional strategies. *Educational Researcher, 39*, 406–412.

Román, P., Soriano, M. F., Gómez-Ariza, C. J., & Bajo, M. T. (2009). Retrieval-induced forgetting and executive control. *Psychological Science, 20*, 1053–1058.

Rosch, E. H. (1978). Principles of categorization. In E. Rosch & B. Lloyd (Eds.), *Cognition and categorization* (pp. 27–48). Hillsdale, NJ: Erlbaum.

Rosengren, K. S., Brem, S. K., Evans, E. M., & Sinatra, G. M. (Eds.). (2012). *Evolution challenges: Integrating research and practice in teaching and learning about evolution*. Oxford, England: Oxford University Press.

Rosenshine, B., Meister, C., & Chapman, S. (1996). Teaching students to generate questions: A review of the intervention studies. *Review of Educational Research, 66,* 181–221.

Ross, B. H., & Spalding, T. L. (1994). Concepts and categories. In R. J. Sternberg (Ed.), *Handbook of perception and cognition* (Vol. 12, pp. 119–148). New York, NY: Academic Press.

Roth, K. (1990). Developing meaningful conceptual understanding in science. In B. F. Jones & L. Idol (Eds.), *Dimensions of thinking and cognitive instruction* (pp. 139–175). Hillsdale, NJ: Erlbaum.

Rothbart, M. K. (2011). *Becoming who we are: Temperament and personality in development.* New York, NY: Guilford.

Rothbart, M. K., & Hwang, J. (2005). Temperament and the development of competence and motivation. In A. J. Elliot & C. S. Dweck (Eds.), *Handbook of competence and motivation* (pp. 167–184). New York, NY: Guilford.

Rothbart, M. K., Sheese, B. E., & Posner, M. I. (2007). Executive attention and effortful control: Linking temperament, brain networks, and genes. *Child Development Perspectives, 1,* 2–7.

Rovee-Collier, C. (1993). The capacity for long-term memory in infancy. *Current Directions in Psychological Science, 2,* 130–135.

Rovira, E., Mackie, R. S., Clark, N., Squire, P. N., Hendricks, M. D., Pulido, A. M., & Greenwood, P. M. (2016). A role for attention during wilderness navigation: Comparing effects of BDNF, KIBRA, and CHRNA4. *Neuropsychology, 30,* 709–719.

Rowe, M. B. (1974). Wait-time and rewards as instructional variables, their influence on language, logic, and fate control: Part I. Wait time. *Journal of Research in Science Teaching, 11,* 81–94.

Rubin, D. C. (2006). The basic-systems model of episodic memory. *Perspectives on Psychological Science, 1,* 277–311.

Rule, D. C., & Bendixen, L. D. (2010). The integrative model of personal epistemology development: Theoretical underpinnings and implications for education. In L. D. Bendixen & F. C. Feucht (Eds.), *Personal epistemology in the classroom: Theory, research, and implications for practice* (pp. 94–123). Cambridge, England: Cambridge University Press.

Rumelhart, D. E., & Ortony, A. (1977). The representation of knowledge in memory. In R. C. Anderson, R. J. Spiro, & W. E. Montague (Eds.), *Schooling and the acquisition of knowledge* (pp. 99–136). Hillsdale, NJ: Erlbaum.

Runco, M. A., & Chand, I. (1995). Cognition and creativity. *Educational Psychology Review, 7,* 243–267.

Rutter, M. L. (1997). Nature-nurture integration: The example of antisocial behavior. *American Psychologist, 52,* 390–398.

Ryan, A. M., & Shim, S. S. (2012). Changes in help seeking from peers during early adolescence: Associations with changes in achievement and perceptions of teachers. *Journal of Educational Psychology, 104,* 1122–1134.

Sadler, P. M., Sonnert, G., Coyle, H. P., Cook-Smith, N., & Miller, J. L. (2013). The influence of teachers' knowledge on student learning in middle school physical science classrooms. *American Educational Research Journal, 50,* 1020–1049.

Sadoski, M., & Paivio, A. (2001). *Imagery and text: A dual coding theory of reading and writing*. Mahwah, NJ: Erlbaum.

Salomon, G. (1993). No distribution without individuals' cognition: A dynamic interactional view. In G. Salomon (Ed.), *Distributed cognitions: Psychological and educational considerations* (pp. 111–138). Cambridge, England: Cambridge University Press.

Saltz, E. (1971). *The cognitive bases of human learning*. Homewood, IL: Dorsey.

Samarova, E. I., Bravarenko, N. I., Korshunova, T. A., Gulyaeva, N. V., Palotás, A., & Balaban, P. M. (2005). Effect of ß-amyloid peptide on behavior and synaptic plasticity in terrestial snail. *Brain Research Bulletin, 67*, 40–45.

Sandoval, W. A., Sodian, B., Koerber, S., & Wong, J. (2014). Developing children's early competencies to engage with science. *Educational Psychologist, 49*, 139–152.

Sarama, J., & Clements, D. H. (2009). "Concrete" computer manipulatives in mathematics education. *Child Development Perspectives, 3*, 145–150.

Scarr, S., & McCartney, K. (1983). How people make their own environments: A theory of genotype environment effects. *Child Development, 54*, 424–435.

Schab, F. (1990). Odors and the remembrance of things past. *Journal of Experimental Psychology: Learning, Memory, and Cognition, 16*, 648–655.

Schacter, D. L. (1999). The seven sins of memory: Insights from psychology and neuroscience. *American Psychologist, 54*, 182–203.

Schacter, D. L. (2012). Adaptive constructive processes and the future of memory. *American Psychologist, 67*, 603–613.

Schank, R. C., & Abelson, R. P. (1977). *Scripts, plans, goals, and understanding: An inquiry into human knowledge structures*. Hillsdale, NJ: Erlbaum.

Schneider, W. (2010). Metacognition and memory development in childhood and adolescence. In H. S. Waters & W. Schneider (Eds.), *Metacognition, strategy use, and instruction* (pp. 54–81). New York, NY: Guilford.

Schneider, W., & Pressley, M. (1989). *Memory development between 2 and 20*. New York, NY: Springer-Verlag.

Schneps, M. H., & Sadler, P. M. (1989). *A private universe* [video]. Cambridge, MA: Harvard-Smithsonian Center for Astrophysics.

Schommer, M. (1994). An emerging conceptualization of epistemological beliefs and their role in learning. In R. Garner & P. A. Alexander (Eds.), *Beliefs about text and instruction with text* (pp. 25–40). Hillsdale, NJ: Erlbaum.

Schommer, M., Calvert, C., Gariglietti, G., & Bajaj, A. (1997). The development of epistemological beliefs among secondary students: A longitudinal study. *Journal of Educational Psychology, 89*, 37–40.

Schommer-Aikins, M. (2004). Explaining the epistemological belief system: Introducing the embedded systemic model and coordinated research approach. *Educational Psychologist, 39*, 19–29.

Schommer-Aikins, M., Bird, M., & Bakken, L. (2010). Manifestations of an epistemological belief system in preschool to grade twelve classrooms. In L. D. Bendixen & F. C. Feucht (Eds.), *Personal epistemology in the classroom: Theory, research, and implications for practice* (pp. 31–54). Cambridge, England: Cambridge University Press.

Schraw, G. (2006). Knowledge: Structures and processes. In P. A. Alexander & P. H. Winne (Eds.), *Handbook of educational psychology* (2nd ed., pp. 245–263). Mahwah, NJ: Erlbaum.

Schraw, G., McCrudden, M. T., Lehman, S., & Hoffman, B. (2011). An overview of thinking skills. In G. Schraw & D. R. Robinson (Eds.), *Assessment of higher order thinking skills* (pp. 19–45). Charlotte, NC: Information Age.

Schraw, G., & Moshman, D. (1995). Metacognitive theories. *Educational Psychology Review, 7*, 351–371.

Schunk, D. H. (1989). Social cognitive theory and self-regulated learning. In B. J. Zimmerman & D. H. Schunk (Eds.), *Self-regulated learning and academic achievement: Theory, research, and practice* (pp. 83–110). New York, NY: Springer-Verlag.

Schunk, D. H., Hanson, A. R., & Cox, P. D. (1987). Peer-model attributes and children's achievement behaviors. *Journal of Educational Psychology, 79*, 54–61.

Schunk, D. H., & Pajares, F. (2004). Self-efficacy in education revisited: Empirical and applied evidence. In D. M. McNerney & S. Van Etten (Eds.), *Big theories revisited* (pp. 115–138). Greenwich, CT: Information Age.

Schunk, D. H., & Pajares, F. (2005). Competence perceptions and academic functioning. In A. J. Elliot & C. S. Dweck (Eds.), *Handbook of competence and motivation* (pp. 85–104). New York, NY: Guilford.

Schunk, D. H., & Zimmerman, B. J. (Eds.). (1998). *Self-regulated learning: From teaching to self-reflective practice*. New York, NY: Guilford Press.

Schwarz, N., & Skurnik, I. (2003). Feeling and thinking: Implications for problem solving. In J. E. Davidson & R. J. Sternberg (Eds.), *The psychology of problem solving* (pp. 263–290). Cambridge, England: Cambridge University Press.

Segedy, J. R., Kinnebrew, J. S., & Biswas, G. (2013). The effect of contextualized conversational feedback in a complex open-ended learning environment. *Educational Technology Research and Development, 61*(1), 71–89.

Seligman, M. E. P. (1991). *Learned optimism*. New York, NY: Alfred Knopf.

Seligman, M. E. P., Railton, P., Baumeister, R. F., & Sripada, C. (2013). Navigating into the future or driven by the past. *Perspectives on Psychological Science, 8*, 119–141.

Semb, G. B., & Ellis, J. A. (1994). Knowledge taught in school: What is remembered? *Review of Educational Research, 64*, 253–286.

Sergeant, J. (1996). A theory of attention: An information processing perspective. In G. R. Lyon & N. A. Krasnegor (Eds.), *Attention, memory, and executive function* (pp. 57–69). Baltimore, MD: Paul H. Brookes.

Serra, M. J., & Metcalfe, J. (2009). Effective implementation of metacognition. In D. J. Hacker, J. Dunlosky, & A. C. Graesser (Eds.), *Handbook of metacognition in education* (pp. 278–298). New York, NY: Routledge.

Shah, P., & Miyake, A. (1996). The separability of working memory resources for spatial thinking and language processing: An individual differences approach. *Journal of Experimental Psychology: General, 125*, 4–27.

Shanahan, C. (2004). Teaching science through literacy. In T. L. Jetton & J. A. Dole (Eds.), *Adolescent literacy research and practice* (pp. 75–93). New York, NY: Guilford.

Sharot, T., Martorella, E. A., Delgado, M. R., & Phelps, E. A. (2007). How personal experience modulates the neural circuitry of memories of September 11. *Proceedings of the National Academy of Sciences, USA, 104*, 389–394.

Shen, H., Sabaliauskas, N., Sherpa, A., Fenton, A. A., Stelzer, A., Aoki, C., & Smith, S. S. (2010). A critical role for α4βδ GABA$_A$ receptors in shaping learning deficits at puberty in mice. *Science, 327*(5972), 1515–1518.

Sherman, D. K., & Cohen, G. L. (2002). Accepting threatening information: Self-affirmation and the reduction of defensive biases. *Current Directions in Psychological Science, 11*, 119–123.

Shimamura, A. P. (2014). Remembering the past: Neural substrates underlying episodic encoding and retrieval. *Current Directions in Psychological Science, 23*, 257–263.

Shors, T. J. (2014). The adult brain makes new neurons, and effortful learning keeps them alive. *Current Directions in Psychological Science, 23*, 311–318.

Siegel, D. J. (2012). *The developing mind: How relationships and the brain interact to shape who we are* (2nd ed.). New York, NY: Guilford.

Sinatra, G. M., Kardash, C. M., Taasoobshirazi, G., & Lombardi, D. (2012). Promoting attitude change and expressed willingness to take action toward climate change in college students. *Instructional Science, 40*, 1–17.

Sinatra, G. M., Kienhues, D., & Hofer, B. K. (2014). Addressing challenges to public understanding of science: Epistemic cognition, motivated reasoning, and conceptual change. *Educational Psychologist, 49*, 123–138.

Sinatra, G. M., & Mason, L. (2008). Beyond knowledge: Learner characteristics influencing conceptual change. In S. Vosniadou (Ed.), *International handbook on conceptual change* (pp. 560–582). New York, NY: Routledge.

Sinatra, G. M., Southerland, S. A., McConaughy, F., & Demastes, J. (2003). Intentions and beliefs in students' understanding and acceptance of biological evolution. *Journal of Research on Science Teaching, 40*, 510–528.

Sligte, I. G., Scholte, H. S., & Lamme, V. A. F. (2009). V4 activity predicts the strength of visual short-term memory representations. *Journal of Neuroscience, 29*, 7432–7438.

Smith, E. E. (2000). Neural bases of human working memory. *Current Directions in Psychological Science, 9*, 45–49.

Smith, E. R., & Conrey, F. R. (2009). The social context of cognition. In P. Robbins & M. Aydede (Eds.), *The Cambridge handbook of situated cognition* (pp. 454–466). Cambridge, England: Cambridge University Press.

Smith, G. E. (2016). Healthy cognitive aging and dementia prevention. *American Psychologist, 71*, 268–275.

Sneider, C., & Pulos, S. (1983). Children's cosmographies: Understanding the earth's shape and gravity. *Science Education, 67*, 205–221.

Soderstrom, N. C., Kerr, T. K., & Bjork, R. A. (2016). The critical importance of retrieval – and spacing – for learning. *Psychological Science, 27*, 223–230.

Soemer, A., & Schwan, S. (2012). Visual mnemonics for language learning: Static pictures versus animated morphs. *Journal of Educational Psychology, 104*, 565–579.

Solomon, P., Kubzansky, P. E., Leiderman, P. H., Mendelson, J. H., Trumbull, R., & Wexler, D. (1961). *Sensory deprivation: A symposium held at Harvard Medical School.* Cambridge, MA: Harvard University Press.

Somerville, L. H., Jones, R. M., & Casey, B. J. (2010). A time of change: Behavioral and neural correlates of adolescent sensitivity to appetitive and aversive environmental cues. *Brain and Cognition, 72,* 124–133.

Southerland, S. A., & Sinatra, G. M. (2003). Learning about biological evolution: A special case of intentional conceptual change. In G. M. Sinatra & P. R. Pintrich (Eds.), *Intentional conceptual change* (pp. 317–345). Mahwah, NJ: Erlbaum.

Sowell, E. R., Thompson, P. M., Holmes, C. J., Jernigan, T. L., & Toga, A. W. (1999). *In vivo* evidence for post-adolescent brain maturation in frontal and striatal regions. *Nature Neuroscience, 2,* 859–861.

Spalding, K. L., Bergmann, O., Alkass, K., Bernard, S., Salehpour, M., Huttner, H. B., . . . Frisén, J. (2013). Dynamics of hippocampal neurogenesis in adult humans. *Cell, 153,* 1219–1227.

Speer, N. K., Reynolds, J. R., Swallow, K. M., & Zacks, J. M. (2009). Reading stories activates neural representations of visual and motor experiences. *Psychological Science, 20,* 989–999.

Spunt, R. P., Falk, E. B., & Lieberman, M. D. (2010). Dissociable neural systems support retrieval of *how* and *why* action knowledge. *Psychological Science, 21,* 1593–1598.

Stahl, S. A., & Shanahan, C. (2004). Learning to think like a historian: Disciplinary knowledge through critical analysis of multiple documents. In T. L. Jetton & J. A. Dole (Eds.), *Adolescent literacy research and practice* (pp. 94–115). New York, NY: Guilford.

Stanovich, K. E., West, R. F., & Toplak, M. E. (2012). Judgment and decision making in adolescence: Separating intelligence from rationality. In V. F. Reyna, S. B. Chapman, M. R. Dougherty, & J. Confrey (Eds.), *The adolescent brain: Learning, reasoning, and decision making* (pp. 337–378). Washington, DC: American Psychological Association.

Steinberg, L. (2009). Should the science of adolescent brain development inform public policy? *American Psychologist, 64,* 739–750.

Stepans, J. (1991). Developmental patterns in students' understanding of physics concepts. In S. M. Glynn, R. H. Yeany, & B. K. Britton (Eds.), *The psychology of learning science* (pp. 89–115). Hillsdale, NJ: Erlbaum.

Sternberg, R. J. (2005). Intelligence, competence, and expertise. In A. J. Elliot & C. S. Dweck (Eds.), *Handbook of competence and motivation* (pp. 15–30). New York, NY: Guilford.

Stevenson, H. C., & Fantuzzo, J. W. (1986). The generality and social validity of a competency-based self-control training intervention for underachieving students. *Journal of Applied Behavior Analysis, 19,* 269–276.

Stevenson, H. W., Chen, C., & Uttal, D. H. (1990). Beliefs and achievement: A study of black, white, and Hispanic children. *Child Development, 61,* 508–523.

Stokes, S. A., Pierroutsakos, S. L., & Einstein, G. (2007, March). *Remembering to remember: Strategic and spontaneous processes in children's prospective memory.*

Paper presented at the biennial meeting of the Society for Research in Child Development, Boston, MA.

Stone, N. J. (2000). Exploring the relationship between calibration and self-regulated learning. *Educational Psychology Review, 12,* 437–475.

Storm, B. C. (2011). The benefit of forgetting in thinking and remembering. *Current Directions in Psychological Science, 20,* 291–295.

Strike, K. A., & Posner, G. J. (1992). A revisionist theory of conceptual change. In R. A. Duschl & R. J. Hamilton (Eds.), *Philosophy of science, cognitive psychology, and educational theory and practice* (pp. 147–176). Albany, NY: State University of New York Press.

Sweller, J. (1988). Cognitive load during problem solving: Effects on learning. *Cognitive Science, 12,* 257–285.

Sweller, J. (1994). Cognitive load theory, learning difficulty, and instructional design. *Learning and Instruction, 4,* 295–312.

Sweller, J. (2008). Human cognitive architecture. In J. M. Spector, M. D. Merrill, J. van Merriënboer, & M. P. Driscoll (Eds.), *Handbook of research on educational communications and technology* (3rd ed., pp. 369–381). New York, NY: Erlbaum.

Sweller, J. (2009). Cognitive bases of human creativity. *Educational Psychology Review, 21,* 11–19.

Talarico, J. M., LaBar, K. S., & Rubin, D. C. (2004). Emotional intensity predicts autobiographical memory experience. *Memory & Cognition, 32,* 1118–1132.

Talarico, J. M., & Rubin, D. C. (2003). Confidence, not consistency, characterizes flashbulb memories. *Psychological Science, 14,* 455–461.

Talmi, D. (2013). Enhanced emotional memory: Cognitive and neural mechanisms. *Current Directions in Psychological Science, 22,* 430–436.

Tang, R., & Tang, Y.-Y. (2012). Brain ventricle volume correlates with effortful control in healthy young males. *Neuroscience, 13*(Supplement 1), 22.

Tennyson, R. D., & Cocchiarella, M. J. (1986). An empirically based instructional design theory for teaching concepts. *Review of Educational Research, 56,* 40–71.

Tessler, M., & Nelson, K. (1994). Making memories: The influence of joint encoding on later recall by young children. *Consciousness and Cognition, 3,* 307–326.

Thanukos, A., & Scotchmoor, J. (2012). Making connections: Evolution and the nature and process of science. In K. S. Rosengren, S. K. Brem, E. M. Evans, & G. M. Sinatra (Eds.), *Evolution challenges: Integrating research and practice in teaching and learning about evolution* (pp. 410–427). Oxford, England: Oxford University Press.

Thiede, K. W., Anderson, M. C. M., & Therriault, D. (2003). Accuracy of metacognitive monitoring affects learning of texts. *Journal of Educational Psychology, 95,* 66–73.

Thiede, K. W., Griffin, T. D., Wiley, J., & Redford, J. S. (2009). Metacognitive monitoring during and after reading. In D. J. Hacker, J. Dunlosky, & A. C. Graesser (Eds.), *Handbook of metacognition in education* (pp. 85–106). New York, NY: Routledge.

Thompson, R. A., & Nelson, C. A. (2001). Developmental science and the media: Early brain development. *American Psychologist, 56,* 5–15.

Thorndike, E. L. (1924). Mental discipline in high school studies. *Journal of Educational Psychology, 15,* 1–22, 83–98.

Tirosh, D., & Graeber, A. O. (1990). Evoking cognitive conflict to explore pre-service teachers' thinking about division. *Journal for Research in Mathematics Education, 21*, 98–108.

Tobin, K. (1987). The role of wait time in higher cognitive level learning. *Review of Educational Research, 57*, 69–95.

Tomporowski, P. D., Davis, C. L., Miller, P. H., & Naglieri, J. A. (2008). Exercise and children's intelligence, cognition, and academic achievement. *Educational Psychology Review, 20*, 111–131.

Tononi, G., & Cirelli, C. (2013). Perchance to prune. *Scientific American, 309*(2), 34–39.

Toplak, M. E., & Stanovich, K. E. (2002). The domain specificity and generality of disjunctive searching for a generalizable critical thinking skill. *Journal of Educational Psychology, 94*, 197–209.

Topolinski, S., & Reber, R. (2010). Gaining insight into the "aha" experience. *Current Directions in Psychological Science, 19*, 402–405.

Torney-Purta, J. (1994). Dimensions of adolescents' reasoning about political and historical issues: Ontological switches, developmental processes, and situated learning. In M. Carretero & J. F. Voss (Eds.), *Cognitive and instructional processes in history and the social sciences* (pp. 103–122). Mahwah, NJ: Erlbaum.

Trachtenberg, J. T., Chen, B. E., Knott, G. W., Feng, G., Sanes, J. R., Welker, E., & Svoboda, K. (2002). Long-term *in vivo* imaging of experience-dependent synaptic plasticity in adult cortex. *Nature, 420*, 788–794.

Trautwein, U., Lüdtke, O., Schnyder, I., & Niggli, A. (2006). Predicting homework effort: Support for a domain-specific, multilevel homework model. *Journal of Educational Psychology, 98*, 438–456.

Tulving, E. (1983). *Elements of episodic memory*. Oxford, England: Oxford University Press.

Turkheimer, E., Haley, A., Waldron, M., D'Onofrio, B., & Gottesman, I. I. (2003). Socioeconomic status modifies heritability of IQ in young children. *Psychological Science, 14*, 623–628.

Unsworth, N., Redick, T. S., McMillan, B. D., Hambrick, D. Z., Kane, M. J., & Engle, R. W. (2015). Is playing video games related to cognitive abilities? *Psychological Science, 26*, 759–774.

Urdan, T. C., & Turner, J. C. (2005). Competence motivation in the classroom. In A. J. Elliot & C. S. Dweck (Eds.), *Handbook of competence and motivation* (pp. 297–317). New York, NY: Guilford.

Valiente, C., Lemery-Chalfant, K., & Swanson, J. (2010). Prediction of kindergart-ners' academic achievement from their effortful control and emotionality: Evidence for direct and moderated relations. *Journal of Educational Psychology, 102*, 550–560.

van de Sande, C. C., & Greeno, J. G. (2012). Achieving alignment of perspecti-val framings in problem-solving discourse. *Journal of the Learning Sciences, 21*, 1–44.

Van Hiel, A., Pandelaere, M., & Duriez, B. (2004). The impact of need for closure on conservative beliefs and racism: Differential mediation by authoritarian submission and authoritarian dominance. *Personality and Social Psychology Bulletin, 30*, 824–837.

VanSledright, B., & Limón, M. (2006). Learning and teaching social studies: A review of cognitive research in history and geography. In P. A. Alexander & P. H. Winne (Eds.), *Handbook of educational psychology* (2nd ed., pp. 545–570). Mahwah, NJ: Erlbaum.

Vaughn, K. E., & Rawson, K. A. (2011). Diagnosing criterion-level effects on memory: What aspects of memory are enhanced by repeated retrieval? *Psychological Science, 22,* 1127–1131.

Veenman, M. V. J. (2011). Learning to self-monitor and self-regulate. In R. E. Mayer & P. A. Alexander (Eds.), *Handbook of research on learning and instruction* (pp. 197–218). New York, NY: Routledge.

Verghese, J., Lipton, R. B., Katz, M. J., Hall, C. B., Derby, C. A., Kuslansky, G., . . . Buschke, H. (2007). Leisure activities and the risk of dementia in the elderly. *New England Journal of Medicine, 348,* 2508–2516.

Verkhratsky, A., & Butt, A. (2007). *Glial neurobiology.* Chichester, England: Wiley.

Vintere, P., Hemmes, N. S., Brown, B. L., & Poulson, C. L. (2004). Gross-motor skill acquisition by preschool dance students under self-instruction procedures. *Journal of Applied Behavior Analysis, 37,* 305–322.

Volet, S., Vaura, M., & Salonen, P. (2009). Self- and social regulation in learning contexts: An integrative perspective. *Educational Psychologist, 44,* 215–226.

von Stumm, S., Hell, B., & Chamorro-Premuzic, T. (2011). The hungry mind: Intellectual curiosity is the third pillar of academic performance. *Perspectives on Psychological Science, 6,* 574–588.

Vosniadou, S. (1991). Conceptual development in astronomy. In S. M. Glynn, R. H. Yeany, & B. K. Britton (Eds.), *The psychology of learning science* (pp. 149–177). Hillsdale, NJ: Erlbaum.

Vosniadou, S. (1994). Universal and culture-specific properties of children's mental models of the earth. In L. A. Hirschfeld & S. A. Gelman (Eds.), *Mapping the mind: Domain specificity in cognition and culture* (pp. 412–430). Cambridge, England: Cambridge University Press.

Vosniadou, S. (Ed.). (2008). *International handbook on conceptual change.* New York, NY: Routledge.

Vosniadou, S., Vamvakoussi, X., & Skopeliti, I. (2008). The framework theory approach to the problem of conceptual change. In S. Vosniadou (Ed.), *International handbook on conceptual change* (pp. 3–34). New York, NY: Routledge.

Vygotsky, L. S. (1978). *Mind in society: The development of higher psychological processes* (rev. ed.; M. Cole, V. John-Steiner, S. Scribner, & E. Souberman, Eds.). Cambridge, MA: Harvard University Press.

Vygotsky, L. S. (1986). *Thought and language* (rev. ed.; A. Kozulin, Ed. and Trans.). Cambridge, MA: MIT Press. (Original work published 1934.)

Vygotsky, L. S. (1987). *The collected works of L. S. Vygotsky* (R. W. Rieber & A. S. Carton, Eds.). New York, NY: Plenum Press.

Walker, E., Shapiro, D., Esterberg, M., & Trotman, H. (2010). Neurodevelopment and schizophrenia: Broadening the focus. *Current Directions in Psychological Science, 19,* 204–208.

Walkington, C., Sherman, M., & Petrosino, A. (2012). "Playing the game" of story problems: Coordinated situation-based reasoning with algebraic representation. *Journal of Mathematical Behavior, 31*, 174–195.

Wang, J., Sperling, R. A., & Haspel, P. (2015). Patterns of procrastination, motivation, and strategy use across class contexts and students' abilities. *Journal of Psychology and Behavioral Science, 3*, 61–73.

Watkins, M. J., & Watkins, O. C. (1974). Processing of recency items for free-recall. *Journal of Experimental Psychology, 102*, 488–493.

Weaver, C. A., III, & Kelemen, W. L. (1997). Judgments of learning at delays: Shifts in response patterns or increased metamemory accuracy? *Psychological Science, 8*, 318–321.

Webb, N. M., Franke, M. L., Ing, M., Chan, A., De, T., Freund, D., & Battey, D. (2008). The role of teacher instructional practices in student collaboration. *Contemporary Educational Psychology, 33*, 360–381.

Weiner, B. (1984). Principles for a theory of student motivation and their application within an attributional framework. In R. Ames & C. Ames (Eds.), *Research on motivation in education: Vol. 1. Student motivation* (pp. 15–38). Orlando, FL: Academic Press.

Weiner, B. (1986). *An attributional theory of motivation and emotion.* New York, NY: Springer-Verlag.

Weiner, B. (1994). Ability versus effort revisited: The moral determinants of achievement evaluation and achievement as a moral system. *Educational Psychologist, 29*, 163–172.

Weiner, B. (2000). Intrapersonal and interpersonal theories of motivation from an attributional perspective. *Educational Psychology Review, 12*, 1–14.

Weiner, B. (2004). Attribution theory revisited: Transforming cultural plurality into theoretical unity. In D. M. McNerney & S. Van Etten (Eds.), *Big theories revisited* (pp. 13–29). Greenwich, CT: Information Age.

Weiner, B. (2005). Motivation from an attribution perspective and the social psychology of perceived competence. In A. J. Elliot & C. S. Dweck (Eds.), *Handbook of competence and motivation* (pp. 73–84). New York, NY: Guilford.

Wellman, H. M. (1990). *The child's theory of mind.* Cambridge, MA: MIT Press.

Wellman, H. M., & Gelman, S. A. (1992). Cognitive development: Foundational theories of core domains. In M. R. Rosenzweig & L. W. Porter (Eds.), *Annual review of psychology* (Vol. 43, pp. 337–375). Palo Alto, CA: Annual Reviews.

Wells, G. L., Olson, E. A., & Charman, S. D. (2002). The confidence of eyewitnesses in their identifications from lineups. *Current Directions in Psychological Science, 11*, 151–154.

West, R. F., Toplak, M. E., & Stanovich, K. E. (2008). Heuristics and biases as measures of critical thinking: Associations with cognitive ability and thinking dispositions. *Journal of Educational Psychology, 100*, 930–941.

Wiley, J., Goldman, S. R., Graesser, A. C., Sanchez, C. A., Ash, I. K., & Hemmerich, J. A. (2009). Source evaluation, comprehension, and learning in Internet science inquiry tasks. *American Educational Research Journal, 46*, 1060–1106.

Willems, R. M., Hagoort, P., & Casasanto, D. (2010). Body-specific representations of action verbs: Neural evidence from right- and left-handers. *Psychological Science, 21*, 67–74.

Wilson, R. S., Scherr, P. A., Schneider, J. A., Li, Y., & Bennett, D. A. (2007). The relation of cognitive activity to risk of developing Alzheimer's disease. *Neurology, 69*, 1911–1920.

Wineburg, S., Martin, D., & Monte-Sano, C. (2011). *Reading like a historian: Teaching literacy in middle and high school history classrooms.* New York, NY: Teachers College Press.

Winer, G. A., Cottrell, J. E., Gregg, V., Fournier, J. S., & Bica, L. A. (2002). Fundamentally misunderstanding visual perception: Adults' belief in visual emissions. *American Psychologist, 57*, 417–424.

Winik, M. (1994). *Telling.* New York, NY: Random House.

Winne, P. H., & Hadwin, A. (2008). The weave of motivation and self-regulated learning. In D. Schunk & B. Zimmerman (Eds.), *Motivation and self-regulated learning: Theory, research, and applications* (pp. 297–314). Mahwah, NJ: Erlbaum.

Winograd, E., & Neisser, U. (Eds.). (1992). *Affect and accuracy in recall: Studies of "flashbulb" memories.* Cambridge, England: Cambridge University Press.

Wiser, M., & Smith, C. L. (2008). Learning and teaching about matter in grades K–8: When should the atomic–molecular theory be introduced? In S. Vosniadou (Ed.), *International handbook on conceptual change* (pp. 205–231). New York, NY: Routledge.

Wixted, J. T. (2005). A theory about why we forget what we once knew. *Current Directions in Psychological Science, 14*, 6–9.

Wolters, C. A. (2003). Regulation of motivation: Evaluating an underemphasized aspect of self-regulated learning. *Educational Psychologist, 38*, 189–205.

Wood, D., Bruner, J. S., & Ross, G. (1976). The role of tutoring in problem-solving. *Journal of Child Psychology and Psychiatry, 17*, 89–100.

Wood, P., & Kardash, C. A. M. (2002). Critical elements in the design and analysis of studies of epistemology. In B. K. Hofer & P. R. Pintrich (Eds.), *Personal epistemology: The psychology of beliefs about knowledge and knowing* (pp. 231–260). Mahwah, NJ: Erlbaum.

Yang, F.-Y., & Tsai, C.-Ch. (2010). An epistemic framework for scientific reasoning in informal contexts. In L. D. Bendixen & F. C. Feucht (Eds.), *Personal epistemology in the classroom: Theory, research, and implications for practice* (pp. 124–162). Cambridge, England: Cambridge University Press.

Yeager, D. S., & Dweck, C. S. (2012). Mindsets that promote resilience: When students believe that personal characteristics can be developed. *Educational Psychologist, 47*, 302–314.

Yerkes, R. M., & Dodson, J. D. (1908). The relation of strength of stimulus to rapidity of habit-formation. *Journal of Comparative Neurology and Psychology, 18*, 459–482.

Young, C. B., Wu, S. S., & Menon, V. (2012). The neurodevelopmental basis of math anxiety. *Psychological Science, 23*, 492–501.

Zacks, R. T., Hasher, L., & Hock, H. S. (1986). Inevitability and automaticity: A response to Fisk. *American Psychologist, 41*, 216–218.

Zajonc, R. B. (2000). Feeling and thinking: Closing the debate on the primacy of affect. In J. P. Forgas (Ed.), *Feeling and thinking: The role of affect in social cognition* (pp. 31–58). New York, NY: Cambridge University Press.

Zaragoza, M. S., Payment, K. E., Ackil, J. K., Drivdahl, S. B., & Beck, M. (2001). Interviewing witnesses: Forced confabulation and confirmatory feedback increase false memories. *Psychological Science, 12*, 473–477.

Zatorre, R. J., & Halpern, A. R. (2005). Mental concerts: Musical imagery and auditory cortex. *Neuron, 47*(1), 9–12.

Zeidner, M., & Matthews, G. (2005). Evaluation anxiety: Current theory and research. In A. J. Elliot & C. S. Dweck (Eds.), *Handbook of competence and motivation* (pp. 141–163). New York, NY: Guilford.

Zelazo, P. D., Müller, U., Frye, D., & Marcovitch, S. (2003). The development of executive function in early childhood. *Monographs of the Society for Research in Child Development, 68*(3), Serial No. 274.

Zhang, W., & Luck, S. J. (2009). Sudden death and gradual decay in visual working memory. *Psychological Science, 20*, 423–428.

Zhao, Q., & Linderholm, T. (2008). Adult metacomprehension: Judgment processes and accuracy constraints. *Educational Psychology Review, 20*, 191–206.

Zhong, C.-B., Dijksterhuis, A., & Galinsky, A. D. (2008). The merits of unconscious thought in creativity. *Psychological Science, 19*, 912–918.

Ziegert, D. I., Kistner, J. A., Castro, R., & Robertson, B. (2001). Longitudinal study of young children's responses to challenging achievement situations. *Child Development, 72*, 609–624.

Zimmerman, B. J. (2004). Sociocultural influence and students' development of academic self-regulation: A social-cognitive perspective. In D. M. McNerney & S. Van Etten (Eds.), *Big theories revisited* (pp. 139–164). Greenwich, CT: Information Age.

Zimmerman, B. J. (2008). In search of self-regulated learning: A personal quest. In H. W. Marsh, R. G. Craven, & D. M. McInerney (Eds.), *Self-processes, learning, and enabling human potential* (pp. 171–191). Charlotte, NC: Information Age.

Zimmerman, B. J., & Kitsantas, A. (2002). Acquiring writing revision and self-regulatory skill through observation and emulation. *Journal of Educational Psychology, 94*, 660–668.

Zimmerman, B. J., & Kitsantas, A. (2005). The hidden dimension of personal competence: Self-regulated learning and practice. In A. J. Elliot & C. S. Dweck (Eds.), *Handbook of competence and motivation* (pp. 509–526). New York, NY: Guilford.

Zimmerman, B. J., & Moylan, A. R. (2009). Self-regulation: Where metacognition and motivation intersect. In D. J. Hacker, J. Dunlosky, & A. C. Graesser (Eds.), *Handbook of metacognition in education* (pp. 299–315). New York, NY: Routledge.

Zimmerman, B. J., & Schunk, D. H. (Eds.). (2001). *Self-regulated learning and academic achievement: Theory, research, and practice.* Mahwah, NJ: Erlbaum.

Zohar, A., & Aharon-Kraversky, S. (2005). Exploring the effects of cognitive conflict and direct teaching for students of different academic levels. *Journal of Research in Science Teaching, 42*, 829–855.

Zusho, A., & Barnett, P. A. (2011). Personal and contextual determinants of ethnically diverse female high school students' patterns of academic help seeking and help avoidance in English and mathematics. *Contemporary Educational Psychology, 36*, 152–164.

INDEX

minimizing distractions, 65
mnemonics, 89
never trusting memory, 8
open-mindedness, 139
organizing information, 8
paper/computer use, 65–66
paying attention, 65
physical exercise, 25
prioritizing information, 65
realistic schedules, 168
recall of information, 66
recent activities review, 111
reflection on learning efforts/outcomes, 126
review and practice, 89–90
seeking others' perspectives, 45–46
self-criticism of opinions, 45
self-reinforcement, 168–169
skepticism, 89
sleep, 26
specifying goals, 167
theory validation, 139
trust in long-term memory, 112
understanding new material, 125–126
worldview assumptions, 46
self-talk, 165
semantic memory, 105
sensory register. *See also* human memory
    system
  connection-making process and, 73–74
  in human memory system, 51–52
shame/guilt, 166–167. *See also* self-regulated
    behavior
shared memories, 1
Shiffrin, R., 50
short-term memory, 56. *See also* human
    memory system; long-term memory;
    working memory
similarity, principle of, 34, 35–36
situational strategies for self-control.
    See self-regulated behavior
skepticism, as learning strategy, 89
sleep, role of, 26
social construction of meaning, 37–39
social influences, in conceptual change, 136–137
specific transfer, 86
stimulation, brain's need for, 30–31
stimulus control, self-imposed. *See* self-
    regulated behavior
storage, of information, 50–51
strategies. *See* instructional strategies (for
    thinking/learning); self-strategies (for
    thinking/learning)
summarizing/organizing principles, for
    thinking/learning, 3–4, 8

superimposed meaningful structure, 83–84
suppression, of neural pathways, 104
symbols/symbol systems, 33
synapses/synaptic connections, 13–14,
    20–21
synaptic consolidation, 15
synaptic pruning, 22–24
synaptogenesis, 22–23
systems consolidation, 15

temporal stability, in attributions, 151
terminal buttons, 12
thalamus, 17–18
theory of mind, 116
theory validation, 139
thinking. *See also* misconceptions (about
    thinking/learning)
  meaning-making and, 4–5
  psychological inquiry and, 5
  summarizing/organizing principles for,
    3–4, 8
thoughts, organization of
  concepts, 39–40
  personal theories, 42–44
  schemas/scripts, 40–42
  worldviews, 44–45
transfer, maximization of, 85–86
truth, as an absolute entity, 121

unencoded information, 52. *See also* encoding

verbal analogies, 140
verbal mediation, 82
visual imagery, 79–81
visual stimuli, 34–36
vivid memories, 108–109, 112

wait time, as instructional strategy, 112
Walters, A. A., 81, 106
ways of knowing. *See* epistemic beliefs
white matter, 12
whole-brain thinking, 18–20
Winik, M., 107
working memory. *See also* long-term memory;
    retrieval; short-term memory
  cognitive load, 65–66
  connection-making process in, 73–74
  "forgetting," 100–101
  in human memory system, 52–56
  recall and, 66, 124–125
  term definition/usage, 6–7
worldviews
  assumptions about, 46
  as organizing tools, 44–45